Contentious Agency and Natural Resource Politics

The looming depletion of non-renewable resources has increased the global land grab in the past decade. So far, however, the question of how and when people can influence economic outcomes has received little attention in the study of social movements.

Based on in-depth ethnographic field research since 2003 in the industrial forestry expansion frontiers in Brazil and elsewhere in the global South, this book presents a novel theory to explain how the interaction between resistance, companies and the state determines investment outcomes. The promotion of contentious agency by organizing and politicizing, campaigning, protesting, networking and engaging in state and corporate-remediated politics whilst maintaining autonomy is central to explaining how impacted people influence resource flows, and block or slow projects they deem harmful to their livelihoods and the environment. The conflicts between globalizing paper and pulp corporations and the landless peasants, indigenous communities and other parties with alternative projects for the planet's future are studied to illustrate how a great transformation can be built upon progressive counter-movements. This systematic comparison of several cases illustrates the broader principles and problems endemic to the global political economy.

Contentious Agency and Natural Resource Politics will be of strong interest to students and scholars of international relations, international political economy, environmental studies, environmental politics, sociology and social movement studies.

Markus Kröger is an Academy of Finland Postdoctoral Researcher at the Department of Political and Economic Studies at the University of Helsinki, Finland.

Rethinking Globalizations

Edited by Barry K. Gills, *University of Helsinki, Finland*

This series is designed to break new ground in the literature on globalization and its academic and popular understanding. Rather than perpetuating or simply reacting to the economic understanding of globalization, this series seeks to capture the term and broaden its meaning to encompass a wide range of issues and disciplines and convey a sense of alternative possibilities for the future.

1 **Whither Globalization?**
The vortex of knowledge and globalization
James H. Mittelman

2 **Globalization and Global History**
Edited by Barry K. Gills and William R. Thompson

3 **Rethinking Civilization**
Communication and terror in the global village
Majid Tehranian

4 **Globalization and Contestation**
The new great counter-movement
Ronaldo Munck

5 **Global Activism**
Ruth Reitan

6 **Globalization, the City and Civil Society in Pacific Asia**
Edited by Mike Douglass, K.C. Ho and Giok Ling Ooi

7 **Challenging Euro-America's Politics of Identity**
The return of the native
Jorge Luis Andrade Fernandes

8 **The Global Politics of Globalization**
"Empire" vs "cosmopolis"
Edited by Barry K. Gills

9 **The Globalization of Environmental Crisis**
Edited by Jan Oosthoek and Barry K. Gills

10 **Globalization as Evolutionary Process**
Modeling global change
Edited by Geroge Modelski, Tessaleno Devezas and William R. Thompson

11 **The Political Economy of Global Security**
War, future crises and changes in global governance
Heikki Patomäki

12 **Cultures of Globalization**
Coherence, hybridity, contestation
Edited by Kevin Archer,
M. Martin Bosman,
M. Mark Amen and
Ella Schmidt

13 **Globalization and the Global
Politics of Justice**
Edited by Barry K. Gills

14 **Global Economy Contested**
Power and conflict across the
international division of labor
Edited by Marcus Taylor

15 **Rethinking Insecurity, War and
Violence**
Beyond savage globalization?
*Edited by Damian Grenfell and
Paul James*

16 **Recognition and Redistribution**
Beyond international development
*Edited by Heloise Weber and
Mark T. Berger*

17 **The Social Economy**
Working alternatives in a
globalizing era
Edited by Hasmet M. Uluorta

18 **The Global Governance
of Food**
*Edited by Sara R. Curran,
April Linton, Abigail Cooke and
Andrew Schrank*

19 **Global Poverty, Ethics and
Human Rights**
The role of multilateral
organisations
*Desmond McNeill and
Asunción Lera St. Clair*

20 **Globalization and Popular
Sovereignty**
Democracy's transnational dilemma
Adam Lupel

21 **Limits to Globalization**
North-South
divergence
*William R. Thompson and
Rafael Reuveny*

22 **Globalisation, Knowledge
and Labour**
Education for solidarity within
spaces of resistance
*Edited by Mario Novelli and
Anibel Ferus-Comelo*

23 **Dying Empire**
U.S. imperialism and global
resistance
Francis Shor

24 **Alternative Globalizations**
An integrative approach
to studying dissident
knowledge in the global
justice movement
S.A. Hamed Hosseini

25 **Global Restructuring, Labour and
the Challenges for Transnational
Solidarity**
*Edited by Andreas Bieler and
Ingemar Lindberg*

26 **Global South to the Rescue**
Emerging humanitarian
superpowers and globalizing rescue
industries
Edited by Paul Amar

27 **Global Ideologies and Urban
Landscapes**
*Edited by Manfred B. Steger and
Anne McNevin*

28 **Power and Transnational
Activism**
Edited by Thomas Olesen

29 **Globalization and Crisis**
Edited by Barry K. Gills

30 **Andre Gunder Frank and Global Development**
Visions, remembrances and explorations
Edited by Patrick Manning and Barry K. Gills

31 **Global Social Justice**
Edited by Heather Widdows and Nicola J. Smith

32 **Globalization, Labor Export and Resistance**
A study of Filipino migrant domestic workers in global cities
Ligaya Lindio-McGovern

33 **Situating Global Resistance**
Between discipline and dissent
Edited by Lara Montesinos Coleman and Karen Tucker

34 **A History of World Order and Resistance**
The making and unmaking of global subjects
André C. Drainville

35 **Migration, Work and Citizenship in the New Global Order**
Edited by Ronaldo Munck, Carl-Ulrik Schierup and Raúl Delgado Wise

36 **Edges of Global Justice**
The World Social Forum and its "others"
Janet Conway

37 **Land Grabbing and Global Governance**
Edited by Matias E. Margulis, Nora McKeon and Saturnino Borras Jr.

38 **Dialectics in World Politics**
Edited by Shannon Brincat

39 **Crisis, Movement, Management**
Globalising dynamics
Edited by James Goodman and Jonathan Paul Marshall

40 **China's Development**
Capitalism and empire
Michel Aglietta and Guo Bai

41 **Global Governance and NGO Participation**
Charlotte Dany

42 **Arab Revolutions and World Transformations**
Edited by Anna M. Agathangelou and Nevzat Soguk

43 **Global Movement**
Edited by Ruth Reitan

44 **Free Trade and the Transnational Labour Movement**
Edited by Andreas Bieler, Bruno Ciccaglione, John Hilary and Ingemar Lindberg

45 **Counter-Globalization and Socialism in the 21st Century**
The Bolivarian Alliance for the Peoples of our America
Thomas Muhr

46 **Global Civil Society and Transversal Hegemony**
The globalization-contestation nexus
Karen M. Buckley

47 **Contentious Agency and Natural Resource Politics**
Markus Kröger

Contentious Agency and Natural Resource Politics

Markus Kröger

LONDON AND NEW YORK

First published 2014
by Routledge
2 Park Square, Milton Park, Abingdon, Oxfordshire OX14 4RN

and by Routledge
711 Third Avenue, New York, NY 10017

First issued in paperback 2016

Routledge is an imprint of the Taylor & Francis Group, an informa business

© 2014 Markus Kröger

The right of Markus Kröger to be identified as author of this work has been asserted in accordance with sections 77 and 78 of the Copyright, Designs and Patents Act 1988.

All rights reserved. No part of this book may be reprinted or reproduced or utilised in any form or by any electronic, mechanical, or other means, now known or hereafter invented, including photocopying and recording, or in any information storage or retrieval system, without permission in writing from the publishers.

Trademark notice: Product or corporate names may be trademarks or registered trademarks, and are used only for identification and explanation without intent to infringe.

British Library Cataloguing in Publication Data
A catalogue record for this book is available from the British Library

Library of Congress Cataloging in Publication Data
Kröger, Markus.
  Contentious agency and natural resource politics / Markus Kröger.
    p. cm. – (Rethinking globalizations ; 47)
  Includes bibliographical references and index.
  1. Natural resources–Political aspects. 2. Land use–Political aspects.
3. Political participation. 4. Social action. I. Title.
  HC85.K76 2013
  333.7–dc23
                    2012050444

ISBN 13: 978-1-138-28792-1 (pbk)
ISBN 13: 978-0-415-65967-3 (hbk)

Typeset in Times New Roman
by Taylor & Francis Books

Contents

List of illustrations		viii
Acknowledgements		x
List of abbreviations		xiii
Introduction		1
1	Theory of contentious agency in natural resource politics	12
2	Accumulation by dispossession in resource exploitation frontiers: The case of industrial forestry in Brazil	36
3	Contentious agency, the Brazilian landless movement and pulp conflict outcomes	58
4	Political games determining resource exploitation pace and style	87
5	Key characters in contemporary global expansion of resource exploitation, illustrated by conflicts over tree plantations	109
Conclusion: The role of resistance in natural resource politics		137
References		153
Index		169

Illustrations

Figures

I.1	Veracel's eucalyptus plantations in cutting phase in Eunápolis, Bahia, Brazil, April 2011	9
1.1	The virtuous cycle of contentious agency promoting strategies	15
1.2	Economic outcomes as a result of political games	24
2.1	The correlation of state financing and pulp/eucalyptus plantation expansion per year in Brazil, 1996–2007	43
2.2	Veracel pulp mill from the inside, Eunápolis, July 2006. The bleached pulp is ready to be shipped to the world	44
2.3	Members of a Brazilian Landless Rural Workers' Movement (MST) camp in northeastern Rio de Janeiro, March 2004	50
2.4	Veracel's outgrower eucalyptus plantation, Eunápolis, Bahia, Brazil, June 2004	53
3.1	La Vía Campesina Women's Stora Enso plantation occupation, Santana do Livramento, Rio Grande do Sul, Brazil, 8 March 2008	72
3.2	Steps of state embedding by a movement: the influence of movement embedding with the state apparatus on resource use	76
3.3	MST camp in Pinheiro Machado, Rio Grande do Sul, May 2008. The MST is pushing for the expropriation of the surrounding land areas, whereas VCP, a pulp company, tried to buy the land for eucalyptus and to extend eucalyptus by outgrowing schemes even within the nearby MST settlements	80

Tables

1.1	Processes, mechanisms and strategies in natural politics	31
2.1	Land access type, land price and dispossession in Brazil, 2006–10	45
2.2	Accumulation by dispossession, and signs of eucalyptus expansion-related dispossession in Brazil (yes or no), 2004–10	46

3.1	Contentious agency promoting strategies and plantation expansion in 13 pulp holding cases, 2004–08	82
5.1	Global "planted forest" expansion by regions, 1990–2010	113
5.2	Countries with over 800,000 ha of forestry plantations, % of introduced species, and conflict existence	125

Acknowledgements

Numerous people have helped me to conduct the research for this book. I wish to thank everyone. I want to thank Teivo Teivainen, Peter Evans and Jussi Pakkasvirta for offering sound advice and encouragement each provided support, encouragement, and critical but kind commentary that both touched on similar issues as well as complementing each other. I thank Jussi for the initial support he gave me to start research at the Finnish National Graduate School for North and Latin American Studies, in which I worked as a full member for four years. Through his expertise in Latin American Studies and the globalization of the paper industry, Jussi was exactly the right person to give advice. He also put me in contact with Teivo, who supported the development of a rigorous hypothesis-based analysis that links the events in Brazil to world politics. He made excellent and critical comments, crucially helping to develop an analysis incorporating democracy and capitalism in the world system, especially in Latin America. Teivo also put me in contact with the right people, without whom I could not have finished this research in its current form, the most important being Peter Evans. Peter gave continuous, meaningful and pertinent commentary and advice whilst I was a visiting researcher at the Department of Sociology of the University of California, Berkeley. With Peter's expert knowledge on state-business-social movement relations, especially in Brazil, and sophisticated theoretical advice, I was able to draft a framework that emphasized the dynamics of contention and establish a hypothesis probing the efficiency of contentious agency in corporate resource exploitation. Talks with Peter developed my general understanding of the globalization of the political economy and development. The political economy aspect of this research gained crucial depth while participating in the seminars Peter gave at UC Berkeley. I could not have wished for better advisors than Jussi, Teivo and Peter.

I am greatly indebted to Sidney Tarrow, Ruth Reitan, Barry Gills, Jun Borras and Jan-Erik Nylund. Sid provided crucial commentaries that pushed me towards an ever more dynamics- and process-based analysis, without which the conceptual framework developed here would be very different. Similarly important were the excellent commentaries and motivating words given by Ruth. Barry's ideas and comments were crucial in turning the

Acknowledgements xi

dissertation into a Routledge book, going beyond the dissertation and making a broader claim. Jun Borras gave excellent comments for several chapters of this book, and discussions with him brought me closer to the general land grabbing scholarship. Jan-Erik Nylund's critical and forestry-specialist commentaries were important in refining and testing the arguments, and working with him in writing research articles was helpful in many senses.

The research seminars on Latin American politics offered by David and Ruth Collier at UC Berkeley offered an excellent platform to develop the conceptual framework and shape several parts of the book with experts in Latin American politics. I want to thank all the seminar participants who commented on the research: your critical comments were important in the process of creating the conceptual framework. Likewise, I have to thank Kim Voss and Cihan Tugal from the UC Berkeley Department of Sociology for advising me on the social movement and contentious politics literature, and offering good guidelines for building up the research. The email discussions with Peter Kingstone were helpful in contesting previous research and shaping the analysis of Brazilian state-business relations, while discussions with Christian Brannstrom and Angus Wright were helpful in looking in more detail into the environmental historical context. I am indebted to all of you.

I want to thank the following colleagues for excellent comments: Biancca Castro, Silvia Zimmermann, Ricardo Carrere, Winnie Overbeek, Fabian Ochsenfeld, Ilse Ruiz Mercado, Débora Lerrer, Carlos Santana, Adam Cohon, Rebecca Tarlau, Juha Mononen, Iagê Zendron Miola, Mariana Affonso Penna, Sascha Lohmann, Marina Barros, Simone Batista, Larry Lohmann, Bruno Bringel, Brian Palmer, Tero Pekki, Marjaana Virtanen, Teresa Perez, Jenni Munne and Juho Partanen. The Director of the Finnish National Graduate School for North and Latin American Studies Markku Henriksson provided a graduate student with all he could wish for. I am indebted to my graduate school colleagues Daniel Blackie, Hanna Laako, Sami Lakomäki, Elina Valovirta, Pekka Kilpeläinen, Janne Immonen and Sarri Vuorisalo-Tiitinen. I am grateful to Phillip Brooks, who made comments on the language and other issues in the thesis. I wish to thank also the many other people who have commented on the language. I thank fellows in Latin American Studies at the University of Helsinki for their inspiration: Pirjo Virtanen, Elina Vuola, Martti Pärssinen, Auli Leskinen, Florencia Quesada, Antti Korpisaari, as well as Mikko Saikku from North American Studies. Marshall Eakin provided useful comments on the early stage of this research project, as I was introducing my research to him at the Brazilian Studies Association Conference, as did Donal Carbaugh, as I submitted a part of the research to him on a course at the University of Helsinki. I thank Michael Watts and Pauliina Raento for brief but important helpful comments. I also want to thank the large number of people who made comments, including colleagues from the UC Berkeley Sociology, Political Science, Anthropology and Geography departments; the members and professors of the Finnish National Graduate School for North and Latin American Studies; and fellow scholars xii *Acknowledgements*

at the conferences of the Latin American Studies Association, the Brazilian Studies Association, International Studies Association, World Congress of Rural Sociology, CEISAL, global land grabbing conferences, and the forest policy and conflict conferences at SLU in Sweden. I would also like to thank for their excellent help all those in the Routledge editorial team, including Alex Quayle, Dominic Corti, Heidi Bagtazo and Alison Neale. Of course, all the remaining errors are mine.

I also want to thank Kaisa Tarna and all others from Stora Enso, João Cordeiro from Pöyry, Keila Reis from INCRA, Ivonete Gonçalves and Melquíades Spínola from CEPEDES, Guttenberg Pereira from ASPEX, and Pertti Simula and Mika Rönkkö from Maattomien ystävät ry, for helping to organize the field research. I am grateful to João Paulo, Igor, Celia, Waldemar, João Lopes, Jocerlei, Raquel, Gelio, Johanna, Eliene and countless others from the MST and other social movements: thanks for letting me sleep at your homes and sharing your time with me during the interviews, and organizing the field trips.

Abbreviations

ABD	accumulation by dispossession
ALBA	Bolivarian Alliance for the Peoples of Our America
BNDES	Banco Nacional de Desenvolvimento Econômico e Social
BRACELPA	Associação Brasileira de Celulose e Papel
CEPEDES	Centro de Pesquisas para o Desenvolvimento do Extremo Sul da Bahia
CONTAG	Confederação Nacional dos Trabalhadores na Agricultura
CPI	Comissão Parlamentar de Inquérito
CPT	Comissão Pastoral da Terra
CUT	Central Única dos Trabalhadores
DOC	Dynamics of Contention
EU	European Union
EZLN	Ejército Zapatista de Liberación Nacional
FAO	United Nations Food and Agriculture Organization
FASE	Federação de Órgãos para Assistência Social e Educacional
FSC	Forest Stewardship Council
FUNAI	Fundação Nacional do Índio
GDP	gross domestic product
GM	genetically modified
ha	hectare
IBAMA	Instituto Brasileiro do Meio Ambiente e dos Recursos Naturais Renováveis
IMF	International Monetary Fund
INCRA	Instituto Nacional de Colonização e Reforma Agrária
ITP	industrial tree plantation
km	kilometer
MLT	Movement for Land Liberation
MMA	Ministério do Meio Ambiente
MNC	multinational corporation
MST	Movimento dos Trabalhadores Rurais Sem Terra
NGO	nongovernmental organization
OAB	Ordem dos Advogados do Brasil
PT	Partido dos Trabalhadores

xiv *Abbreviations*

QCA	qualitative comparative analysis
REDD	United Nations Collaborative Programme on Reducing Emissions from Deforestation and Forest Degradation in Developing Countries
STP	smallholder tree plantation
STR	Sindicato dos Trabalhadores Rurais
TP	tree plantation
UNEP	United Nations Environment Programme
WRM	World Rainforest Movement
WSF	World Social Forum

Introduction

We are living through a world-historical conjuncture of rising corporate resource exploitation and resistance to this. The resistance struggles of displaced people against exploitation are multiple instances of a single world-historical process. Subsistence economies are being incorporated into global capitalism. Resources are being exploited on an unforeseen scale and with unimaginable speed to feed the globalizing world economy. New sources of transnational commodity and capital flows are being created. As investments such as industrial plantations displace huge natural forest, savanna and grassland landscapes in a matter of years, the socio-ecological relations between people and nature are being subjected to chaotic transformations.

Capital has always sought easier territories to incorporate and exploit. The race for resources has recently peaked. Land questions, land grabs, resource scarcity, climate disruption and resilience, food prices, security and sovereignty have vigorously entered the list of key topics in world politics. As the race for the world's last non-renewable resources has intensified rapidly and with drastic consequences in recent years, sharply illustrating the natural limits to current capitalistic expansion (Klare 2012), industrial civilization and capitalism seek prolonged continuance by their transformation into "green capitalism" and a "bio-economy." Forestry is going to increase its significance within this context of the change from non-renewable to renewable resources, as oil and mineral exploitation eventually depletes even the most peripheral but commercially extractable sources. Industrial tree plantation (ITP) conflicts, the interaction between resistance and companies and states, help to understand this world-historical conjuncture in many ways, this dance between the forces pushing, slowing and shaping the style of new types of capitalist accumulation, as well as its disappearing forms.

There is enough evidence that the contemporary global resource use is unsustainable; what is needed is studies of how change, real change, is possible. At the deepest level, this signifies changes in the mindsets and volition driving extraction practices and responses to them. The turn to renewable resources in the form of establishing plantations is not a sustainable solution. According to peer-reviewed studies (e.g. Jackson *et al.* 2005; Fearnside 1998; see Chapter 5) and impacted populations all around the world, short

2   Introduction

rotation industrial tree plantations (ITPs) typically cause severe damage to soil and water quality and stream flows. This signifies that the "green" and "bio"-economies based on ITPs may not be truly green, bio or renewable resource extraction settings, but could be classifiable as nonrenewable nature relations.

With this in mind, the cases in which dispossessed local people have surprisingly been able to change the resource extraction style and pace, even stopping not only low-profile but also high-profile investment projects, is of particular interest. This calls for research on how these outcomes were possible: findings can suggest whether, how and to what degree the main process is being increasingly shaped by the underdogs.

Resistance, which can happen anywhere, can slow the expansion.[1] There are always possibilities and opportunities for agency. The desire and will to decry injustices, voice suffering and propose changes, are universally available human actions. Examples of movements largely achieving their objectives range from mining resistance against Vedanta in India's Orissa state to landless rural workers halting eucalyptus plantation expansion in southern Brazil. Examples reveal that struggles are more likely to lead to the desired outcome if a combination of resistance strategies is used. Although agency matters most, political-natural conditions, context, political actors and the dynamics involved and the investment project play a role in the degree to which movements attain their goals. History is not made in a void.

Change in the actual course of events in natural resource politics can and should happen because otherwise even more trouble is ahead for all of us. Industry, consumers and states need a new plan. We all need a new plan. The large-scale, multinational corporation-based extraction and trade in resources is not a preferred plan because it creates so much misery and so many security problems. The land, resource, climate, ocean and water questions here and now are of much greater importance and more urgent than fixing the global and regional financial meltdowns. Can we stop this global resource grab? How? How should we study how some movements have managed to stop the local part-processes of this global change? What theories can help us in understanding and explaining the role of resistance in resource politics? How should these theories be combined into a generally usable framework?

This book crafts a framework to help in investigating the natural resource politics of various industrial sectors in myriad political contexts. Particular focus is on explaining the role of strategies used by the resistance. The theory is constructed using developments in many fields, particularly scholarship on social movements. I combine a broad theoretical argument and specific, detailed empirical case studies, producing a theory of when and how contentious agency can slow down or reverse the expansion of corporate resource exploitation.

How have some social movements managed to slow or even discontinue destructive projects and investments? I argue that a theory of contentious agency can help answer this vexing, urgent and important question. Bringing

Introduction 3

social movements into the heart of explaining political and economic processes was abnormal in natural resource exploitation – its actual governance and its study – remaining in the shadows until a few years ago. However, no politics can be explained without seeing what is going on in the streets, fields, forests, mountains, waters and air; by looking at what ordinary and less-ordinary people are doing, and how they are relating to nature.

The book is based on analysis of the influence of social movements on primary-sector investments, for which there is a lack of rigorous global comparison, and on which there is limited research, mainly as separate case studies (Perreault and Valdivia 2010; King and Pearce 2010). To provide a larger number of comparable cases, forest industry-related tree plantation expansion and conflicts are surveyed globally, and a systematic comparison of all paper pulp investments, conflictive or not, is offered by a detailed study of pulpwood expansion politics in Brazil, arguably the most rapidly and significantly growing site currently.

In the literature on resource politics, and even in the more specific substudy of bottom-up resistance to corporate resource exploitation, scholars have seldom concentrated on the question of how conflict outcomes were achieved. Trajectories of large-scale investment projects can be understood only by explaining the politics of resource exploitation in general, including the role of resistance or its absence.

The work of Polanyi (2001 [1944]), which focuses on the interplay between politics and the economy, especially in the struggle for and against the commoditization of land, money and labor, has resurfaced as an explanatory framework for counter-hegemonic globalization of this type (see Munck 2007 for an example of a Polanyian study). Simultaneously, scholarship on movement influence on investment and economic outcomes (King and Soule 2007; King 2008; Soule 2009; Vasi 2009; Sherman 2011) has emerged, demanding further analysis of the causalities between protests and business within the dynamics of contention (McAdam *et al.* 2001, 2008; Luders 2010). As a response to both of these calls (Polanyi and the movement scholarship), this book considers natural resource politics as an interaction between movements wanting (or not wanting) to influence investment, and governments and target companies/industries. The book identifies the generalizable and specific processes, strategies, mechanisms and political games by which movements influence the style and pace of resource exploitation and transform the local-global political dynamics in areas where increasing transnationalization of resource flows has taken place.

I argue that particular movement strategies foster contentious agency, which can markedly influence economic outcomes in investment. Formation of agency and the political games in which economic outcomes are defined are greatly influenced by the strategies and relations between movements, targets and the state. What strategies secure continuity and success for social movements, albeit relative and transitory? What contextual and strategic factors explain differences in resistance outcomes?

4 *Introduction*

Considering the odds, it is intriguing that some of the new "poor people's movements" are becoming influential in modifying the style, governance and policies of resource exploitation in the global peripheries that are their homes. A detailed study of resistance has become increasingly topical. The attention of the world and research on large-scale land deals, particularly in the global South, also dubbed a "global land grab," has boomed in the past five years. Consistent with the urgency of the problem and the limited number of specialists dedicated to the study of the causal relations and consequences related to the phenomenon of resistance spearheading action in the impact areas, focused research, concepts and a theoretical framework are required.

A delimited, well-studied and illustrative set of research cases is required to start explaining the causal complexes behind the push for ever-larger resource exploitation investments and resistance to them in more depth. A systematic analysis of investment conflicts over industrial- and smallholder-scale tree plantation serves this purpose.

The world-historical conjuncture of rising resistance is tied to the rise of the so-called BRIC (Brazil, Russia, India, China) countries, particularly the massive Chinese resource demand that drastically reshapes world commodity chains, as well as that for timber (Dauvergne and Lister 2011). Investigating this contemporary global process in its local dynamic could use the comparative strategy of incorporated comparison suggested by McMichael (1992: 362), where the goal is to understand how global processes are interpreted, expressed and realized locally. Comparative case-by-case variation is not assumed a priori, but is illuminated across space as well as embedded in the distinct histories of the contexts. This produces a cross-sectional comparison between segments of a contradictory whole, in which segments are comparable through the political-economic meta-process of mounting resistance to increasing resource exploitation.

Besides the interaction of resistance movements and the industrial forestry companies, I also explore the complex role of the various state actors and institutions. Brazil has been accorded most attention as it is arguably among the world's most important industrial plantation and forest resource countries, producing 25% of the world's food[2] and containing about 14% of the world's forests (FAO 2001). Global natural resource politics cannot be understood without locating its struggles in the political-environmental contexts where resistance emerges and where much of the ongoing expansion and commoditization of the environment and socio-ecological relations takes place. The Brazilian Rural Landless Workers' Movement (MST, or Movimento dos Trabalhadores Rurais Sem Terra), established officially in 1984 and a progenitor and unifying movement within the Brazilian anti-ITP front, is given special attention. Since the 1980s, it has turned into a sustained grassroots movement with almost 30 years of experience. The strategies it has used in ITP conflicts illustrate what is required for resistance to make a difference. Comparative examples are drawn from across the globe. It is argued that some movements, including sub-groups of the MST, have managed to influence investment outcomes even in very difficult circumstances because they have built and used a combination of critical strategies and mechanisms that can foster contentious agency.

Theoretical bases

The Marxist dialectic tradition, where "Peasant[s] make their own history, but not just as they please" (McMichael 2008: 205), and Karl Polanyi's (2001) work on the double movement dynamic between the expansion of market capitalism and the reaction of civil society to that expansion, are precursors in explaining how movements influence the economy. The recent scholarship on peasant movements has argued that autonomous, food sovereignty-based innovative movements such as the MST and La Vía Campesina have the potential to challenge the dominant model of large-scale, capitalist and export-based agriculture (Wittman 2009; Martínez-Torres and Rosset 2010; Schneider and Niederle 2010).[3] I assess these claims on the capacity of the movements to counter capitalist expansion and commodification through a systematic comparison across closely observed pulp and other forestry conflicts, which are cases of resistance by the MST, La Vía Campesina, their allies and others to corporate resource exploitation.

The latest contentious politics research has argued that movement outcomes are the fruit of many simultaneously utilized, concatenating and intersecting strategies, processes and dynamics, in which targets and third parties also play key roles (McAdam *et al.* 2001; Soule 2009; Silva 2009; Luders 2010). Within this dynamic and relational approach, I develop consideration of specific strategies and techniques of mobilization the assessment of which, Hobson (2003), Goodwin and Jasper (2004), Luders (2010), and Soule (2009) argue, has been absent.

Some research has already been done in this theoretical vein. Movement scholarship has offered empirically grounded and methodologically solid studies on movement outcomes (such as Piven and Cloward 1978; Giugni 2004). However, there is still far to go in developing an assessment of economic outcomes (Soule 2009) and measuring cause-effect mechanisms (McAdam *et al.* 2008). The analysis of economic outcomes is not nearly as well understood as policy outcomes; studies of how movements affect both industry development (Vasi 2009) and corporate social responsibility (Soule 2009) have been especially rare. Since claims on a movement's influence on economic outcomes are mainly based on individual cases or are not supported by rigorous methodology, a central objective is to develop both theory and methodology.

The modes of action most commonly used across the globe, for example, by environmental movements, have been studied (Dalton *et al.* 2003). Although these studies have not generally been linked with outcomes, they reveal interesting points about agency and strategies. In a survey of environmental groups across 56 nations, Dalton *et al.* (2003) found that attempts to

6   *Introduction*

influence public opinion and the media were the most common action, followed by networking with other citizen-based movements and meetings with government officials. Environmental groups use protests and direct action markedly less than conventional political action. Protesting was most frequent among better organized and staffed groups, not among the more marginalized political groups. Overall, movements have multiple goals and often use multiple strategies and repertoires of action, across the globe (Dalton *et al.* 2003). When movements use both routine and unconventional strategies, they were more likely to influence environmental policy (Hochstetler and Keck 2007). Contentious acts often attract more attention and make people more aware of problems. Based on these findings, further examination of the links between outcomes and conflicts where protests are or are not used is needed, taking into consideration the simultaneous (non)usage of the other actions mentioned above as well.

Although having a strong environmental focus, the movements engaged in land-based forestry conflicts considered here are more socio-economic justice and human rights-based than environmental. The social justice focus can boost unconventional and radical agency. Ideology and identity influences the use of strategies, in that challenger groups that criticize the dominant economic paradigm protest more (Dalton *et al.* 2003). This explains why protesting was quite frequently used by strong peasant organizations. Dalton *et al.* find that national political context matters very little: both conventional and unconventional strategies are available for use and were used across dramatically different contexts. This is an important finding, implying that agency matters more than context, and thus should be explored more carefully. This finding is in sharp contrast to the practice over recent years of social movement research, where most emphasis has been on political opportunities (e.g. Tarrow 2011). However, investigating the political-environmental context is also essential, as the role of context cannot be taken for granted. Thus contexts are also considered here, attempting to assess the explanatory power of different dynamics and factors.

In order to understand why corporate resource exploitation is slowed, discontinued, reversed or transformed in some cases but expands unchecked in others, it is necessary to know how these outcomes occurred. Therefore, tracing processes and causal process analysis in order to relate various mechanisms to expansion outcomes will be utilized. The study of the process of mobilization from within presents an opportunity to specify the connective mechanisms and understand how the chain of causation operates. A variety of outcomes pinpoints possible differences in the actions and whether there are connections between resistance outcomes and mobilization processes will be determined.

The pushing process, globalization of capitalism, has to be investigated as well. Few world-system scholars have stressed the key relevance of the nature, environment, natural resources, global-local space and the scale of operations in globalization. Bunker and Ciccantell (2005) build an approach they call

Introduction 7

new historical materialism, arguing that material environmental conditions are the most important factor in explaining globalization, development and capitalism. The environment has agency and imposes the boundaries on the scale of primary-sector operations. Low-cost and abundant commodities are necessary for emerging nation-states to become globally dominant. Bunker and Ciccantell (2005) emphasize that a struggle for hegemony between ascending global powers is taking place in the race for resources. They claim that Arrighi (1994) and Harvey (1983) stress politics and finance too much, without considering the primary importance of resources. To assess corporate resource exploitation, I will utilize all of these authors, without subscribing to Bunker and Ciccantell's important but perhaps overtly environment-centered historical materialist view. I place primary explanatory importance on the political processes, which are built in particular environmental settings that political struggles also condition. For example, large-scale industrial plantations do provide more rapid growth rates and higher timber yields when situated in conditions of tropical rainfall and good soil, but only when the political-legislative setting allows for this by permitting extensive conversion of biodiversity-rich landscapes into fenced, corporate-controlled plantations where pesticides, fertilizers and intensive harvesting techniques and cycles are used. I will thus build on the same theoretical vein as Moore (2011), who has studied capitalism as world ecology, a relational bundle in which capitalism in the environment, the production of the environment and the accumulation of capital are inseparable. Opening up new commodity frontiers to produce timber, for example, relies on historically and spatially specific movement of humans and the rest of the environment. This socio-ecological crafting of commodities is capitalism. Similar arguments have been made also by others studying global political ecology (e.g. Peluso and Watts 2001; Hornborg 2001; Vandergeest and Peluso 2006; Hornborg *et al.* 2007; Peet *et al.* 2010).

Methodology and research material

The research is based on the ethnographic case study approach, which has been a natural basis for the analysis of environmental, natural resource-related conflicts (Lewicki *et al.* 2003). The strategy of collecting rich empirical material, typical of participant observation, makes it possible to develop innovative theories and ideas by induction. The methodology included process tracing, triangulation, discourse analysis, media analysis, semi-structured interviews and a qualitative comparative analysis (QCA) of empirical cases on a large set of dependent variable outcomes, political games and movement strategies. A total of 160 semi-structured interviews were conducted between 2004 and 2012 with the key informants, mostly in MST-paper industry conflicts in Brazil and Europe, including governmental officers, company directors and social movement activists; these were in business and state offices,

8 *Introduction*

encampments, settlements, rural and indigenous communities and towns, and particularly in pulp investment areas.

It is also worth noting that researchers are not outsiders to what they study, but influence the phenomenon by directing attention to it. The role of the researcher is to be laid bare and explained. This is particularly true of research on agency and making investment policy suggestions. As a Finnish scholar and citizen, I have found it a natural choice to direct my intellectual inquiry toward the transformation of the increasingly globalized forest industry. I started to conduct research on the paper and pulp industry while writing a master's thesis on the MST in Latin American Studies and Intercultural Encounters (Kröger 2005). While doing ethnographic research in Rio de Janeiro's lush countryside on a 20-year-old land reform settlement in April 2004, members of the MST occupied a section of a eucalyptus plantation of Veracel Celulose, a joint venture between Aracruz Celulose and the Swedish-Finnish Stora Enso in the state of Bahia. It was a logical step to go to Bahia to redefine my master's thesis as a study of the interaction between the paper and pulp industry and the Brazilian landless movement. I have been on that road ever since. After finishing the master's thesis on the Veracel case in 2005, I continued by expanding the study to cover other Brazilian states and pulp conflicts. The result of these years of research was a doctoral dissertation (Kröger 2010). In this book, a further step is taken in situating the Brazilian conflicts in the global context, particularly in the expansion of tree plantations, which was surveyed globally. A lot is happening in the field of tree plantations right now, with a very limited number of researchers engaged on the topic by doing fieldwork in the actual expansion and conflict sites in rural peripheries and considering the magnitude of this change in the global agrarian political economy.

I went to all kinds of research sites, even those that seemed irrelevant at first sight. An understanding of the rural mosaics started to emerge as I probed through various territories controlled or marked by this or that entity. Visits to indigenous villages, large and small city suburbs, middle-class neighborhoods, various industrial sites, farming facilities and agribusiness investments, traditional and new areas and groups, provided a heightened understanding of the specificity of movements and political contexts. An eye for the local territorial differences developed in the field. The extreme south of Bahia was my starting point and was followed by Espírito Santo, Rio Grande do Sul, São Paulo and other pulp investment states, including Rio de Janeiro, Pará and northeastern states such as Maranhão where there are no large pulp conflicts. During this period, I moved into comparing pulp production with other agribusiness operations, in order to see the paper and pulp sector specificity. I interviewed the executives of the paper and pulp industry, not only in Brazil, but also in Finland. To conduct research in multiple locations was crucial. I investigated other social movements in the countryside and cities to understand the distinctiveness of the MST. I did field research and participant observation within rural movements and nongovernmental organizations

Figure I.1 Veracel's eucalyptus plantations in cutting phase in Eunápolis, Bahia, Brazil, April 2011
Source: Photograph © the author

(NGOs) in Venezuela, Uruguay, Argentina and Colombia. I also compared the forestry conflicts to other resource conflicts – for example, those in mining in the Amazon and in India and Finland.

I had several roles. My position as a researcher was that of a critical insider in relation to the resistance movements and an outsider in relation to the industry. At the end of the dissertation research period in 2008, following research and experiences in the Latin American countryside, I helped to establish Maattomien ystävät ry, a Finnish solidarity association interested in the condition of landless people around the globe. Most were open to my research. I also acted during the research period as a freelance journalist, writing articles and news for the Finnish and transnational media about the phenomenon I was studying. I gave public and academic lectures and actively participated in the debate over the paper industry transformations, writing several research and op-ed newspaper articles.

Theory building was guided principally by empirical observations and participant observation. In the interviews I conducted with the key informants, governmental officers, company directors and social movement activists all saw the movement resistance efforts as the biggest challenge to pulp investment continuation. For example, in a foresters' seminar at the University of Helsinki that I attended as a student and an ethnographer, Stora Enso

10 *Introduction*

director Weine Genfors worried that if resistance like that in the state of Rio Grande do Sul since 2005 expanded to the rest of Brazil, there would no longer be large tree plantations (n.a. 2007). The prognosis was true in the sense that up till 2012, all companies attempting to build a large-scale pulp investment in the state have failed, largely due to fierce resistance from movements and progressive state actors. In the view of Bracelpa, Brazil's paper and pulp front organization, the MST, organized indigenous peoples and most recently the Afro-descendant *Quilombola* communities are the greatest threat to the advance of the industry's power (author's interview with Ludwig Moldan, Bracelpa, June 25, 2008). I will assess whether, how and by the utilization of what resistance strategies this claim holds true.

Chapter 1 will outline a theory for the study of the role of contentious agency in impacting economic outcomes in natural resource politics. Chapter 2 demonstrates resistance to the global phenomenon of the current push for land grabbing, by a discussion of the illustrative Brazilian tree plantation expansion cases. Although modern mechanisms of land appropriation have emerged, the expansion is still marked by accumulation by dispossession, focusing on enclosing zero- or low-cost, large-scale land areas. Chapter 3 shows how the theory can be applied, by explaining how social movements in Brazil fostering contentious agency, such as the MST, have managed to slow down plantation expansion. Chapter 4 continues using the Brazilian cases, discussing the role of the interactive political games determining resource exploitation pace and style, political spheres where contentious and corporate agency meet, in more detail. Both state-remediated and private political dynamics of corporate outreach via corporate social responsibility are discussed.[4] Chapter 5 takes the discussion to the global level, reviewing the current state of knowledge of the expansion of tree plantations and the impact of resistance on this around the world. The concluding chapter summarizes results and discusses some illustrative cases from other industries across the world, where the mobilization against growing corporate resource exploitation is apparent.

Contentious Agency and Natural Resource Politics has several important theoretical and political implications. Politically, the research implies that an efficient social movement can utilize a mix of strategies to promote awareness and consciousness of its position, potential and agency among its members. This research should be understood as a study of the initial phase of the growing conflicts over corporate resource exploitation, including growing ownership of the environment in the contemporary world. It is possible that the strategies creating contentious agency will be used more widely in the world, challenging global capitalism. Theoretically, the research implies a need to shift attention from structural or rational choice theories to the relations, dynamics and processes that explain politics. Until now, there has been no clear, comprehensive theory focusing on dynamics and processes on when and how contentious agency can slow down or reverse the expansion of corporate resource exploitation. The original contribution of this research is to provide such a theory, and utilize it to offer an extensive explanation of the conflicts over large-scale investment projects, the globalization of the forestry industry, and the slowing of industrial plantation expansion. This theory, with its generally applicable conceptual and methodological framework, can be used to determine when, how and why resistance can slow down or reverse or at least influence the expansion of resource extraction. The theoretical framework, research design and results of this study apply, with due precautions, at least to corporate resource exploitation-based conflicts. Another matter for discussion is that major contextual differences between societies and times may shape the functioning of the generally observable characters of strategies, processes and the dynamics of struggle.

Notes

1 Resistance to expansion pressure is defined as those responses whereby people do not select a strategy of (loose or tight) incorporation into the investment model or proposed business (e.g. by outgrower farming of trees), or conflict avoidance (e.g. by silently fleeing from the site of convulsion), but where they fight (violently or non-violently, visibly or silently) to defend their autonomy, to retain or increase their control over territorial, social and symbolic space. This conceptualization of resistance and power relations draws on Scott (2009: 209) and Bourdieu (1991).
2 Brazil ranks first in the export and production of several food commodities, such as sugar (42% of global exports), ethanol (51%), coffee (26%), orange juice (80%), tobacco (29%), and ranks in the top four in the export and production of beef (24%), poultry (35%), soybeans (35%), soy meal (25%), corn (35%) and pork (13%) (USDA 2005).
3 La Vía Campesina is a transnational movement of peasants, small and medium-sized producers, landless, rural women, indigenous people, rural youth and agricultural workers, with about 300 million members. It is one of the largest global networks resisting neoliberalism and capitalist resource exploitation. For insightful studies on its importance, see Ruth Reitan's *Global Activism* (2007: 148–88) and Borras (2010).
4 "Corporate social responsibility" implies "the commitment by business to behave ethically and contribute to economic development while improving the quality of life of the workforce and their families as well as of the local community and society at large" (World Business Council for Sustainable Development 2002, cf. Soule 2009: 20).

1 Theory of contentious agency in natural resource politics

In this chapter, I generate a framework for analyzing when and how resistance can slow or reverse corporate resource exploitation, or secure other objectives of social movements. Sustained corporate strategies create capacity for corporate agency, and sustained mobilization strategies create capacity for contentious agency. Capacity is not enough, since one has still to have willingness to act, and act, believe that change is possible and desire it. The support given by the state to movements and corporations, and vice versa, is also important. The interaction of these three processes (corporate, contentious and state agency) forms the dynamics that explain natural resource politics. The state and civil society should be studied relationally, since focus on their relationship to other power networks offers a more flexible analytical tool than, for example, state-centered explanations, as Silva (2009) has demonstrated in his study on the occurrence and outcomes of anti-neoliberal mobilizations.

In the social sciences, agency refers to the capacity of individuals to act independently and to make their own free choices (Giddens 1984). I suggest that the creation of particular social action, strategies, mechanisms and relations can foster human agency, the capacity of humans to act and to make choices, and get involved and participate in politics. Mechanisms are better understood as strategies in most cases, as they involve direct human intervention: I use "mechanism" and "strategy" as the same concept. Extending and going beyond the dynamics of contention (DOC) research program started by Doug McAdam, Sidney Tarrow and Charles Tilly (2001), who urge scholars to go beyond the structure/agency debate, I agree that what happens within political trajectories and conflicts can better be understood as the result of the intersection of a number of causal mechanisms. My major theoretical point is to show how such intersections create specific types of human agency.

I use the concept of contentious agency to refer to contentious changing of the social relations by social actors. The agency is contentious if it challenges the orthodox, accepted trajectory of development promoted by more powerful actors, that extend resource exploitation operations.[1] Resource extraction is political action and cannot be extended by nature or "free markets" alone,

Contentious agency in natural resource politics 13

since they are always a sign of strong human intervention, that is, agency on the part of somebody.

In order to analyze the strategies systematically, I utilize the partition approach, which breaks processes into their constituent mechanisms. Besides disaggregation, the partition approach tackles one mechanism or strategy at a time, does it well, and then moves on to the next, "searching for interactions and interdependencies, concatenations and combinations, among the mechanisms" (Lichbach 2008: 348). Following this approach, I can muster evidence on the existence of strategies promoting contentious agency that is causally relevant to the slowing of or change in the style of resource exploitation. I seek to respond to the call by Lichbach (2008: 350) for accounts of how social systems emerge from causal processes of contention, how they solidify, and how they come to structure social, economic and political life. I assess how the social systems of the movements and the industry emerge, solidify and structure social, economic and political life while clashing in the contentious episodes occurring in the course of projects. Moreover, I consider the outcomes of these contentious episodes, pointing out the new processes set in motion by the expansion or slowing of resource extraction and focusing on the social movement aspect.

To construct the right strategies and link them is essential as the instruments of protest and means of contention "are not easy to establish when they are not already there, and they certainly require a good deal of initiative and acumen" (Drèze and Sen 2002: 369). Since development theorists Drèze and Sen do not analyze the strategies by which contentious agency can be promoted, I consider specific strategies of mobilization. McAdam *et al.* (2001: 37) also note the scarcity of the type of analysis provided here: "the classic approach to social movements concentrates on mobilization and demobilization; it provides relatively weak guides to explanation of action, actors, identities, trajectories, or outcomes." I seek to provide heuristic tools to assess these issues.

I build on multiple-mechanism, joint-effect outcome assessment, in which outcomes are the fruit of many strategies. Multiple methods of measurement can produce a better representation of the phenomena studied than single-method research (McAdam *et al.* 2008). In his *Freedom is a Constant Struggle*, Kenneth Andrews (2004: 22) maintains that movements should engage in multiple means of influence to obtain the best outcomes. Marco Giugni identifies four interrelated variables that have influenced the outcomes of conflict involving social movements historically. These are *movement organization* and *protest activities* within changing *political opportunity structure*, and the impact of *public opinion* (Giugni 2004: 4). Combining ethnographic induction with deduction from Giugni, McAdam *et al.* (2001) and other social movement theorists' proposals above, the active making of the first two variables I conceived as strategies denominated (a) (organizing and politicizing a movement) and (c) (protesting), respectively. The last two I combined into strategies (d) (networking with allies) and (e) (the embedded autonomy of

14 *Contentious agency in natural resource politics*

the movement vis-à-vis the state and targets), as well as into the analysis of the control process (corporate resource exploitation).

Peter Evans (1995: 12) originally used the concept of embedded autonomy to refer to a developmentalist state that embeds with the society (particularly industry) whilst maintaining autonomy, escaping capture by private interests but still listening to them. I extend and flip the concept here to analyze social movements and companies, arguing that effective groups are those that embed with the society and the state whilst maintaining autonomy. Even though autonomy cannot be expected when embedding with the state, I argue that this interaction has allowed the MST, for example, to manage to maintain considerable autonomy by distinct strategies, considering the level of embedding it has in relation to the state (as is done in Chapter 3). Besides utilizing the concept of embedded autonomy to assess the interaction of a movement with the state, I also use it to assess the interaction between corporations and the state. The embedded autonomy of corporations and movements explains a large part of the state-remediated dynamics between movements and corporations.

The uniting of agents and structures into relational strategies allows one to escape the theoretical dichotomy between "movements" and their "political opportunity structures," for which there has been great demand (McAdam *et al.* 2001; Luders 2010; Tarrow 2011). To complement Giugni's set of variables, I made them dynamic by focusing on the action in these, studying the action leading to the phenomena observed by Giugni as "variables" as formed by strategies. Going beyond variable-based research, I imbued particular qualities to strategies (a), (c), (d) and (e) and created a new strategy concept (not covered by Giugni's variables): campaigning by heterodox framings (b), a cognitive mechanism creating targeted campaigns within the movement, among other things.[2] By a systematic comparison of cases, I investigate whether there is a causal relation between contentious agency formed by a virtuous cycle between strategies a–e (see Figure 1.1) and resistance outcomes.

Only action maintains movements: perhaps their most typical feature is that they campaign and/or protest. For a social movement, the deepening virtuous cycle of contentious agency promotion envisioned in Figure 1.1 can ensure actions and support the advancement of their mobilization and agenda.

The strategies come in a sequence: (b) follows from (a) (or quite often (a) follows from (b), when a movement has not yet been established but is forming by dint of an initially rag-tag campaign on a specific issue), after which the movement can utilize (c), (d) or (e), or all of them. If a movement uses all of c–e, or some of them particularly well, this is more likely to foster further organizing, politicizing and campaigning than using only one of these strategies, the theory goes. In such a case, a loop, a virtuous cycle is created between the strategies. This cycle will maintain the contentious agency and make it grow. The territorial, social and symbolic space for independent

Contentious agency in natural resource politics 15

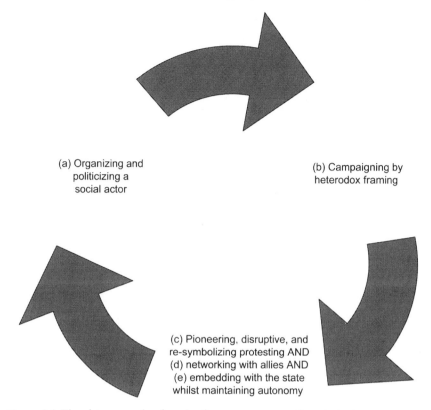

Figure 1.1 The virtuous cycle of contentious agency promoting strategies

and heterodox movement action and choice is increased; that is, contentious agency can be promoted more efficiently.

The disaggregation of the main process, contentious agency promotion, as deriving from strategies a–e serves to assess what type of process is more prone to lead movements to attain their objectives. Without the disaggregation, this research would be able to say that movements matter or do not matter, but not exactly when and how. I will show that strategies a–e are best used in a particular sequence, and roughly simultaneously. They are techniques and phases of contentious agency promotion. At the base are strategies (a) and (b). Typically, only after these two phases have been completed can the social movement initiate further actions. A movement may utilize protests (c), networking (d), or embedding whilst retaining autonomy (e), or all of them to further its goals. It may also use direct dialogue and negotiation (f) with a company in private politics without state actor participation to negotiate about the style and pace of resource exploitation.[3] However, I have not added strategy (f) to the virtuous cycle, as engagement in private politics has frequently led to diminishing contentious agency and radicalism. Strategy (f)

16   *Contentious agency in natural resource politics*

(direct dialogue with a company) might even be mutually exclusive with some elements of a–e. The larger dynamics in which these strategies and their users are situated are bound to vary, but in their technical form the strategies that resistance can use and often uses in political endeavors are generalizable across contexts.

Specific strategies creating a specific type of human agency, contentious agency, foster the spread of contentious action through time and across space. Any social actor can utilize general contentious agency. What is contentious depends on the definer, the powerful and the level of definition. Thus, contentious agency could also be developed by state and multilateral institution actors, if these were to challenge contentiously the prevailing global orthodoxy to gain more space for their independent and heterodox decision making. For example, an international system-focusing analysis of contentious agency could focus on the challenge posed by the Bolivarian Alliiance for the Peoples of Our America (ALBA) to the capitalist world system. In this type of international-level analysis, one would consider how and whether ALBA governments utilize particular strategies to create contentious agency in the world-system processes, and whether this challenge has resulted in attaining their desired goals, possibly including countering abusive resource exploitation and fostering discontent over this in the international system.

A concatenation of strategies a–e provides strength for the resistance. The activeness of the strategies, as well as their combination and interaction in the given context, determines the depth, pace and spatial transmission of resistance promotion. For example, if one takes protest acts away, the MST landless movement is more likely to gain less or no land in the political context of Brazil, which weakens its organizational base, the daily, politicized practices and campaigning by heterodox framing, as well as the networking and embedding strategies. Likewise, if the networking and embedding strategies deteriorate, the power of land occupation decreases: these might even be made constitutionally illegal because of the lack of embedding with the state apparatus.[4] The daily, politicized practices and heterodox framing as well as organizing would be harmed by a weakness in the embedding strategy, as the movement would not obtain resources like school funding, and because the reduced autonomy would allow the dominant system to overrule the contentious movement strategies. If politicized practices or organizing strategies were curtailed, the embedded autonomy and protest would be harmed.

The organizing and politicizing work forms a social movement organization and is essential in fostering such things as interpersonal trust between members. Trust is a key element explaining the use of protests by movements: the more militant and dangerous a protest act, the deeper the required trust usually is (Benson and Rochon 2004). This finding applies across contexts and in both democratic and non-democratic states, with higher trust levels correlating with more protests (ibid.). Trust allows the intensity of participation to be raised, which means that a wider array of strategies becomes available: in this form, everything begins from the organizing grid of a movement.

However, protests also feed back into trust levels, since unified protesting binds participants together, and was the most efficient site of contentious agency creation for those interviewed. When mental processes are voiced they become stronger, and they become strongest by impact when made physical, i.e. in protesting by moving bodies and key objects from one place to another.

In fact, a strong organizing strategy, which creates a strong organizational base, is a necessary condition for developing and implementing ever more contentious, challenging and pioneering protest acts. Pioneering protests against resource exploitation also depend on the heterodox framings of a project as a principal enemy of genuinely sustainable development. The ideological strategizing work done by leaders, converted into heterodox framings in campaigning, is a necessary condition of protesting. Networking and embedding whilst maintaining autonomy are not necessary conditions, but if these are not active, the expected outcomes of the protests for a movement are worse.

The hypothesis suggests that if contentious agency is promoted, a process starts by which the resistance can manage to impact resource exploitation. This happens either soon, or in the future when the process has created enough strength for the resistance in the dynamics with corporate agency in given political systems.

Agency, development and democracy

I argue that groups of people promoting contentious agency effectively, such as the self-denominated members of the MST and Vía Campesina can make a difference in resource conflicts, and even more generally, on the road towards strengthening democracy, if this is the goal of the groups. Democracy is understood here as the power of the people to make decisions that alter their lives, like the principle that everybody has one vote that has the same value in decision making, including economic and socio-environmental issues. Situations in which this rule is not followed, where people do not have the power or where one person's vote counts more than somebody else's, are less democratic than those polities or investments in which people have more power and there is a greater equality between the votes.[5] Agency distribution is skewed in such settings.

Contentious agency is a useful concept in highlighting the importance of heterodox discourses and protest, resistance and conflicts in general, on the road towards democracy and development. Many scholars have emphasized the importance of heterodoxy and the courage to disagree. For example, Amartya Sen (2005: 30) sees them as pivotal in science, the fostering of public reasoning, and the establishment of democracy. Even though contentious agency might appear as increasing conflicts, conflictive mobilization is often used to resolve the deeper, underlying, real conflicts and harmful situations that have not been addressed. The attempt is to create the potential for dialogue by equalizing power disparities, creating mechanisms and

18   *Contentious agency in natural resource politics*

spaces for discussion, introducing contentious ideas and buttressing these by accompanying political acts.

In contexts where expert or elite decision making is preferred and the participation of others is seen as a hindrance or framed as a nuisance, the activist promotion of greater democracy and dialogue takes the form of contentious agency. In such struggles, agency is framed as contentious and is principally concerned with incorporating and emphasizing the active role of the underdogs in social transformations. The have-nots will also be involved, after gaining more access, self-confidence and knowledge in assessing priorities, scrutinizing values, doing things, and crafting and executing policies that influence them.

Sound policy making benefits from contention, since without outside contentious pressure the state would be less efficient in its policy making and in implementing processes. Hochstetler and Keck (2007: 18) argue that "the policy process requires a political mobilization all the way down. Even then, enforcement remains a difficult problem." Thus, one has to place the study of contention influence in a prominent position. For example, Brazilian policy institutionalization "depends substantially on the voluntarism of committed individuals, and owes as much to short-term improvisations (*jeitos*) as to a longer-term process of embedding procedures" (ibid.). Contentious agency is a required element of adequate policy-led social transformations.

This is particularly true in state contexts that are found wanting. For example, "the weak enforcement capacity and low levels of institutional continuity characteristic of the Brazilian state" (Hochstetler and Keck 2007: 19) mean that turning policy into practice requires contentious agency promotion. In the natural resource politics setting, "Not only the early stages, but also the maintenance of institutional processes frequently required the continuing active agency of actors outside the institutions themselves" (ibid.: 224). When state institutions and policies are extremely mutable, consistent citizen support for the continuation of a given policy or institution offers stability, even if the contender is created by and influences society by disruptive and at first sight even destructive mechanisms, such as land occupations/invasions. In achieving sweeping policy changes, being vigilant in taking advantage of sudden disruptions matters much more than institutional continuity (ibid.: 227). Resistance movements can empower people and offer constant venues to contest and thus construct contentious agency. Such movement organizations offer social organizational continuity and pressure where state institutions falter or change.

Contentious agency is required to raise developmental and moral questions if they challenge the prevailing power relations. This is the case, for example, in top-down development projects that displace people. Particularly in such cases, dialogue on ethical praxis can lead not only to more sustainable economic outcomes, but also to resolving conflicts and enhancing well-being. In general, Gibson-Graham (2006) argues that economic development is the by-product of discussions on and answers given to practical ethical issues. The

Contentious agency in natural resource politics 19

key questions are what is necessary for personal and social survival; whether and how social surplus is to be appropriated and distributed, produced and consumed; and how a commons is produced and sustained (ibid.). Questioning arising from contentious agency is thus a pre-condition for sustainable development.

Agency, identity and emotions

Contentious agency also refers to the personal and group-level identity in social action. Grievances lock in negative emotions, and there is a need to let them out. Mobilization and often conflict is needed as a tool to change or free emotions, become aware of them by their conscious expression. Discussions with dozens of activists in protest situations in 2004–11 in Brazil suggested that the participants felt the full gamut of emotions while staging a roadblock or land occupation. Protesting allowed the users of this strategy to become aware of their power and suppressed feelings.

Protest situations are also potentially dangerous, being easily derailed into violence. This is why strong social movement organizations with embodied moral guidelines are required for keeping protests disruptive yet peaceful. For example, in the MST guidelines, no physical violence against humans is allowed, in a pragmatic political calculation that was and is typical of many other non-violent but radical resistance movements around the globe. Fostering of blind rage and violent expression of it do not promote freedom of individual choice but are destructive. Particular tactics and strategies foster different types of typically repeated, learned action and reaction.

People can promote agency by particular practices, actions and communication. Once movement strategies a–e are in action, for example, they foster the education of contentious subjects, those activists with a contentious habitus. Pierre Bourdieu has briefly described habitus as socialized subjectivity (Bourdieu 1998). Bourdieu's agents socialize into a habitus, which regulates their actions but also defines who and what they are. Bourdieu has three premises for habitus: 1 it becomes active only in relation to a field, and thus depends on the state of that field; 2 habitus always either strengthens – when expectations encounter opportunity – or may weaken: it transforms endlessly; 3 habitus is controllable by socio-analysis and consciousness (Bourdieu 1990: 116).[6]

Activists can use specific communication tools to create mobilization and manage emotions in conflicts. In resource politics, these tools are tied into the core objects over whose use and social symbolization the struggles exist. The environment often has sacred significance to locals resisting the commodification of nature into natural resources. The resource commodities central to a struggle are the pinnacle of cultural relations between social actors with different socio-ecological relations. A central feature boosting mobilization are emotionally charged discourses that decommodify the land or resource under a purposeful and necessary commoditization in the process by which

20 *Contentious agency in natural resource politics*

a capitalist agency converts a region's environment into natural resources. For many MST members, as well as indigenous and traditional rural populations across the global South, "land" is sacred and has sacred characteristics, which makes attempts to commoditize it a profanation. Poetic forms charged with emotions build up the counter-movement against commoditization all around the globe. Ideological, identity building and ethical discourses, and the actions of activists, company directors and state actors struggle over decision-making power.

Concepts for the study of agency and control of space

To understand resistance, one has to determine how group members identify themselves, construct their cause and the schism. To tap into the ideological set of resistance, Bourdieu (1991, 1998) can be used to assess how a symbolic system organizes meanings inherent to the movement and reflects both a social space and a territorial space, an autonomous space for counter-hegemonic resistance. Bourdieu (1991, 1998) argued that one has to make heterodox claims to challenge the established order. Only competing discourses and symbolic acts can make the issues at hand visible and frame them. The established truth is transformed into a battle between heterodoxy and orthodoxy when the issue is discussed instead of remaining suppressed. Those whom Bourdieu nominates as controlled parties will then want to show the artificiality of the existing order, while those in control try to maintain it (Bourdieu 1991: 165, see graph).

The heterodoxy has to contest the prevailing orthodoxy; in the case of ITPs, the legitimacy of expanding trees in a corporate-controlled monoculture. I point out how one needs to turn knowledge into practice to do this, how subjects become active participants in the processes they formulate, and how power always includes resistance in itself. These points on contentious agency also rely partly on Michel Foucault (1994) and Gramsci (1971); however, I do not engage explicitly with a Foucauldian or Gramscian analysis, even though their contribution remains in the background.

Agency and struggles are tied into the control of space. I argue that the structure and positioning of agents and changes in society always take place as simultaneous, relational shifts and transformations in the social, symbolic and territorial spaces (building on Bourdieu 1990: 113–14; Bourdieu 1991: 43; Wacquant 2008, 2013). If something happens in the territorial space, this change must come with equal, correlated changes in the social and the symbolic spaces of the area in question. For example, when a plantation expands (territorial space), this change must correlate, now or later, with changes in the social and symbolic space. Extractive investments come with a change not only in the territorial space but also in the local social space by involving the creation of landlessness in many cases and exclusion of alternative uses in most cases and, in the symbolic space, producing a pro-exploitation investment policy. This basic guideline helps in connecting changes to all aspects of life.

Local communities and corporate resource investments typically belong to very different systems, which both try to win over the same territorial, symbolic and social space. At a deeper level, the ensuing conflicts are about different human-land relations and cultural transmission mechanisms. Theories on cultural motion can help in analyzing these typical differences between local resistance and expanding capitalist resource exploitation. As resources and land are finite, there is a zero-sum game (Hornborg 2001) and a global race for the remaining resources (Klare 2012).

To understand the logic of the various players in this resource game, the cultural motion analysis of anthropologist Greg Urban (2001) helps to identify two ways in which culture moves: dissemination and replication. Urban (2001) is used to show how the resistance can institutionalize a questioning psychology; how the promotion of contentious agency needs replication, the organizational spread of an inquiring, contesting attitude; and how initial resistance organizations have spread their strategies into the network of allies resisting expansion.

Culture moves in two ways, argues Urban (2001: 64), by replication and dissemination. I argue that power relations are formed in a distinctive way for actors following these. Networking attempts by replication promote and offer to others the same replicating patterns in their spheres of action. Agency-fostering resistance spreads by replication, grouping people into patterns of replication based on strategies a–e, for example. In many landless movements under these principles of replication people can produce their living compounds by themselves, and start to farm for their subsistence instead of being dependent on outsiders. In the MST, they can and are given incentives also to engage in collective mobilization of the movement, in effect spreading the strategies of mobilization further themselves by the metaculture of replication by teaching others. The replication-type cultural motion is a key to creating agency-space for self-aware and organized, lasting contention.

Contentious agency can be created only by strategies that promote and spread the metaculture of replication. Replication promotes creativity, innovation, and empowers people to be autonomous and do things themselves. Dissemination attempts to create consumers, passive receivers of cultural transmission, not innovative replicators but masses with unified ideas and absence of say in making important decisions regarding, for example, production and use of common spaces. Corporate agency typically depends on and moves itself by the metaculture of dissemination. Commodity producing and selling industries rely on this metaculture. Cultural transmission by dissemination "focuses only on the demand for things, not on the replication of those things" (Urban 2001: 64). No paper company will teach local people how to produce paper if not forced to, since they sell paper and want to secure timber-supply for their own mills. This is metaculture of dissemination par excellence, trying to limit and gain a monopoly over the production of an

22   *Contentious agency in natural resource politics*

object while maximizing demand for it. Companies rely on hierarchical internal and external order where the disseminated orders of owners and executives are to be obeyed.

The mere existence of cultural motion based on replication is an obstacle to a metaculture of dissemination operating within the same social space. The paper industry representatives have often labeled their opposition ideological, a characterization that may refer precisely to a fundamentally different metaculture. The negative views, however, which *Sem Terras* (as the MST members are called) have of agribusiness in general, have a lot to do with the strategies based on the metaculture of replication that the movement seeks to expand throughout the same social and territorial space. This is why the MST vehemently opposes patented genetically manipulated seeds owned by companies like Monsanto, since these are perhaps the most drastic contemporary form of cultural transmission by dissemination. Such technology delimits not only local human agency but also the agency of nature to replicate itself by its own innovation. Contentious landless workers, many of whom are former landed peasants having undergone rural exodus, know by experience that if the agents of dissemination once destroy the patterns of replication, or make them disappear for some time, it might become impossible to regain the metaculture of replication. For example, colonization destroyed most of the highly sophisticated pre-Colombian food production systems in Latin America (Miller 2007).

In the end, resource conflicts are a question of power relations and about control of one's own life, a question about social practices, if these are operated and designed by somebody up the ladder of dissemination or are replicated by oneself. Investment decisions are questions of power. Contentious agency attempts to point up these drastic power relation and cultural transmission pathway differences. The strength of resistance organizations is in promoting an alternative territorial, social and symbolic system and remaining the most viable, continuous and stable option for the locals to impact their lives and society.

Political games and their impact on natural resource exploitation

Government strategies such as the creation of corporate commodity export-based industries are contested and molded in the political games through which the strategy passes before becoming an executed policy with particular economic outcomes. Corporate and contentious actors use distinct but interactively linked strategies to influence economic outcomes via political games with dynamics that are largely state remediated.[7] For example, movements protest against corporate land access through land occupations (contentious politics). Movement members use voting power to counter corporate electoral campaign financing (electoral politics). Both movements and corporations seek to embed the state institutions and structures whilst maintaining autonomy (institutional and structural politics). Besides this, movements and companies may interact directly without state remediation (private politics).

In natural resource politics, land conflicts where local people and companies and state authorities clash in physical mobilizations, either violent or non-violent, are situated within the field of contentious politics. Incumbents, such as conservative politicians, elites and companies condemning talk about the political tactics used by contesters in contentious politics, often attempt to frame these acts as contentious, illegal, immoral, non-developmental, backward, unacceptable, destructive, violent, chaotic and abusive. The pushing side demands "strong" action to punish resistance and stop contentious actions, in such forms as police or paramilitary violence. Such counter-mobilizations often attempt to foster a process of resistance criminalization.

Besides contentious politics, there may be and typically are other political games in which economic outcomes are determined in the clash between incumbents and challengers. These are less contentious, typically much more routinized games, electoral, institutional and structural politics belonging to this subset. They are the means primarily suggested by conservatives for political participation in democratic political systems. There may be political actors with anti-democratic tendencies seeking to curb even these forums of resistance. In the conflicts involving anti-democratic actors, the resistance participation in electoral and institutional politics is also framed as contentious and unacceptable. Private politics, on the other hand, are direct interactions between companies and their challengers, taking place in the form of corporate social responsibility, outreach, dialogue, stakeholder relations and so on (Soule 2009).

Whether state-remediated or not, contentious or not, strategies used by the actors within these games can foster contentious agency, that is, support turning passive people into active citizens who do not remain silent but participate in and create politics, forcefully drawing attention to problems and solutions. The myriad and complementary, yet to some extent presumably generalizable and limited ways in which this may and may not happen are the object of scrutiny here.

Figure 1.2 illustrates a general theoretical framework for the study of economic outcomes of resistance-industry interaction. The numerous corporate and contentious actors, structures, strategies and mechanisms, both at the domestic and transnational levels, are situated in the dashed boxes named "corporate" and "contentious" agency. The lined boxes are the main political games in which economic policy, outcomes, and investment pace and style are determined by the struggle between actors. Government strategies are influenced by contentious and corporate agency and influence these both directly (the narrow two-headed arrows) and indirectly in the policy-making processes (via the overlapping political games).

The size of the arrows leading to economic outcomes in the framework suggests that the games situated within the state are generally more

24 *Contentious agency in natural resource politics*

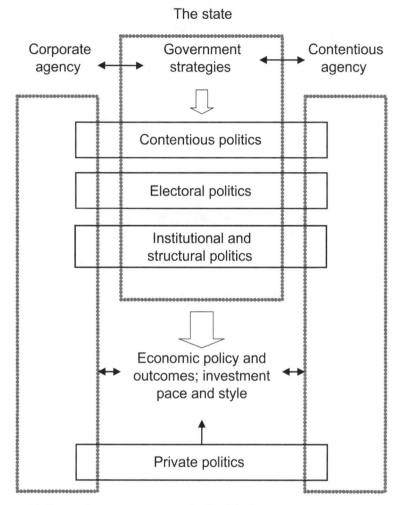

Figure 1.2 Economic outcomes as a result of political games

important in influencing economic outcomes than "private politics." Figure 1.2 suggests that contentious agency loses explanatory power to the degree that corporate agency weighs more, in which sense this is a zero-sum game. Crucial to resource exploitation, for example, is the struggle for limited land as well as state support. Contextual natural and political limitations are thus inherent to the games, and are reflected within the political strategies of the actors.

Politics outside the state, "private politics," are a rising trend, offering opportunities for conflict and problem resolution via corporate social responsibility and stakeholder dialogue, and exerting greater influence on economic policies and outcomes via associative civil society networks.

However, state-remediated and government-driven politics continues to be the mainstay, and shows even further consolidation in the neomercantilist and neodevelopmentalist national strategies and globalization driven by many contemporary governments, including that of Brazil (see Chapter 4).[8] Besides private and state politics, contentious and corporate actors may influence government actors directly, without interacting with each other via political games, as suggested by the direct two-headed arrows between economic outcomes and contentious and corporate agency. The framework can be used to assess the interaction and influence of the state and government, business and contentious agency in economic policy-making processes.

This theoretical framework can be used contextually to delineate varying sets of political games used by resistance to influence resource exploitation and thus to explain differences and commonalities in natural resource politics. At the broad level, some projects are embroiled in conflicts, while in others the discontented does not protest, although disagreeing about the claimed benefits of the project. The framework explains both conflictive and non-conflictive politics.

This theory has parallels in the social scientific inquiry. Bourdieu sees the social world as constructed of various fields, the agents of which fight for control, resources and capital.[9] In these fields, agents invest in order to maximize capital, "all fields are the site of competition and conflicts" (Bourdieu 2000: 183). Fields are a conjunction of habitus struggling to gain capital by the field-specific rules. A field imposes rules: looking into a wider social structure than the field allows one to see how specific a given field's rules are. Bourdieu follows Max Weber in stating that one has always to consider the agents, the division of a system into fields, and the interests and interactions these agents and fields have, be they conflict, competition or cooperation (Bourdieu 1998: 57; Bourdieu 2000: 177). McAdam *et al.* (2001) suggests scholars should concentrate on dynamics of contention. The several political games in which those pushing and resisting particular resource exploitation policies meet are the sub-fields of natural resource politics.

The idea of political games in which contentious and corporate actors struggle for the resource exploitation policies preferred by them is similar in theoretical terms also to the recent theoretical framework of strategic action fields suggested by Fligstein and McAdam (2011). Drawing on social movement scholarship and Bourdieu, Fligstein and McAdam (2011: 3) also define strategic action fields as the fundamental units of collective action in society:

> A strategic action field is a meso-level social order where actors (who can be individual or collective) interact with knowledge of one another under a set of common understandings about the purposes of the field, the relationships in the field (including who has power and why), and the field's rules.

26 *Contentious agency in natural resource politics*

The idea in Figure 1.2 is to place emphasis on fields (political games), and the interaction between incumbents and challengers in the context in which they are embedded, that is, corporate-movement-state interaction in overlapping political systems. Fligstein and McAdam (2011) recommend pursuing broad theory and explanation, as the previous theories have not attempted to explain stability and transformation simultaneously. Adding contentious and private politics as separate games in the framework is one example of attempting to capture not only field stability, but also transformation and emergence. The concept of contentious agency, in particular, links agency with the study of political games or fields where particular rules apply yet may be contested and changed by strategic action.

The more embedded a contentious actor is in the political games in relation to industry embedding, the more likely it will achieve its goals – other strategies supporting it. Likewise, the more embedded the corporation is in relation to resistance embedding, the more likely it can achieve its goals, for example expand at a rapid and unchecked pace. The comparative analysis of these two process types during various times demonstrates the struggle for the state, and can help to explain the differing investment outcomes between projects. The actors also influence contentious politics directly. An ITP company accesses land as it buys and outsources land for tree plantations. The resistance may weigh acts of protest, such as land occupations, against the plantation expansion.

The sub-mechanisms corporations utilize when embedding with the state depend on the political game in question. Embedded autonomy by a corporation can be split into the following sub-mechanisms: contributions to politicians (within electoral politics), and utilizing and lobbying for structural and institutional support mechanisms linking the state and corporations (institutional and structural politics). Within contentious politics, companies may also use legal or paramilitary violence or non-violent means of exclusion to control land/resources. Corporations are not alone in these political games, but they do meet with resistance (if the resistance is not completely anarchistic, that is, not involved in state embedding attempts but seeking simply to foster autonomy), which also forms part of the interactive dynamics.

The framework also applies the other way around: companies can and do try to influence the pace and style of resisting populations' resource use. This can happen as a by-product of securing a particular parcel of land or resource for corporate use, which then delimits alternative resource uses; or be an integrated expansion strategy, if a company wants both land and to create labor by curbing alternative economies and thus "freeing" people from other activities, fostering, for example, a "proletarianization" and/or smallholder capitalist-creation process displacing subsistence farming.[10] For example, in industrial forestry this increasingly takes place in the spread of outgrower schemes where smallholders replace food production on their lots with the planting of fast-growth trees to be sold for forest industry purposes, at industry terms.

Mobilization and the dynamics of contention

Any theory of social movements or resistance has to involve a discussion of mobilization. Bourdieu forms the theoretical basis here for the study of contentious agency, but to add temporality and a deeper explanation of change to Bourdieu, it is helpful to turn to the Dynamics of Contention (DOC) research program offered by McAdam *et al.* (2001, 2008). I see the territorial, social and symbolic spaces as snapshots, topography in a given time and place of the environmental, relational and cognitive mechanisms that McAdam *et al.* (2001) argue are the three categories into which mechanisms explaining social change fall. Thus, environmental mechanisms operate in the territorial space, relational mechanisms in the social space, and cognitive mechanisms in the symbolic space. This merging of DOC and spatial analysis is a novel theoretical development.

The changes in the externally generated influences on the conditions of social life in environmental mechanisms do not explain mobilization automatically or alone. Besides these, we also have to look at the relational and cognitive mechanisms of contention, since the interaction of all three explain the causal chain. Environmental and relational mechanisms alone are unable to explain mobilization. In the case of corporate resource exploitation, mobilization against it need not depend at all on environmental mechanisms (e.g. the advance of plantations and dispossession), but relies on cognitive mechanisms (a social actor's consciousness, awareness, articulation, conceptualization and valuation of what is happening and what needs to be and can be done), and relational mechanisms (relationships of actors in the social space, including possible interpersonal relations between movement-company-state personnel and organizational relations tied to politics more broadly).

The material dimension in building mobilization

The projected or actual use of and relative change in physical space is central to mobilization in natural resource politics. Ruth Reitan (2007: 56) found that the trenchant strength of transnational activist networks lies in the fact that communities in physical places feel under attack. These communities have an identity seriously threatened by neoliberal globalization. Thus Reitan (2007: 56–57) also argues that environmental, cognitive and relational mechanisms explain contention. Both McAdam *et al.* (2008: 45) and Reitan (2007: 281–82, footnote 56) note that environmental mechanisms are not necessarily "outside" a movement, but can be analyzed into other mechanisms. I therefore suggest that it is best to break down the assumed process into constituent government and corporate strategies, dynamics and agency. This reveals that, for example, the "structural violence of neoliberal globalization" is a more complex phenomenon than assumed, and does not come only from outside, but is created in political dynamics, where potential contenders also have agency, even in cases where this agency is passive and not contentious.

28   *Contentious agency in natural resource politics*

Marxist scholars provide ways to spot the changes in the environmental, relational and cognitive mechanisms, focusing especially on the relational mechanisms, such as class dynamics.[11] Where capital accumulates via a process of predatory capitalism, which Marx called primitive accumulation, dispossession and resistance may follow. Polanyi (2001) saw the rise of the "organic society" made of progressive regulation-creating state and civil society actors as an almost automatic defense mechanism of the society to protect itself from self-destruction by over-commodification of nature, human life and money. Polanyi focused on the macro level and a case of movement success; going to the micro level and comparing cases, as here, automatic social self-defense cannot be assumed, self-destruction remaining a plausible alternative if agency is not used. This view becomes clearer when incorporating the agency of nature, as Moore (2011) and Bunker and Ciccantell (2005) suggest should be done to get the full picture of capitalism and its limits.

Drawing on other Marxist examples, the books by Tania Murray Li (2007), who has studied landless resistance in Indonesia, and Beverly Silver (2003), who studied global capital moves and resistance can offer insights into how changes in the relational mechanisms may feed mobilization. Li (2007: 20) explains that "interventions that set the conditions for growth simultaneously set the conditions for some sections of the population to be dispossessed." Apart from noting this broad process of change, Li (2007: 280) also emphasizes the importance of the practice of politics. The "primary mode of engagement is political: asking questions, provoking debate, and conducting analysis that helps to expose unfair rules, greed and destruction." Her research is an amalgam in which environmental, relational and cognitive mechanisms explain mobilization. In the spirit of these accounts, the concept of contentious agency can shed light on how changes in the relational and environmental mechanisms influence mobilization, as well as how they do not automatically lead to mobilization. There are many empirical cases of dispossession not leading to resistance, even when the local people have had the means and the opportunity whilst faced with sets of clues about great threats.[12] Cognitive promotion of contentious agency by pinpointing a relative worsening of conditions, or lack of it, offers an explanation of why there is such variance.

Environmental mechanisms (expansion of exploitation), cognitive (framing the types of corporate control as a problem), as well as relational mechanisms (change in the investment area class, ethnic, gender, age and other social relations) explain the origins and dynamics of resource conflicts. The externally generated influences on the conditions of social life – environmental mechanisms – may stimulate critical analysis (Li 2007: 26), as may relational mechanisms, but to grasp the dynamics of contention and the causal chain underlying mobilization in their totality, the changes in and the operation of cognitive mechanisms are also to be analyzed. In fact, the cognitive mechanisms framing relative grievances seem to be the most crucial initially mobilizing causal mechanism. I have summarized the causal influence of the

Contentious agency in natural resource politics   29

cognitive mechanism as the "importance of the area/issue to the actor." This causal mechanism, which triggers the other mechanisms by which the actors promote their agency, draws on framing grievances caused by the investment, particularly on relative grievances criticizing change.

Typical grievances in corporate plantation conflicts

Neither the arrival of capital in the form of investment, nor the supposedly large number of people dispossessed explains mobilization alone. Grievances play a role but are not equal to mobilization. Grievances can be classified into three sub-categories, situated within particular social change mechanisms: industry and/or investment *model-specific grievances* (a relational mechanism); *relative grievances* in which people put the change brought about by a large-scale project into an historical and contextual relationship to what it replaces (a cognitive mechanism); and *objectively observable grievances* such as ecological and state capacities for receiving the proposed investment (an environmental mechanism). I will briefly exemplify this, as well as how grievances relate to mobilization in corporate plantation conflicts.

First, there is a set of *specific grievances* typically arising against corporate plantations: pollution of soil and waters in the investment area; expansion into traditional communities' lands; rural mechanization and ensuing unemployment; industrial pollution; increased traffic due to logistical operations; outsourcing and the degradation of working conditions; creation of food insecurity by monocultures and land concentration in areas of intense rural exodus, lack of agrarian reform, public policies and no titling of traditional territories. A universally applied investment model, such as the large-scale pulp model, tends to create a set of broadly similar industry-specific grievances across different contexts.[13] These are McAdam *et al.*'s (2001) relational social change mechanisms. Investments change social structures in specific ways, depending on the pace and style of expansion, including the style of corporate outreach used by locally embedded company staff.

Second, there are *relative grievances*, which set the specific grievances in a contextual and historical setting. Local people judge new projects by past experiences, evaluating methods of insertion and potential benefits and losses in land-use change based on what is considered a just way of distributing land access in the local "moral economy" (see Wolford 2010a). These are cognitive mechanisms that frame whether the change has been positive or negative.

Third, there are also the more *objectively observable grievances* such as state capacity and the ecological suitability of a region to receive a massive investment, since if the investment surpasses the objective limits, grievances are likely to arise. The state infrastructure for receiving a massive investment in peripheral areas, with the massive impacts of the size of a pulp project producing a megaton per year, is typically underdeveloped (Carrere and Lohmann 1996). Peripheries where large-scale resource deals take place have typically the least capacity to avert potential problems such as rural exodus

30 *Contentious agency in natural resource politics*

caused by these environmental mechanisms of social change. Ecologically, at least from the point of view of expanding companies, the lands are typically deemed suitable for exploitation in a business-wise sustainable way, at least for a time, otherwise they would not be there, if not for misjudgment or speculation (Nylund and Kröger 2012).

A systematic comparison of conflicts (and their absence) in all the major pulp investments in Brazil and in tree plantation expansion worldwide in the succeeding chapters suggests that grievances do not automatically or even mostly explain mobilization. More important is the use of both contentious and routine political strategies, both of which turn passive people into active contesters, demanders of rights. Politicization is required as the economic structure does not determine the views of the poor on inequality. In fact, over time, the poor have become more accepting of skewed economic distribution, even in the very unequal societies of Latin America (Cramer and Kaufman 2010). What matter most are the *relative grievances* tied to the importance of a change in area/issue to a social group. After conflict potential has been triggered by cognitive framing of relative grievance, mobilization may ensue, depending on the use of strategies.

Disaggregating processes and strategies

Table 1.1 explains more in detail what is to be studied in disaggregating resource politics. Table 1 disaggregates the strategies, mechanisms and processes promoting contentious and corporate agency. I have followed the disaggregation table in Falleti and Lynch (2008: 335) as an example in producing this table. Three top-level process types influence resource use-style: resistance, interaction within the state, and corporate exploitation. These upper-level processes are results of specific relational games and mechanisms, summarized for both of the main processes in Table 1.1.

The valuation of the importance of change in the investment area by the actors (e.g. relative grievances) is a mechanism-as-cause boosting or triggering the willingness to start corporate resource exploitation and resistance. Exploitation and mobilization willingness can gain strength following this mechanism. The mechanism has a specific quality, as it is causal (see Falleti and Lynch 2008: 335, table 1). The conceived importance of the proposed or actual change in the area to the actors may influence top-level processes. If the actors have capacity to act, it triggers the constituent strategies, such as protests (c), or corporate land/resource access (j), by which exploitation is resisted or expanded. If a movement considers a given area or issue important, this can lead to framing of relative grievances and then to protests and the use of strategies such as extending embedded autonomy seeking in the area in question – strategies (a), (b), (d) and (e) permitting, i.e. being available for use and wanted. If strategies a–e are active, the movement should have the contention capacity to turn its judgment on the importance of the area into action and be able at least to attempt to slow corporate resource exploitation,

Contentious agency in natural resource politics   31

Table 1.1 Processes, mechanisms and strategies in natural politics

Top-level process (what explains resource use style)	Resistance	Interactive processes within the state	Corporate exploitation
Process as type (what relations produce the top-level processes)	*Direct government influence; Contentious, electoral, institutional and structural, and private politics*		
Mechanism-as-example (what mechanisms create the processes above)	*Indirect strategies:* a) Organizing and politicizing b) Campaigns w/ heterodox frames d) Networking with allies f) Dialogue with companies *Direct mechanisms:* c) Protesting e) Movement embedding with the state whilst maintaining autonomy (EAM): contributions to state actors, advocacy with institutions linking the state and movements		*Indirect strategies:* g) Capital accumulation h) Industry formation, cooperation and competition, lobbying i) Corporate social responsibility *Direct mechanisms:* j) Corporate land/resource access k) Corporate embedded autonomy with the state: contributions to state actors, utilizing structural and institutional support mechanisms linking the state and corporations
Mechanism-as-cause (what causes the example mechanisms to be active)	Importance of a change in area/issue to a social group (relative grievances)		Importance of a change in area/business to a corporation
Mechanism-as-indicator (how can the sample mechanisms be observed to be active in the case, here in ITP investment politics)	*Indirect strategies:* a) Existence of alternative space AND revolutionary attitude b) Targeted heterodox discourses d) Existence of a strong local resistance network OR replication of the progenitor movement model by other social actors in the area OR transnational networking f) Movements receiving material benefits from companies, cordiality *Direct mechanisms:* c) The number of directed, pioneering, re-symbolizing, disruptive and massive land occupations and other protests e) Embedding: voting, the congruity of state actor discourses and decisions with the resistance. Autonomy: movement-controlled decision-making and utilization of external resources		*Indirect strategies:* g) The business profits or invests h) Industry coalitions exist and act i) The company seeks real dialogue and is ready to make real changes *Direct mechanisms:* j) Surge in the area covered; e.g., by eucalyptus in the investment area k) Direct election financing by companies, investment project support by government discourses and policies, government-controlled credit given to companies

32 *Contentious agency in natural resource politics*

and even discontinue it. For example, in the case of southern Brazil's Rio Grande do Sul state, the MST deemed the area the most important strategically in the nation for the movement, and consequently managed to block plantation expansion as strategies a–e were active, as I will show. In the case of corporations, the judgment that a given area/issue is important leads to corporate resource access and deepening government-industry alliance seeking, available corporate strategies and environmental-political permitting.

The specific viewpoints and strategies of actors vary a great deal depending on the ideology, culture, symbolic system, social position, habitus, correlation of forces, conflict dynamics and irrational elements. The reasons for decisions are hard to spot before the decisions have been made, but after observing the actors' actions in the world, these can be used as references to indicate some, although not all, sources of decisions.

I will assess the sources of the resistance strategizing across global industrial forestry conflicts. I also assess many of the forest industry and its government alliance's sources of strategizing. Bourdieu's concepts of symbolic system and habitus, as well as historical institutional analysis probing the institutional trajectories of entities operating in the political economy, are used to analyze the specificities of social actors and the reasons for their strategizing. The explication of causal mechanisms serves partially to answer the question why, although complete answers cannot be achieved.

The ideology of corporations becomes apparent in analyzing the judgments and strategic decisions corporations make on the importance/suitability of an area for a resource exploitation project. The strategic importance of the area as well as expansion costs for the industry are influenced by many factors, including land prices and the exploitation efficiency rate/costs – these depend on the regulatory framework set by the state, not merely on the available land or on natural conditions. As John Zysman (1994: 243) puts it, "Markets do not exist or operate apart from the rules and institutions that establish them and that structure how buying, selling and the very organization of production takes place." Whatever the complex rationality and irrationality behind the decision, the relative importance of the investment area to the actors activates and directs their actions. The ITP industry privileges lands closer to the sea, transportation routes and, in the fastest tree-growth areas, qualities defined in political processes and not purely by nature. Likewise, some areas are more important to social movements than others; this assessment is based on several interviews with the movement and corporate leadership. This framework allows an empirically grounded theoretical claim on the role of contentious agency in natural resource politics.

Concluding remarks

I assess the hypothesis that corporate resource exploitation can be slowed down more effectively and more certainly when the resistance is formed

Contentious agency in natural resource politics 33

by, utilizes and promotes contentious agency. A theoretical framework studying contentious agency in its interaction with a control process, corporate agency, can explain the resistance role in natural resource politics. The framework draws on Bourdieu, McAdam, Tarrow, Tilly, Evans, Urban, social movement studies, institutional analysis and other strands of social scientific theory.

Resistance exists where people have, first, *desired* and, second, *managed* to build strategies promoting contentious agency. What one primarily has to look for is not the dispossession of rural populations or environmental havoc, but the promotion of contentious agency. As development theorists Drèze and Sen (2002: 379) point out, "the political salience of selective misery depends not only on the specific number of sufferers, but also on the effectiveness of public discussions that politicize the sufferings involved." Awareness of one's potential to be active in changing the world leads to the realization and implementation of one's human capabilities. Paulo Freire (2000: 53; see Teivainen 2003) argued that to change the world or a societal setting implies knowing that this is possible. People have to start seeing the world as something they can change, no matter what the difficulty of the task.

This power-relational, transformative realization of possibility that is always there is an experience resistance movements making an impact offer people, including the incapacitated and agency-stripped people. Resistance endowed with such agency may offer real and existing alternatives that help in building another type of world from the bottom up, if able to put democratic principles into practice. Aside from building a new world and blocking the destructive conversion of existing socio-ecological relations and nature, movements formed around such transformative agency can be effective social assistance and social work organizations. Alternative land use-based movements gather marginalized people into alternative territorial, social and symbolic spaces and organize them to work in such things as self-organized, self-supporting units. Such agency can restore people's dignity, initiative and capabilities – they may become able to organize and start to produce, as in the case of many settlements and camps of the Brazilian landless movement.

The next chapter illustrates the typical socio-economic and political-environmental changes brought by the expansion of corporate resource exploitation to new frontiers in recent decades. It does this by looking closely at the expansion of tree plantations in Brazil, arguing that this process relies on accumulation by dispossession. Resistance formation to this expansion is not discussed at length here, but in the chapters following it. The next chapter offers a view of what resistance movements are facing when industrial tree plantations expand, which is essential to understanding the pushing process and the strategies developed by the resistance to counter this. This Brazilian case aptly illustrates the general contemporary corporate resource grabbing, analyzable only via detailed scrutiny of the constituent sectors of this ongoing global process.

34 *Contentious agency in natural resource politics*

Notes

1 According to Pierre Bourdieu (1991), the term "orthodox" can be used to describe the standpoint and discourse of the actor that currently occupies the better position – more capital, i.e. power – in a given setting.
2 Using pre-existing categorizations to address complex local problems related to abrupt changes, framings never completely describe the phenomena in play (Snow and Benford 1992), but allow politicization via a discursively transmissible conceptualization of eucalyptus, for example, as "producing hunger," as the MST has done in Brazil.
3 I define as state actors all persons in the executive, legislative and judicial spheres of the federal, state and municipal levels of the political system. Resistance or companies can gain the sympathy of some courts, judges and public prosecutors (by embedding with the judiciary), as well as some elected representatives (or otherwise selected political powerbrokers) at the federal, state and municipal levels who can draft legislative frameworks regulating investment. In some cases, since the state agents may be people who belong to the movements or companies, the categories are not mutually exclusive but complementary and possibly simultaneous and active as well as overlapping.
4 In Brazil, the 1988 Constitution allows occupation of land not fulfilling the social purpose requirement set out for the definition of productive property in articles 184–86. The Constitution also stipulates that the land appropriation process cannot be slowed down, interrupted, or made more difficult in any other way. However, the MST laments that this slowing down of agrarian reform happens all the time. The slowness of the courts has practically forced the landless to seize land (Taylor 2008). (Furthermore, social function is obviously an ideological question, one of values, and maintaining values requires action promulgating particular views. The municipal *planos diretores* currently decide what satisfies the social function.)
5 For helpful discussion on democracy in the realm of political economy and globalization, especially on the role of economism in diminishing the sphere of democracy, see Teivainen (2002: 15–32, 172–94) and Robinson (2008: 272–81).
6 For example, a pulp industry mechanical engineer habitus: 1 becomes active only in relation to the field of mechanical engineers in the industry; 2 strengthens as the expectations of a career coincide with objective opportunity – people have a real chance to rise up the career ladder if they succeed; 3 can transform into a *contentious habitus* or be controlled in other ways by those with this habitus, or others, when socio-analysis and consciousness of this habitus increase.
7 In Weberian terms, since the state is a set of institutions and the collection of individuals in those institutions, the state and government differ: "The state is, in many ways, a broader concept, which includes government, but also the legislature that votes on public rules, the political system that regulates elections, the role that is given to opposition parties, and the basic political rights that are upheld by [the] judiciary. A democratic state makes it much harder for the ruling government to be unresponsive to the needs and values of the population at large ... we have to ask questions not merely about the nature of the actual government in office, but, going beyond that, also about the nature of the state of which the ruling government is only one part" (Drèze and Sen 2002: 45).
8 Neomercantilism is defined as "noninstitutional restrictions on imports using exchange rates, regulation of financial flows, and active promotion of exports" (Abu-El-Haj 2007: 109). Neodevelopmentalist manoeuvres reorder the territorial, socio-political and economic fabric through large-scale infrastructure, energy and export-growth augmenting projects and industrial restructurings, so that the larger goals of neomercantilism are secured.

Contentious agency in natural resource politics 35

9 Bourdieu (1991: 163-170) differentiated separate forms of capital (economic, social and cultural being the main forms) and, respectively, powers, which correspond to these capitals. Bourdieu's capital (and power) is a resource, a characteristic and a relation. The distribution of power and style of power relations can be empirically spotted by looking at who gets to change landscape in a way fathomed as the most suitable by him/her, and where and how this occurs.

10 There is a wide variety of companies and smallholders. The analysis of these concrete social producers in differing contexts, in historically specific political economies with their own dynamics and laws of emotion, yields an understanding of the heterogeneity and unity of their practices. A smallholder is defined here as having control over the rights and power in the deployment of labor and means of production in a space which spans a few hectares territorially. Smallholders here differ from peasants (as distinguished by Watts 2009: 524) in that smallholders, in contrast to peasants, are not necessarily self-sufficient at all (all of the smallholder's land may be planted with trees sold for money that buys food, whereas a peasant is at least partly self-sufficient according to the definition by Watts, adopted here); furthermore, smallholders may not be subordinate actors in larger political economies such as national timber markets (peasants are subordinate), and may be autonomous and not fulfilling obligations to holders of political and economic power.

11 Wright's (2005) narrow and Marxist definition of class relations as social relations of production is adopted. In this, class relations exist when there is inequality in the distribution of rights and powers with respect to deployment of productive assets (labour power and/or means of production) in production. Exploitative class relations are fundamentally spatial and "this spatial organization is critical to understanding the nature of uneven development", as for example work in radical geography has compellingly shown (Gidwani 2009: 98).

12 I am criticizing here the "political opportunity structure" framework and argument. According to Sidney Tarrow (2011: 32–33), political opportunities are consistent sets of clues that encourage people to engage in contentious politics. Political threats are those factors that discourage contention. In the framework, according to Tarrow, *political opportunity structures* are the principal causal determinant from which contentious politics emerge. They may lead ultimately to social movements. I argue this depends on capacities and will, agency and strategies of activists, alongside the political games in which they engage. The difference in claim I make in comparison to the political opportunity structure framework is that what matters most are not the outside clues or factors per se, but the internal processes within the human mind. The mind and thoughts can change even though social structures and thus the "set of clues" remain the same. The will to mobilize can emerge completely independently of any outer clues, based on internal processes of one mind. The process starts inside the mind, not outside it. The framing of grievances about changes in situations depends ultimately on the framer, although in terms of realism, generally most mobilizations tend to follow from a worsening of relative grievances, such as the arrival of a dispossessing investment, as will be shown.

13 One cannot speak of just *pulp mills*, as the current investment model essentially includes large areas of surrounding fast-wood tree plantations, making them thus *pulp projects*, not just pulp mill investments. In the current model, the production of pulp is concentrated in large units controlled by a limited number of engineers and paper workers – forestry operations and land ownership are also concentrated in the hands of companies instead of farmers.

2 Accumulation by dispossession in resource exploitation frontiers

The case of industrial forestry in Brazil[1]

This chapter canvases the primary context and sector used as examples to analyze the role of resistance in natural resource politics. The expansion of tree plantations in Brazil is an illustrative case of the rising corporate resource exploitation in the global South. The chapter assesses what mechanisms support the rising role of corporate agency and its support by states, and what kind of impacts this accumulation has had in investment areas. Such analysis of the context and the pushing processes are required better to situate the resistance movements' actions. The subsequent chapters will use the theoretical framework to illustrate the role resistance can play in this process still largely determined by corporate-state alliances.

Brazilian agrarian change is playing an increasingly important role in global natural resource politics. Rising levels of natural resource extraction in Brazil, particularly the expansion of the export-oriented plantation economy, is pushing land cover changes, social changes and market transformations. An increasing proportion of the Brazilian territory is being used for industrial plantations,[2] including trees, agrofuels and genetically modified soybean (IBGE 2006a). In 1995, 41.8 million ha of Brazil's land area were used for fields (*lavouras*); in 2006, the figure was 76.7 million ha (ibid.). Much of the increase was from the expansion of industrial plantations, which covered 70.5% of fields in 2006 (the rest being used by family farms) (IBGE 2006b). Charcoal and pulpwood plantations use fast-wood forestry of eucalyptus trees (with a rotation of two to ten years) to produce fiber for charcoal and paper pulp production.[3] In 2006, Brazil had over 3.5 million ha of eucalyptus plantations (Piketty *et al.* 2009: 181), which meant that eucalyptus accounted for 6.6% of all industrial plantations that year. In 2011, there were 5 million ha of eucalyptus. All tree plantations amounted to 7 million ha (ABRAF 2011: 44). Brazil will soon be the leading global exporter of chemical pulp, with the main destinations being China, the USA and Germany (Finnish Forest Industries Federation 2009). The rising demand from China alone will maintain heavy pressure on Brazilian land, encouraging rapid eucalyptus expansion.

This chapter assesses the different mechanisms, the unifying logic and the consequences of the process by which tree plantations have expanded in

Brazil. Most mechanisms are driven by the state-industry alliance, though mounting resistance since 2004 has started to influence the pace and style of expansion, as the next chapters will discuss. The main argument presented here is that "private" pulp corporations continue to expand largely because the state is providing them with land to do so,[4] and that this land is being taken from users who have common or collective claims. There is evidence that the main process is characterized by primitive accumulation, or accumulation by dispossession, following the financial logic dominant in the current phase of capitalism. Harvey (2003) and Sassen (2010) argue that Marx's primitive accumulation is still prevalent in the expanding resource frontiers of most extraction industries, and dispossession and financialization have become its central mechanisms. According to this theory, while expanding tree plantations over state, indigenous, peasant, Afro-Brazilian and other publicly or commonly inhabited or uninhabited land, companies are able to seize zero-cost or low-cost land assets and turn them to private, profitable use. The state has largely preferred to provide land titles to key corporations rather than to smallholders. Corporate land access that directly or indirectly causes the exclusion of poor, non-documented tenant farmers and rural populations that comprise indigenous, extractive and other traditional communities – which are then fenced off from these lands – can be characterized as accumulation by dispossession.

The goal of the chapter is to present, as holistically as possible, the central correlations and causal relationships operating in the illustrative Brazilian pulpwood and eucalyptus plantation parcel of the actual process of global land grabbing. For this, both statistical inference and qualitative analysis are used, going through the entire body of interviews and primary material, and analyzing for dominant themes, patterns, exceptions and contradictions in order to explore and explain the causes and consequences of eucalyptus expansion.

Tree monocultures and rural exclusion

Primitive accumulation

With the concept of primitive accumulation, Marx illustrated a process of "taking land, say, enclosing it, and expelling a resident population to create a landless proletariat, and then releasing the land into the privatized mainstream of capital accumulation" (Harvey 2003: 149). Harvey summarizes the classic mechanisms of primitive accumulation:

> These include the commodification and privatization of land and the forceful expulsion of peasant populations; the conversion of various forms of property rights (common, collective, state, etc.) into exclusive private property rights; the suppression of rights to the commons; the commodification of labour power and the suppression of alternative (indigenous)

38 *Accumulation by dispossession*

forms of production and consumption; colonial, neo-colonial, and imperial processes of appropriation of assets (including natural resources); the monetization of exchange and taxation, particularly of land; the slave trade; and usury, the national debt, and ultimately the credit system as radical means of primitive accumulation.

(Harvey 2003: 145)

Harvey redefines the process as "accumulation by dispossession," given that the mechanisms of primitive accumulation have changed: "Some of the mechanisms of primitive accumulation that Marx emphasized have been fine-tuned to play an even stronger role now than in the past ... above all we have to look at the speculative raiding carried out by hedge funds and other major institutions of finance capital as the cutting edge of accumulation by dispossession in recent times" (Harvey 2003: 147). New mechanisms, such as the patenting and licensing of genetic material and wholesale commodification of nature in all its forms, are typical of accumulation by dispossession.

The alternative is accumulation without dispossession (see Arrighi *et al.* 2011; Hart 2002), in which domestic markets expand, reproduction costs decrease, and the quality of the labor force is raised by rural development and industrialization that do not drive people off the land; classic examples are China and some East Asian countries.[5] A forestry-based example is found in the decentralized agroforestry system in the Nordic countries, where forests – which are mostly not monoculture tree plantations but include multiple species – are owned predominantly by a wide array of families (see Kuisma *et al.* 1999; Nylund 2009).

Harvey (2003: 145–46) argues that the primitive accumulation identified by Marx is still powerfully present, as "many formerly common property resources, such as water, have been privatized (often at World Bank insistence) and brought within the capitalist logic of accumulation" and "family farming has been taken over by agribusiness," especially in the global South. For Sassen (2010: 25), the focus of the current logic of capitalism is not "the 'valuing' of people as workers and consumers, but the expulsion of people and the destruction of traditional capitalisms to feed the needs of high finance and the needs for natural resources."

Sassen's point on labor/capital has recently been confirmed and strengthened by Li's (2011) work on "recentering labor in the land grab debate." Li's labor perspective highlights the lack of jobs generated, illustrating that large-scale land acquisition, promoted by the World Bank and many governments, is unlikely to result in poverty reduction: "In much of the global South, the anticipated transition from the farm to factory has not taken place and education offers no solution, as vast numbers of educated people are unemployed" (Li 2011: 281). Agribusiness expansion "excludes" traditional rural communities from customary land rights (and thus jobs), intensifies the power of financial capital, and in the best case, only leaves conditional options for "incorporation" (Li 2011; Sassen 2010). Far larger numbers of people are "expelled" than "incorporated," however. The expansion of eucalyptus plantations and the simultaneous dispossession and curbing of agrarian reform in Brazil is a case in point.

Dispossession

Between the 1960s and 1980s, tree plantation companies acquired Brazilian land through harsh means. In many regions, the land access mechanisms depicted in a Ministry of the Environment report are still common:

> Before the company establishes itself in the region, men arrive wearing the clothes of rich farmers, driving pick-ups and wanting to buy land from small producers. Even though it was argued that there were no cases of death or explicit physical violence, the non-articulation and non-organization of local farmers put them into too vulnerable a position to take an informed decision.
>
> (MMA 2005: 37)

The Pastoral Land Commission (CPT) has extensively documented since its finding in 1975 both indirect and direct brutal rural violence (including murders, slavery, criminalization of resistance and deprivation of livelihoods) inherent in (tree) plantation expansion.[6] For example, in the state of Amapá, the court found Champion, a company exporting trees for pulp production, guilty of acquiring land illegally, using *grileiros* and extortion (MMA 2005: 37).[7] Some of these accounts led to the transfer of tree plantation lands back to traditional communities.

In the states of Pará, Amapá and Maranhão, particularly, plantations destined to produce pulp or charcoal drove ancient communities and small-scale farmers from their lands. A Parliamentary Investigation (CPI)[8] in 2004 recommended that 370,000 ha of state land occupied by the eucalyptus plantations of the multinational corporation Jarí Celulose be parceled and distributed to subsistence farmers in an attempt to resolve the land conflicts resulting from massive dispossession (MMA 2005: 40). During the 1960s and 1970s, the Jarí Project in Brazil invaded indigenous land, "like most other MNCs [multinational corporations]" (Arruda *et al.* 1975: 164). This occurred all around the world, not just in Brazil; as Marchak (1995: 14) alleges, "where there are still indigenous peoples, both forestry in natural stands and plantations deprive them of land. Typically, they are dispersed or pushed to the margins of the forest." According to the North American Congress on Latin America (NACLA), the company Aracruz Celulose in Espírito Santo:

> Illegally appropriated land from the Tupinikim and Guarani, building its first factory in an *aldeia* called Macacos. This was easy, since there were no formal registers of indigenous populations or their lands. Moreover, the corporation had the full support of municipal, state, and federal

40 *Accumulation by dispossession*

governments, and was able to acquire land through a variety of ways, including *grilagem*, or falsifying deeds.

(Kenfield 2007: 10)

During the military dictatorship (1964–84), pulp companies such as Aracruz enclosed peasant, Indian and Quilombo lands, driving communities out of forests (Ferreira 2009; Myllylä and Takala 2011). This has left a legacy of complex land conflicts surrounding contemporary pulp businesses in the places where rural populations were displaced and where resistance movements have managed to mobilize and bring their grievances to public knowledge, as the next chapter argues. These conflicts are the result of both predatory schemes and latent conflicts given impetus through the introduction of forest companies into the areas.

Illegal land grabbing, or *grilagem*, is a commonly used mechanism for creating private property in Brazil, particularly in the "pioneer" frontiers where capitalism expands into "Deep Brazil": many military government officials supported and/or used it as an unofficial tool for creating large-scale properties for themselves or others (Asselin 2009). All of the ninety-five activists interviewed, as well as two of the ten contract farmers and eleven of the twenty-one public officials interviewed, suggested that pulp companies accessed land through *grilagem* which led to dispossession. None of the twenty-four pulp industry representatives interviewed said directly that companies would have used *grilagem*, even though firms (such as Veracel), which have been caught planting on community lands, have claimed they were unaware of having bought land illegally grabbed previously by the seller (Kröger and Nylund 2012). Ferreira (2009) has done extensive and well-documented research in notary offices in Espírito Santo showing in detail how communal land ended up in the hands of Aracruz via *grilagem*. Another example is the new Suzano pulp venture at Imperatriz in the Eastern Amazon state of Maranhão which used a thickly forested land populated by indigenous and traditional communities (now mostly deforested) to expand its eucalyptus plantations within a land grab trajectory that started in the 1970s (author's fieldwork, spring 2011). The "grilagem arrived as the best instrument of [capital's] domination, turning the so-called 'free' lands into capitalism's privileged means of incorporation" (Asselin 2009: 29). Multilateral agencies and governments have supported this process by offering extensive incentives for plantations.

Governments have also controlled who is defined as a "landowner" or a "squatter," and the procedures by which one could "legally" ratify a landholder status; the Quilombo and indigenous populations living in forests were in the worst position to be able to defend their case. The forest land they used was seized at zero cost by companies backed by governments. To prevent this from happening, the communities would have had to demarcate and register their lands in notary offices, and the state Department of Lands and Cartography would have had to approve their claims. In Espírito Santo, for

Accumulation by dispossession 41

example, the state was much more inclined to name the community lands as "unused" and as having no owner with land deeds (*terra devoluta*), and thus state land, available to be given to Aracruz. This was a form of juridical expropriation, an institutionalized and legalized *grilagem* (Ferreira 2009).

While similar effects were visible with other forms of agricultural expansion, the creation of a tree plantation-based paper industry was a key developmental goal of the military dictatorship (Kröger and Nylund 2012), and the role of the state was more prominent. Whereas cattle ranch expansion on the northern pioneer frontier was often organized by private farmer groups from the south (Jepson 2006),[9] eucalyptus expansion was more clearly a state-led project. The dispossession was therefore more complete, leaving fewer or no clear channels for embedded autonomy of movements in political games: state institutions – the last resort for claims – were not impartial. For example, during the dictatorship, the state of Espírito Santo created the Institute of Agroforestry Development (IDAF) to oversee the process. In spite of requests by the National Institute of Colonization and Agrarian Reform (INCRA) and indigenous movements, IDAF has not opened up its archives to explain how *devoluta* lands were defined (Ferreira 2009).

Brazil's industrial forestry policy

In my analysis of corporate agency, profit, investment and market gains and losses are not independent of the influence of the state, which has a central role. The "free markets" were planned, as Polanyi (2001 [1944]) already has claimed. As a Canadian pulp company director argued, "Adam Smith's invisible hand will not build pulp mills" (George Landegger, cf. Carrere and Lohmann 1996: 103). Plantation expansion is explainable by the strategic decisions of companies and their allies in the government, which evaluates the importance of a given area for investment purposes, and activates support policies in order to promote corporate agency and thus expand exploitation.

The working model of policy makers in developing the forest industry sector is clearly stated in a National Development Bank (BNDES) report as a cooperation between state, multinationals and national investors: "In the 60s, 70s and 80s, BNDES was an instrument guaranteeing the triple alliance between state, multinationals and national private investors. The planning, the follow-up and the financing of the pulp and paper industry by the Bank are a good example of this model" (Juvenal and Mattos 2002: 1). This followed Brazil's general industrial policy (Evans 1979). The state provided policy support through national forestry and pulp and paper industry plans, legislation and other regulative structures and, above all, through access to credit on relatively easy terms (Bull *et al.* 2006). The establishment of ITPs was essentially "free" and even had the potential to provide a net gain: due to fiscal incentives, the rate of return for landowners planting eucalyptus was 663% (assuming zero land cost) (Bull *et al.* 2006: 19, 25–26).[10]

42 *Accumulation by dispossession*

The Center for International Forestry Research (CIFOR) argues that incentives to the paper industry led to market distortions and ecological hazards: "Subsidies led to a greater concentration of land ownership and an increase in deforestation" (Cossalter and Pye-Smith 2003: 38). According to the Brazilian Ministry of the Environment (MMA 2005: 52),[11] the military government imposed the industrial plantation model with an iron fist, and "all attempts to rectify the situation were treated with the same formula of ignore-deny-suffocate." Under the dictatorship, especially the Geisel government, rural development was based on large enterprises. This removed "petty production units, intensifying the proletarianisation of the Brazilian countryside and, simultaneously, marginalizing a large sector of the rural population" in a labor-transforming process in which the pulp entrepreneurs (such as the Norwegian Lorenzen of Aracruz, and Jarí's owner, the American Daniel Ludwig) played "an important role as a corporate agent" (Arruda *et al.* 1975: 185).

Brazil's governments have continued to pursue a macroeconomic policy in which developmental projects are focused on resource exports. In 2009, the BNDES lent US$69 billion, most of it going to the developmental projects of large corporations – an amount that far exceeded the World Bank loan book (*The Economist* 2010). BNDES financing has been the main force behind the highly capital-intensive pulp projects that have territorialized Brazil with such vigor since the late 1990s. Eucalyptus plantations require higher investments than the expansion of other industrial crops (Fingerl and Filho 1998): a new million-ton pulp investment costs over €1 billion, while plantations cost €250–300 million. As a result, establishing production capacity is largely dependent on available state financing. Brazilian pulp entrepreneurs are in a privileged position (Kingstone 1999: 234–35). Figure 2.1 shows the finance provided by the Brazilian government-controlled BNDES to the paper and pulp industry (BNDES 2009),[12] and the annual expansion of eucalyptus plantations destined for pulp production (Bracelpa 2009).[13] Particularly since 2000, the dramatic expansion of eucalyptus plantation lands has been paralleled by the surge of state funding: there is co-movement over time between state funding and expansion.

Pulp investments using fast-wood eucalyptus have managed to repay BNDES loans in record time (four to eight years), so financially it makes sense to invest in the expansion. BNDES provided half of the investment credits for Bahian Veracel Celulose and most of the credit for founding the new pulp giant Fibria, which enabled Votorantim Celulose e Papel (VCP) to buy Aracruz in 2009 (*Correio Braziliense,* "Demissões nas papeleiras," May 4, 2009). The state financing of "Big Pulp" is in line with the general political economic strategy of Brazil (Kröger 2012b). Lessa (2010), a prominent Brazilian economist and former BNDES president, argues that Brazil's economic stability in the past decade is principally based on the high prices of commodities. Structural questions such as extreme inequality are not discussed or addressed and the private sector is dominated by a rentier oligarchy

Accumulation by dispossession 43

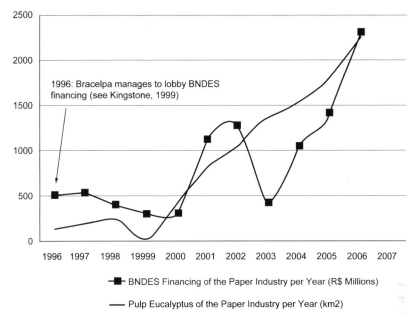

Figure 2.1 The correlation of state financing and pulp/eucalyptus plantation expansion per year in Brazil, 1996–2007
Note: Values on the y-axis are nominal; BNDES credits are shown in millions of reais; plantation expansion is shown in km^2
Source: For financing, BNDES 2009; for plantation expansion, Bracelpa 2009)

that is neither interested nor willing to invest its own money, and therefore looks for speculative, state-backed opportunities. These are all signs of the dominance of the financial logic of accumulation by dispossession in the current phase of global and Brazilian capitalism, which will be confirmed in the following broadly systematic and more detailed analyses of the data.

Systematic comparison across states

The best data available from state, industry, civil society and research institutes have been collected in Tables 2.1 and 2.2, allowing us to draw statistical inferences and assess correlations and anomalies across the major eucalyptus pulp-producing states. In Table 2.1, corporate land access types were divided into owned, rented/partnership and outsourced, to see if these different forms show any relation to signs of primitive accumulation in areas of states where eucalyptus pulp plantations expanded in 2004–10. The numbers include only eucalyptus plantations of pulp companies, not those of other industries or plantations of other tree species. Table 2.1 also shows the relationship between land price and dispossession, based on general state-level data on land prices and displacement.[14]

44 Accumulation by dispossession

Figure 2.2 Veracel pulp mill from the inside, Eunápolis, July 2006. The bleached pulp is ready to be shipped to the world
Source: Photograph © the author

Table 2.1 shows a correlation between low land prices and higher displacement of families by land conflicts: the three states with the highest displacement in 2010 (Maranhão, Pará, Bahia) had the lowest pasture land prices in 2006. According to the pulp companies, most eucalyptus expansion was onto former pasture lands: as companies moved into the peripheries with low land prices, rural families with unclear land tenure relations have been pushed, directly or indirectly, off the lands. Higher land prices, on the other hand, which are a sign of less peripheral settings, act as a barrier against accumulation by dispossession, which is by definition interested primarily in seizing control of assets at zero or low cost (Harvey 2003). Paraná is an example of high land prices and relatively low expulsion rates; the process is happening there as well, but to a lesser degree. The limited primitive accumulation in Paraná also correlates with the distribution of corporate-owned and rented/outsourced eucalyptus land: this is the state in which access is most equally distributed between the three categories (52% of total eucalyptus land is rented or outsourced, the rest is corporate owned), signifying that revenues from sold wood or land use are more equally distributed.

Table 2.2 reduces the information in Table 2.1 into one column, labeled "accumulation by dispossession" (ABD), which is the price of land divided by

Accumulation by dispossession 45

Table 2.1 Land access type, land price and dispossession in Brazil, 2006–10

State	Planted area ('000 ha) by corporate land access type in 2009: a) owned, b) rented, c) outsourced[1]			Average price of pasture land in 2006, reais per ha[2]	Families displaced by all land conflicts in 2010[3]
	a	b	c		
Bahia	369	9	121	1,297	4,327
Espírito Santo	129	1	41	3,882	1,335
Maranhão	47	0	0	184	13,071
Mato Grosso do Sul	89	65	1	1,613	784
Minas Gerais	155	16	49	3,100	2,457
Pará	48	0	1	601	9,225
Paraná	51	12	45	5,900	585
Rio Grande do Sul	150	17	19	3,128	111
São Paulo	224	88	58	7,500	1,646
Total	1,286	211	340		

Notes:
1 Data on pulpwood extension and ownership type in '000 ha on 31 December 2009 (Bracelpa 2010: 12); only states with more than 16,000 ha of eucalyptus plantations were included in the analysis.
2 Source: Gasques *et al.* 2008: 9.
3 Includes all conflicts involving dispossession, expulsion, shootings and takeover of capital, ITP and non-ITP related (CPT 2011).

the number of families dispossessed: the lower the number, the higher the ABD in the state. The ABD is then compared with the nature of the dispossession, in terms of the presence (or absence) of typical signs of ABD in the eucalyptus pulpwood areas of that state. Fieldwork observations on four central and illustrative traits of primitive accumulation by eucalyptus expansion were coded in as columns in Table 2.2 (yes or no signifying their existence or not): occupation of agrarian reform lands/expulsion of peasants; planting on indigenous or Afro-Brazilian territories; killing of or violence against rural people directly linked to companies and the police (at times directly financed by the pulp companies); and replacement of native vegetation (forests, cerrado, pampa) by plantations. The particular indicators for each observation are listed in footnotes.

Table 2.2 shows that Maranhão (ABD 0.014), Pará (ABD figure 0.065) and Bahia (0.299) are the states where accumulation by dispossession has been most common: the land prices have been the lowest and the number of dispossessed families the highest. Next follow Minas Gerais, Mato Grosso do Sul, Espírito Santo and São Paulo, with ABD figures ranging from 1.261 to 4.556. Paraná (10.085) and Rio Grande do Sul (28.180) are in a rank of their own, with the least sign of general accumulation by dispossession. It is interesting to compare these figures with the pulp conflicts. Fieldwork and

46   *Accumulation by dispossession*

Table 2.2 Accumulation by dispossession, and signs of eucalyptus expansion-related dispossession in Brazil (yes or no), 2004–10

State	Accumulation by dispossession (the lower the figure, the higher the ABD in the state in general)	Nature and existence of dispossession in pulp investment areas			
		Peasants expelled/ agrarian reform land occupied	Planting on indigenous or Afro-Brazilian territories	Killing of/ violence against rural people	Plantation replaced native vegetation
Bahia	0.299	Yes[1]	Yes[2]	Yes[3]	Yes[4]
Espírito Santo	2.907	Yes[5]	Yes[6]	Yes[7]	Yes[8]
Maranhão	0.014	Yes[9]	Yes[10]	No[11]	Yes[12]
Mato Grosso do Sul	2.057	Yes[13]	No	No	No
Minas Gerais	1.261	Yes[14]	Yes[15]	Yes[16]	Yes[17]
Pará	0.065	Yes[18]	Yes[19]	No	Yes
Paraná	10.085	No[20]	No	No	No
Rio Grande do Sul	28.180	Yes[21]	No	Yes[22]	Yes[23]
São Paulo	4.556	Yes[24]	No	No	No

Notes:

1 Responsible companies Veracel, Fibria and Suzano; location extreme south of Bahia; thousands of peasants expelled and agrarian reform impeded (Kröger and Nylund 2012).

2 Veracel planted on Pataxó indigenous lands near the Monte Pascoal (author fieldwork 2004–11).

3 A Quilombola man killed by the armed security force of Fibria in 2010.

4 Thousands of hectares of Atlantic rainforest cut down by Veracel (ex-Veracruz) in the 1990s (Fase *et al.* 1993).

5 Responsible company Fibria (ex-Aracruz); author fieldwork 2004–09; see also de'Nadai *et al.* (2005); MMA (2005).

6 More than 8,000 Quilombola families expelled by Aracruz, 1970s–2005; tens of thousands of hectares of indigenous land occupied by Aracruz (Ferreira 2009).

7 Indigenous people beaten by police at the orders of Aracruz (13 were wounded in 2006); Quilombos mistreated by the police (Ferreira 2009; www.cddh.com.br).

8 Massive destruction of rainforest since 1970s by Aracruz (MMA 2005).

9 Main company Suzano, located in the Imperatriz and Baixo Parnaíba regions; observation of peasant exodus and agrarian reform impediment during fieldwork (March 2011).

10 Afro-Brazilian territories occupied by Suzano (author fieldwork March 2011, see also Barros 2008).

11 Suzano not involved in this activity, according to fieldwork (March 2011). The 'no' in here and other cases does not necessarily signify the issue has not occurred; it means that it was not observed in the field or reported in the material covered in this research.

12 Rural population and state authorities reported Suzano would be cutting rainforest in some places.

13 Pulp expansion and agrarian reform impediment at Três Lagoas, main companies Fibria, International Paper (Kudlaviz 2011) and Eldorado Paper under construction, owned by JBS-Friboi, a Brazilian meat company.

14 Main companies Cenibra and International Paper; over 60% of the state's municipalities have long had tree plantations, with severe problems related to rural exodus (MMA 2005: 118–68).

15 Quilombos expelled (see MMA 2005).

16 Slavery, child labor and other drastic violations of human rights still exist in the tree plantations of Minas Gerais (though mostly on charcoal plantations) (MMA 2005: 118–68).

17 Source: MMA (2005).

18 The parliament recommend that company Jári, located at the border with Amapá state, return 370,000 hectares of occupied lands to communities (MMA 2005: 39).

Accumulation by dispossession 47

19 Jári planted on indigenous lands (MMA 2005).
20 The data did not reveal that Paraná would have had considerable expulsion of peasants by pulp eucalyptus in the past years; the main company is Klabin, and its mills are small scale.
21 Tens of thousands of hectares of agrarian reform land (already marked by state authorities) occupied together by Aracruz and Votorantim (now Fibria) and Stora Enso; expansion located in the southern half of the state (pampa).
22 Killing of a landless movement activist in 2009 by police in a conflict with Aracruz; beating of demonstrators by police in 2008 by Stora Enso; orders of eviction (author fieldwork 2008–09).
23 Planted eucalyptus on fragile pampa areas (fieldwork observation May 2008, also Miola 2010).
24 Several communities displaced; agrarian reform made difficult; plantations located close to the state capital (MMA 2005).

interviews revealed that in the latter two states, the landless movements were mostly attracting people from the cities' *favelas* (shanty towns) as there were no longer many rural dwellers. In Rio Grande do Sul, disputes were centered on trying to occupy large tracts of unused *latifúndio* farms (latifundia, "The predominance of large, sometimes extremely large landholdings" (Miller 2007: 101)) to push for direct action land reform where INCRA is pushed to establish agrarian reform settlement before a pulp company could buy the same land tract for eucalyptus planting. However, the other, more specific signs of dispossession were present in pulp conflicts, particularly in the form of pre-emptive enclosure of suitable land and the use of violence against activists.

Within the pulp industry, Bahia, Espírito Santo and Minas Gerais show the strongest signs of primitive accumulation, with all four sub-categories of the process active during the observation period. Expansion by pulp companies in Rio Grande do Sul, Pará and Maranhão showed mid-range primitive accumulation, with three of the four signs observable. Even though high in general ABD terms, Maranhão and Pará did not experience notable pulp plantation expansion between 2004–10, and killing of/violence against rural people was not present. However, the situation has changed since 2010, with massive new investment in Maranhão (and most of the neighboring states) principally by Suzano. In São Paulo one sign was active, in Mato Grosso do Sul one, and in Paraná none. These three states also have a more balanced distribution of corporate access between owned, rented/partnership/outsourced plantations (39%, 42% and 52%, respectively) than the states where more numerous signs of primitive accumulation were observed (Bahia = 26% of total eucalyptus land rented or outsourced; Espírito Santo = 24%; Minas Gerais = 29%). This suggests a correlation between corporate land concentration and primitive accumulation and dispossession. Yet, there are new large-scale pulp projects in the pipeline in these states, potentially altering the situation.

Dispossession was influenced by the large-scale investment style and by context. In the states with fewer signs of primitive accumulation, the context of plantation expansion was important: in these areas, there were fewer (or no) indigenous and Afro-Brazilian communities to dispossess, and less native vegetation to be replaced in the flat, fertile land of these pulp project

48 *Accumulation by dispossession*

areas. With the exception of Paraná and Pará, in all the other cases investment was on a large scale – projects larger than 800,000 tons of pulp per year, requiring at least 80,000 ha of eucalyptus plantations, plus a similar amount in conservation areas which are thus blocked for other uses by rural populations.

Primitive land access: dynamics and consequences

Across Brazil, forest companies are still expanding into dubious land tenure areas such as state lands (*terra devoluta*) and planting eucalyptus; however, these companies are now increasingly finding themselves involved in land conflicts with resistance movements and the dispossessed wanting to reclaim or redistribute these state lands. Traditional populations want their lands back, supported by some state institutions within the now democratic Brazil, though the conservative and authoritarian minded – such as the Ministry of Agriculture and Ministério da fazenda, and both military and federal police forces – side with the companies. As Chapters 3 and 4 discuss, the federal government and state institutions have a complex role vis-à-vis tree plantations, as state institutions represent contradictory platforms of interest mediation. The main cleavage point is between a technocratic developmental ideology relying on massive corporate-state investment as the promoter of development, and a grassroots ideology emphasizing local democracy and agro-ecological human capital and livelihoods to preserve the model of accumulation without dispossession (Nylund and Kröger 2012).[15]

According to Oliveira (2011), about 60% of Brazilian rural "properties" do not have legal titling: these are illegally held and fenced lands, and legally belong to the state. Large tracts of land used for eucalyptus monocultures probably fall into this category of state land; however, it is hard to prove correct titling, as this relies on accounts of local citizens forced out of their lands, on company accounts, or on haphazardly and confusingly collected state or government data. Even so, some advances have been made by progressive prosecutors and movements within this area, as illustrated in the next chapters.

The state, particularly in the form of state-owned companies, facilitated the flow of land and nature (natural resources) from communities to corporations. According to locals, the firm Aracruz cut tens of thousands of hectares of Atlantic rainforest in Espírito Santo in the 1970s. In 1992–93, Veracruz, predecessor of Veracel and at the time a subsidiary of the Odebrecht Group, also felled thousands of hectares of forestland. Locals and activists from the NGOs Fase, Greenpeace and Ibase took aerial photos, gathered personal accounts from locals, logging company contracts and other documents to demonstrate that between 1992–93 Veracruz cut extensive areas of Atlantic forest within the 47,000 ha area Veracruz had acquired in 1991 from the Brazilian iron-ore company Vale do Rio Doce (CVRD, now Vale). The data were assembled by the NGOs into an extensive dossier (Fase *et al.* 1993) and used as a legal document.[16] CVRD, state-owned until 1997, was a central

Accumulation by dispossession 49

agent in almost all eucalyptus expansion areas, playing a key role in facilitating the conversion of state forest lands into ITP concessions operated by charcoal and pulp companies. This relationship still continues today (under Vale), for example in Maranhão, where Vale sold tens of thousands of hectares of eucalyptus plantations to Suzano, agreed to transport the pulp by the railroads it operates, and defended the pulp company against resistance.[17]

Besides environmental destruction, dispossession and repression of small-scale farming, debt slavery and other "modern" forms of slavery that are dominated by the financial logic of capitalism still exist in the Brazilian countryside. Companies such as Jarí, Votorantim, Suzano de Papel e Celulose (the second largest maker of paper and cardboard products in Brazil), Eucatex (the fourth largest wood products company), and Ripasa Celulose (which was the fifth largest paper producer) have been accused of enslavement within the paper and pulp industry (Rose 2005: 224–25). However, most cases of slavery are related to the production of charcoal in the northern pig-iron milling regions of the country.[18]

The expansion of tree plantations is still subject to brutal violence and occasional murders. In February 2007, an armed guard of the French-German steel producer and tree planting company Vallourec and Mannesmann (VM), murdered Antonio Joaquim dos Santos on a eucalyptus plantation certified by the Forest Stewardship Council (FSC) in Minas Gerais. Antonio Joaquim dos Santos was a thirty-two year-old agricultural worker from the Canabrava community which had been dispossessed of its land and denied access to basic natural resources through the expansion of tree plantations since 1975. "Seizing Antonio Joaquim, the two armed guards hired by VM, known as C and J de Casmina, tied him up, hit him and fired two shots into his mouth in front of his daughter," according to a communiqué on 27 February 2007 by the Alert against the Green Desert Network (WRM 2007), the most vehement opponent of tree plantation expansion. The company Aracruz, currently Fibria, has also been involved in manslaughter cases: the armed security force of Fibria killed a local villager, a young Afro-Brazilian man from a Quilombola community, in southern Bahia in March 2010 after he collected firewood from the plantation (Socio-Environmental Forum of the Extreme South of Bahia and Alert against the Green Desert Network 2010). The Quilombola community had been excluded from its lands by pulp companies which did not allow traditional wood collection on "community lands" to continue after enclosure of the eucalyptus enclaves on these former community holdings (Ferreira 2009). In terms of ethno-territorialism, pulp companies have been accused of racist attitudes towards indigenous and Afro-Brazilian communities, which is evident in many company practices and director discourses (Ferreira 2009; Myllylä and Takala 2011).

As a consequence, many (but not all) pulp companies face growing resistance: Veracel is currently experiencing the most pressure. The company claims to have incurred severe losses due to twenty-seven current occupations of their land: opponents claim the land is state land and illicitly occupied by

Figure 2.3 Members of a Brazilian Landless Rural Workers' Movement (MST) camp in northeastern Rio de Janeiro, March 2004
Source: Photograph © the author

Veracel. For example, on 4 April 2011, the landless movements occupied another land area allegedly owned by Veracel, cut down eucalyptus trees and blocked the company's access to a wide area of fiber urgently needed to run the mill.[19] These protests are having an increasingly direct impact on business profits.

The Baixa Verde camp of the MLT (Movement for Land Liberation) near to Eunápolis is another example. In the 1960s and 1970s, the area's forest land was cleared and settled by cattle ranchers, wood loggers and small-scale tenant farmers, and part of the land was registered as private property. However, the land had *terra devoluta* status – that is, it was state land to be used for parceling for farming families, as later confirmed by the relevant authorities of Bahia, the Coordination of Agrarian Development (CDA). In 2000, the alleged owner Veracel forced the settlers to move and the area was planted with eucalyptus.[20] Eucalyptus plantations were quickly extended to the settlement lands. By 2006, the area was completely occupied by eucalyptus, which had even been planted on a communal cemetery, without the required permits and without respect for the local community. All the villagers' houses were demolished and the residents were forced to live in poor urban conditions. MLT coordinators united desperate families ready to return

Accumulation by dispossession 51

to the countryside, and during a "blitz" occupation in November 2008, the locals returned and took over the area where the company grew eucalyptus. Black plastic bag shelters housed dozens of families, waiting for the return of lands which, having officially been declared as state land, could not be appropriated by the company for its own use. According to the CDA, the land in question (Fazenda São Caetano, an area of 1,333 ha) does not belong to Veracel, even if the company alleges it does: this state land is to be delivered back to the farmers in the form of a settlement. The resistance used all strategies a–e in this case (see Chapter 1), leading to re-conversion of corporate land back to community agriculture.

The financial logic of expansion and exclusion

Not all tree plantation expansion involves dispossession, corruption, repression, slavery and murder. Some expansion occurs in the form of business transactions where land changes hands through markets, although some "proprietors" (land grabbers) sell their land to pulp companies illegally.

In the early phase of expansion during the military dictatorship, outright fraud in land sales was common, and the main reason for smallholders to sell was the promise of getting legal land titles promised by brokers. There has been a constant effort since the dictatorship to seduce rural families to move to cities: the "brokers" involved typically argued that life would be better in the city, particularly for the children. They offered to take care of the whole process, legalizing land for dwellers that had a right to it by law, but in fact stealing land by demarcating a smaller area for the families than that to which they actually had rights, and then selling the stolen land to pulp companies. If there were no legal documents showing land ownership, the "right to use" land was sold. If the rural dweller did not want to sell the "right to use" land and plant on it, then the company asked for land directly from the state (Ferreira 2009).

In the area where Veracel is situated, as in most other expansion areas, large unproductive landowners used (and still use) the arrival of the pulp company to liberate themselves profitably from the historical burden of land grab, turning the grabbed land into cash by selling it and thus escaping the risk of land appropriation.[21] Usually, the act of selling land is legally endorsed, even though the land might be state land. It was beyond the scope of this research to gather sufficient information from the thousands of smallholders who had sold their lands in the expansion areas to analyze systematically the reasons for contemporary selling: however, the few interviews gathered illustrate individual reasons for selling, and these are discussed below. Those most aware of the rural exodus phenomenon, such as public officials and rural organization leaders, were interviewed to get a general picture.

Some of these small-scale sellers, as well as rural workers whose tenant relations with the large farms where they used to live and work are severed

52 *Accumulation by dispossession*

when the owners sell lands, end up in landless camps or settlements, although most find themselves in urban *favelas*. For example, in Eunápolis municipality, where the Veracel mill is located, 7,000 rural families left their homes between 1996 and 2000: for example, most of the 800 people on a land area bought by Veracel had to leave their houses, thereby also losing their livelihoods (Lerrer and Wilkinson 2012). Visiting dozens of urban and rural peripheries in almost all eucalyptus-expansion areas allowed for personal observations, and interviews illustrated the causal mechanisms in rural exodus. Some sell their land because they want to, and understand the results of the decision, i.e. the difficulty or impossibility of returning to the land as a farmer. Others sell because life becomes increasingly difficult for them, isolated in a sea of silent eucalyptus trees, as often happens in pulp and charcoal investment areas. In charcoal areas, pollution is another reason to move out, and complaints about water depletion were documented by the author at almost all rural communities close to eucalyptus.

For people whose neighbors have moved out, the pressure to follow is great. The main theme that surfaced in the fieldwork was the same as in the 1970s and 1980s: farmers were seduced to sell their land for the sake of a better future in a city, particularly for their children, rather than on a farm increasingly surrounded by walls of eucalyptus and with fewer neighbors and public services. This domino effect was the main reason for "voluntary" contemporary selling.[22] Tree plantation companies recognize this: they benefit from a domino mechanism of buying one farm and then waiting for the others to fall. The effect is revealed in the personal histories of people faced with eucalyptus plantations in their area. Many rural residents do not want to live next to eucalyptus plantations, as they perceive them to be ugly and potentially dangerous. People are concerned that the pesticides and fertilizers used will spread to their lands and water, and that eucalyptus offers excellent hideouts for criminals. Eucalyptus is aesthetically ugly to many and is associated with subordination. For the local MST activists, the plant represented "multinational companies with money" and "capital, which condemns," and the monoculture is seen as a "Babylon of capital."[23] Rows of orderly trees blocking the extended view do not fit traditional pastoral ideals.

Besides the isolation, a further reason for selling land to companies is debt. Farmers take extensive risks on "Green Revolution" agriculture, where financial logic rests uneasily with the volatility of agriculture. Soils may erode and the intensive use of fertilizers and herbicides (often demanded by lending institutions) harm the land; as a result, farmers' incomes drop and they often become bankrupt; banks then foreclose on the lands and the plantation industry buys them. The debt problem is intensified by Brazil having one of the world's highest interest rates, which means that farmers have little time to look for the best offer when the downturn comes. In comparison to agribusiness, the access to credit for non-corporate agriculture is still limited, even though the Ministry of Agrarian Development has given more credit to small-scale farmers since the mid-1990s (Wolford 2010a).

Figure 2.4 Veracel's outgrower eucalyptus plantation, Eunápolis, Bahia, Brazil, June 2004
Source: Photograph © the author

Exclusion by rising land prices

A rise in land prices is causing a pre-emptive barrier to land distribution attempts.[24] Land prices in Brazil have soared dramatically.[25] In 2006, the land price in Bahia's eucalyptus zones was four to six times higher than a few years previously.[26] Field research interviews with company officials and locals revealed land prices rose from 200 reais per hectare to 6,000 reais per hectare in pulp project areas in the ten years up to 2006 (see also Koopmans 2005; Souza and Overbeek 2008). In general, in many places across Brazil large-scale land acquisition during the past decade rendered family-sized to medium-sized food-producing agricultural units unviable and made agrarian reform difficult, if not impossible, as the state land reform agency could not compete with industry in the buying of land.[27]

Particularly in the 100-km perimeter around pulp projects, land reform and tree plantations struggle for good land, not because land is lacking, but because increases in the price of land mean that landowners, principally cattle ranchers, are unwilling to sell their land for INCRA's agrarian reform at the lower price offered by the state. The prospects for land reform are further weakened by the introduction of temporary and outsourced wage work that fosters the creation of rural landless would-be workers instead of smallholders

54 *Accumulation by dispossession*

controlling or owning lands, based on family and collective farming. Sassen (2010) argues that in primitive accumulation traditional capitalisms are destroyed to transnationalize natural resources. In the mix of market-based agrarian policies and violent forms of land access that are the hallmark of the advance of Brazilian eucalyptus primitive accumulation, landless populations are the losers as the financial logic offers corporations more room to maneuver.

Concluding remarks

The advance of industrial tree plantations is an example of the current phase of global capitalism, which is dominated by financial logic and exploits resource peripheries (Sassen 2010), a process Harvey (2003) calls accumulation by dispossession. The rise of agribusiness and new pulp investments provide empirical evidence to support the claim that land is increasingly considered a financial asset, especially in the government and business sectors but also in many rural communities, through the sale of land. Corporate land access and expansion take place through a mixture of violence and financial mechanisms, most of which lead to capital accumulation through direct or indirect dispossession of traditional communities.

Fast-wood expansion is carried out by traditional forms of primitive accumulation (in which human and other life forms are expelled, commons enclosed, alternative modes of wood production suppressed, neo-colonial-type settings such as free-trade areas established, and even slavery used in some cases), as well as by new mechanisms of accumulation by dispossession (in which tree variants are cloned and patented, the need of rural and industrial labor is minimized through mechanization, and major state and multinational banks support the process by lending to large-scale corporations or investing in resource extraction that either directly or indirectly displaces traditional forms of capitalist and non-capitalist communities). There have been isolated attempts in Brazil to promote accumulation without dispossession, but it is hard to see how they could succeed without considerable changes to the agrarian structure, government/corporate policies, the general political economic dynamics behind industrial plantation expansion, and the expansion model in which the majority of land is corporate owned or controlled. Entrenched power relations in rural areas have instead contributed to the strengthening of primitive accumulation via new mechanisms of accumulation by dispossession, providing a coherent explanatory framework for contemporary plantation expansion.

Systematic comparison of pulp eucalyptus expansion across Brazil, the presence or absence of four signs of primitive accumulation, and general data on land prices and differences in corporate land access type (Tables 2.1 and 2.2) suggest there are differences across contexts and/or companies. Signs of accumulation by dispossession were in general more common than their opposite,

Accumulation by dispossession 55

i.e. accumulation without dispossession. The large-scale, monoculture-based pulp investment model correlated with primitive accumulation. The lower the pasture land price in the state, the higher the dispossession of rural populations has been. The context heightened the impact: in general, the more companies outsourced or rented land instead of directly owning it, the fewer signs of primitive accumulation. However, even though this typically implies wider distribution of income and decreases in accumulation by dispossession, a more detailed look at the specifics of partnership and contract eucalyptus farming is needed to track particular causalities and developmental gains or opportunities. In many places, contract planting has been a middle-class business strongly controlled by companies, with peasants excluded or lacking autonomy. Chapter 5 will discuss the differences between smallholder and corporate tree planting, reviewing global expansion of tree plantations and resistance to them.

The ITP industry is exerting growing power over markets, national governments and states. Companies such as Stora Enso are such large players they can create markets through constructing huge pulp mills, such as Veracel: as one wood supply executive from Stora Enso expressed it, "I am the market." The new Brazilian pulp giant Fibria has considerable power in Brazil, as have had the steel giant Vale and local land markets, in the expansion of eucalyptus monocultures. The state plays a key role in giving preferential land titles and access to eucalyptus companies instead of peasants. Despite broad electoral campaign support from the pulp companies (see Chapter 4), however, Brazilian state actors do not totally favor industrial plantations. This is partly explained by the companies' own mistakes in running plantation operations and advocating the expansion of plantations in dubious ways, as shown by several disastrous cases. Yet, there is still room for things to get worse: the push by companies and large landholders to make environmental legislation more flexible is constant (Miola 2010; Gautreau and Vélez 2011). In 2012 they managed to impose a new forest code radically diminishing environmental protection and easing tree plantation (TP) expansion possibilities.

The dangers represented by eucalyptus expansion accompanied by dispossession of rural populations, violence, environmental degradation and decreasing employment are clear, and speak to a wider global phenomenon. In the words of Li (2011: 296), "the truncated trajectory of agrarian transition in much of the global South, one in which there is no pathway from country to city, agriculture to industry, or even a clear pathway into stable plantation work that pays a living wage, is the crucial scale at which to review the land grab debate." A patch of would-be eucalyptus monoculture land which remains in the hands of a peasant or indigenous tribe is a crucial safety net in the context of global capitalism where off-farm jobs that pay a living wage are scarce. However, primitive accumulation is being increasingly resisted across the globe in many areas. Corporate resource exploitation will continue to expand – if resistance is not present, as the next chapter argues.

56 *Accumulation by dispossession*

Notes

1 Parts of this chapter are developed upon analysis in Kröger (2012a).
2 Industrial plantations are defined as large-scale, non-family farms of four rural modules or larger. The size of rural modules varies according to municipality and state; four rural modules is a maximum of 440 ha, more typically 20 ha.
3 Brazil is the primary country globally in the planting of short-rotation *Eucalyptus grandis* and hybrids (Cossalter and Pye-Smith 2003: 7), the most common of them being *urograndis*.
4 The reason for this continuing state support to "national champions" such as pulp companies is that the Brazilian government has been engaged on a strategy of neo-mercantilist capitalism, as a way of increasing the clout of the most powerful national economic and political groups in the international political economy (Kröger 2012b).
5 Accumulation without dispossession can also be accumulation through productive investment, which still relies on individual ownership and labor exploitation (albeit to a lesser scale than primitive accumulation), even though forceful expulsion of rural populations does not occur.
6 See the CPT website: www.cptnacional.org.br.
7 A prevalent land acquiring mechanism – and the cause of many Brazilian land conflicts – is *grilagem* (illegal land grab), in which a *grileiro* falsifies documents to appropriate land illegally. The *grileiro* is normally a powerful patron with a prominent political, legal and economic position. *Grileiros* use different names and register smallholdings as individual farms, even though they belong to one family or enterprise and thus form a *latifúndio* farm (Asselin 2009).
8 CPI is a principal way of doing politics and investigating wrongdoings in Brazil, and is the focus of major political debates.
9 Although with some large state projects as well, such as the Projeto Grande Carajás in the eastern Amazon (Asselin 2009).
10 Capital inputs were minimal for landowners, given the banking arrangements whereby they received loans for silviculture with no borrowing costs (0% interest rate). The costs to the landowner would relate to the capital in the land purchase or the opportunity costs of capital. The rates of return for pine were lower because pine trees have a longer rotation age and lower yield.
11 The MMA has been one of the few state institutions, alongside the Public Ministry (Ministério Público) and the Ministry of Agrarian Development, that at some times and in some places has been critical towards the expansion, and embedded by movements.
12 The statistics on annual lending by BNDES are publicly available at: www.bndes.gov. br/SiteBNDES/bndes/bndes_pt/Institucional/BNDES_Transparente/Estatisticas_Ope racionais/setor.html. The Bank calculates the annual expenditure of resources from the BNDES System by sectors, including the paper and pulp industry.
13 Bracelpa is the lobby organization of the paper and pulp industry in Brazil, with a website offering data freely. The figures it gives are based on information it has received from its member companies. Thereafter, the figure does not include all eucalyptus expansion in Brazil (non-member companies and charcoal eucalyptus are excluded). Bracelpa is a powerful, but still relatively quite limited organization in comparison to, for example, the Finnish forest industry lobby Metsäteollisuus ry, which includes also the furniture, panel and construction sectors. Bracelpa limits itself to pulp and some paper. Bracelpa's political power vis-à-vis Brazilian government policy has been a significant factor behind the rapid expansion of pulp investments since the end of the 1990s (see also Kingstone 1999).
14 The last rural census in Brazil was conducted in 2006.

Accumulation by dispossession 57

15 There is a wide variety of alternative practices offered by the latter group, some more "socialist" in orientation (such as MST settlements) and others more "green capitalist" (such as forest communities and their advocates wishing to capitalize on standing forest through the carbon markets). The dynamics and blurring of the lines between peasants and agrarian capitalism are also present in other sectors, such as biofuels. For Fernandes *et al.* (2010: 816), even though some agrarian reform communities have benefited from entering into agrarian capitalism through agrofuel projects, the state/industry-peasant relationship is still hegemonic, as "no single production or nutritional policy in Brazil today has been developed in conjunction with or left under the administrative control of peasant organizations." In the case of eucalyptus plantations, attempts to incorporate peasant communities as producers have been rare, and have either been resisted outright, interrupted by state authorities as violating settlement legislation, or have failed in other ways. Most non-corporate tree plantation capitalism is carried out by middle-class, middle-sized farmer entrepreneurs closely tied to the industry. For further discussion on the cleavage between traditional communities and developmentalist projects, see Zhouri (2010).

16 After denunciations, the minister of the environment at the time, Fernando Coutinho Jorge, blocked the project turning Atlantic forest into eucalyptus plantations, demanding the federal environmental agency conduct studies prior to restarting the project; however, the state agency delegated the task to a private forestry consulting company, the Finnish Jaakko Pöyry, which, unsurprisingly, found no problems, and the project continued (Silvestre 2008).

17 This paragraph is based on interviews and field research in the area in March 2011.

18 Interview with Felicio Pontes, Federal Public Prosecutor, Pará, Belem (March 2011).

19 See press releases at www.mst.org.br and www.veracel.com.br.

20 Interviews with residents of the MLT Baixa Verde camp (26 March 2011).

21 Interviews with Arnoldo and Eduardo Prado, lawyers, medium-scale landowners and eucalyptus cultivators in Veracel's outgrower program (26 March 2011); interview with the coordinating prosecutor Silva Neto, Eunápolis (27 March 2011).

22 However, typically smallholder land selling constitutes the minor position of the overall land acquisition by companies, according to almost all those interviewed (activists, public officials, industry representatives, contract eucalyptus farmers): the main mechanism is large-scale land transaction involving cattle ranchers and possession of public lands.

23 Interviews with landless movement militants, Eunápolis, Bahía (June 2006).

24 Interviews with land institute officials (2004–11).

25 Between 2006 and 2008, land prices in Brazil increased due to the general commodity boom in world markets. In the south of Brazil, where three new huge pulp projects (Stora Enso, Votorantim, Aracruz) started to buy land for eucalyptus, land prices rose by 43.3%. In the south-east, prices rose by 36%, and in the north-east by 43.9% (Reuters News 2009).

26 Interviews with trade union leaders at the STR Eunápolis (2006).

27 Interview with Mozar Dietrich, Superintendent of the National Land Institute in Rio Grande do Sul (May 2008).

3 Contentious agency, the Brazilian landless movement and pulp conflict outcomes[1]

How do movements produce a growing sense of agency and self-worth, encouraging people to contest the prevailing development and seek major transformations? To answer this question, this chapter assesses how, and with what economic policy influence, an alternative social, symbolic and territorial system emerges, solidifies and fosters contentious agency – *sem terra* habitus in this case – while clashing in the contentious episodes occurring over investment projects.

This chapter summarizes the research results on how resistance influenced pulp investment in Brazil during 2004–08, and discusses the implications of the findings to the theory of contentious agency-role in natural resource politics. Research material collected by participant observation and in-depth interviews is ordered into a dataset by a qualitative comparative analysis (QCA) of resistance influence on the economic outcomes of all (thirteen) Brazilian large-scale pulp projects in 2004–08. The QCA methodology, developed by Ragin (1987), utilizes Boolean algebra to produce truth tables that allow for drawing causal inferences on a large number of explanative variables (strategies here) in a small N comparative case study. Although well known, QCA has not been widely used, as most social scientists opt for either non-systematic qualitative analysis or quantitative analysis, instead of attempting to fit small numbers of cases into rigorously systematic analyses of key factors (McAdam *et al.* 2001: 81). The technique allows the analysis of multiple causation and interaction effects. Ragin (2009) writes:

> Boolean methods of logical comparison represent each case as a combination of causal and outcome conditions ... The goal of the logical minimization is to represent – in a shorthand manner – the information in the truth table regarding the different combinations of conditions that produce a specific outcome.

The research applies the methodology and provides truth tables for the thirteen investment cases. As this is a logical and not a statistical technique, the comparable variables (in this case strategies) can have only two values (1 = active; 0 = inactive).

The Brazilian landless movement 59

There were three main reasons for adopting this methodology. First, I had a relatively small number of cases (N = 13), which made it hard to perform a quantitative analysis. Second, I wanted to make a comparison of different strategies and their relation to economic outcomes as comprehensive as possible. This technique answers both of these calls. It alleviates the small N problem by allowing inferences to be drawn from the maximum number of comparisons that can be made across the cases under analysis. Third, QCA fits well with strategy analysis, as strategies are best understood as being active (1) or inactive (0). The traditional QCA followed here does not allow evaluating the strengths of variables, or their probabilistic, statistical explanatory power, but relies on logical inference based on induction. In the case of variable-based research this is a problem; in a strategy- and process-based analysis this does not matter. Normally QCA has been applied on variable-based research; the methodological novelty here is to apply it in strategy and causal process analysis, by a relational approach to social dynamics for which there is great demand in social sciences.

The MST, contentious strategies and pulp investment outcomes

At dawn on April 4, 2004, MST activists cut the barbed wire leading to a eucalyptus plantation of Veracel in southern Bahia; these activists stepped in, uprooted 4 ha of eucalyptus and planted beans and corn. The movement justified this action of three thousand five hundred landless workers by noting that, "you cannot eat eucalyptus"; the framing was prominently reproduced by Brazil's largest daily newspaper *O Globo* (April 5, 2004). The protest was disruptive and aimed to transform public opinion on pulp investments and industrial plantations: "To cut the eucalyptus of a paper and pulp multinational is a symbolic gesture as was, some years ago, the destruction of a transgenic soy field in Rio Grande do Sul," explained a movement coordinator (*O Globo,* April 6, 2004). The response to the occupation and its results were swift. The government promised to appropriate land for MST families in the region in which Veracel operates, and thus the landless left the plantation (*O Estado de São Paulo*, April 9, 2004).

The Veracel occupation of 2004 managed to slow down plantation expansion, and several MST settlements established on the lands gained in the protest are now standing proof of this. Without the protest, these lands would have turned into eucalyptus plantations for Veracel, as the company was just about to plant trees in these areas. Due to this successful outcome, other MST groups around Brazil continued these protests, and other civil society actors aligned themselves with the MST's framings and campaign by creating ties with the movement and replicating its strategies. The findings here offer evidence suggesting that this has led to further cases of plantation expansion slowing, especially since 2007 and in the latter half of 2008. The expansion of plantations has not only been slowed or discontinued, but the lands saved

60 *The Brazilian landless movement*

from eucalyptus have also been earmarked for "food sovereignty" and "ethical" uses that Vía Campesina and others stipulate.

There is a wide body of research that gives an impetus to scrutinize in detail the strategies used by resistance movements to corporate resource exploitation, by analyzing such exemplary cases as the MST in a major resource extraction context such as Brazil. There's a helpful, contextually attuned literature on which to build. The scholarship on the relation of civil society and the state in Brazil (Abers 2000; Dagnino 2002; Avritzer and Wampler 2004; Dagnino *et al.* 2006), has argued that movements do best in the current political environment if they collaborate with the state but leave room to protest. Protests have a long history as effective political tools in Brazil, and it has gained currency particularly after the 1984 democratization (Avritzer 1994; Keck 1995; Dagnino 2002; Hochstetler and Keck 2007), peaking in 1997 (Ondetti 2008).[2] The earlier research on environmental policy and conflicts in Brazil by Hochstetler and Keck (2007) emphasized how an amalgam of routine and contentious actions has led to the desired outcomes. Meszaros (2007: 5) goes even further, arguing that the success of the MST has been borne exactly by the more contentious strategies its leaders created:

> In fact, the alternatives had been tried and found wanting. The MST was born of a strong sense of past failures, including the assassinations of rural trade union leaders, the glacial pace of land reform, and the excessively debilitating legalistic culture of existing rural organisations.

The empirical evidence presented here on the dynamics and outcomes of the MST-paper industry conflict support these arguments. Joining the effort of Wolford (2003) and others to explain what happens after individuals join, I shed light on a number of issues not considered before. Where for Wolford (2003: 514) "the MST's ability to maintain participation turns on its presentation of the movement as the primary mediator between a cruel State and its members," I argue that crucial participation boosters are strategies that endow contentious agency and influence the "structures." The claim made by Wolford is a part of my explanation, but it alone cannot explain the outcomes of resistance – the variety between conflict outcomes of the local resistance groups. An analysis of various key strategies can explain the differences between local resistance groups. Thus, I analyze the local resistance as being formed by zero to five of the concatenated strategies promoting contentious agency: a) organizing and politicizing, b) campaigning by heterodox framing, c) protesting, d) networking, and e) embedding vis-à-vis the state whilst maintaining autonomy.

In the Brazilian context, the analysis of the last strategy (e) builds on the significant debate about autonomy in peasantry and Latin American social movements, with some arguing movements have been co-opted by state engagement, and others that a more nuanced view is needed, also as the state context for embedding has changed (Alvarez *et al.* 1998). Hellman (1992)

The Brazilian landless movement 61

illustrates how Latin American social movements generated a "fetishism of autonomy" in fear of losing their identities. It has been a long process since then for the movements to rework their relations with the state. Fox (1993), studying food policy in Mexico, argued for a theoretical framework focusing on reciprocal interaction between actors inside and outside the state. Evans (1995), studying industrial transformation in Brazil, showed how these actors are often embedded and play multiple roles. Borras (2001) continued going beyond the dichotomous views, arguing that redistributive land reform can be implemented in a politically hostile situation when initiatives by state reformists "from above" positively interact with social mobilizations "from below." The findings here confirm these claims, and continue developing the interactive framework of Fox and Borras, flipping and utilizing the concept of "embedded autonomy" by Evans (1995) to assess how movements and companies embed the state whilst retaining autonomy.

The truth table (see Table 3.1 in this chapter) on the movement strategies and correlating outcomes suggests that the movements' ability to maintain internal control and influence the public and state officials – the strategies by which they are able to self-propagate – are central in explaining the outcomes. By studying strategies, one can explain how the resistance to investment has slowed corporate expansion. Next, I outline one by one an illustrative set of the strategies that foster contentious agency, in this case also building the ideal "MST model," and influence economic outcomes, providing empirical accounts from the conflict cases.

Organizing and politicizing

An ideal resistance model is based on a strong organizing and politicizing of those who enter a social actor group, such as a movement. Contentious agency can be promoted by transforming the structural positions – that is, by creating an alternative social space, a new organization. Within the MST's organization, movement "members" live in a social space quite different from Brazilian society's dominant social space.[3] Organizing and politicizing positions people in ways that allow them to participate daily in group activities. The coordinators encourage and ask campers and settlers to act in sectors (like health, education) and at different levels (base unit, brigade, state, national, transnational), changing their positions frequently. The aim is to form an effective positioning grid to strengthen the organization, a pyramidal structure permitting both bureaucratic and ideological steering at the top and local initiatives at the base. As contradictory as it might sound, this strategy aims for promoting both a direct democracy and a hierarchical and bureaucratic movement.[4] When positions are rotated, work within sectors fosters capacity for personal agency in many fields, which supports contentious agency.

After a typical period of camping for three or more years, the campers pass into agrarian reform settlements. This is a crucial moment. The spirit of

62 The Brazilian landless movement

solidarity, material scarcity and harsh conditions, suffering under the plastic bag shacks, cold water, severe weather, bugs, insecurity, mud and dirt, and the feelings of brotherhood and a shared struggle in the camp, turn into something new. People obtain land and state loans to build housing and increase production. At this point, some opt not to continue within the MST, as they have acquired land. The MST's goal is to assure that this does not happen. It does this principally through politicizing ideological and emotional practices (strategy a) and campaigning by ethical, heterodox framing (b), which aim to tie people together, fostering a shared agency in protest acts (c), and allowing activity in society (d) and the state (e) whilst requiring activism, loyalty and autonomy.

Because settlements were formed in the process of land conflicts, the struggle lives on: for Medeiros and Leite (2004: 47–49) these are the reason for the formation and continuity of the MST. Guidry (2003: 190), who has studied space, citizenship and social movements in Brazil, argues that space is essential: "movement success means changing how people conceive of equality in the spaces of everyday life, work, and leisure, as well as making new conceptions of equality tangible and concrete in everyday spatial practice." Daily rural practices, such as planting and harvesting, working on the land and within the movement-marked territory, allows for an interlinking of territorial, social and symbolic practices to create a radical alternative.[5] These acts are essential in the promoting and diffusing of a contentious habitus.

The movement seeks a change in people's behavior and symbolic systems through daily, politicizing practices, such as collective laundries, kindergartens and other practical tasks and social gatherings, alongside discussions of new values. The MST has its own words for organizing and politicizing work, which is called *formação*, formation, and the product of which, the movement grid composed of people together, is called *organicidade*. The politicizing practice of *Mística* is one of the most marked identity formation tools and essential rituals. According to Pertti Simula (various interviews, MST SP, 2007–09),[6] without mystical, strongly emotional rituals, the MST would not have the contentious force it has. *Mística* is extremely important as a clue uniting radically different people, not only through the struggle for land within the MST, but also internationally in La Vía Campesina (Martínez-Torres and Rosset 2010: 164). The struggle of the movement gains depth through these practices.

In *Mística*, the MST members perform a drama displaying symbols that tell a teaching history that people can re-live. Normally the plot starts with a story of subjugation of the indigenous people, prisoners or slaves. The drama offers a scene of torture, followed by the reaction of the oppressed, who liberate themselves by a victorious fight. Words written on paper and displayed in solemnity, concepts like "solidarity," "peace" and "love," end the *Mística* play, Simula relates. Each base unit has to prepare a *Mística* for a specific day, which means that everybody both acts and watches, participates in the spectacle almost daily. These are daily, politicized practices. *Mística* is a key

The Brazilian landless movement 63

contentious agency fostering ideological practice, as it leads to the experiencing of one's past, present and potential future agency and power relation positions in the emotional, spiritual and collective spheres, and as a part of a great mystical utopia and epic poem. *Mística* has mystical dimensions, and specific meanings within the MST. Leonardo Boff, a central ideologist behind the movement, writes:

> Mystical signifies a combination of deep convictions, of grand visions and strong passions that mobilize the people and movements in their desire for change, or that inspire practices that are capable of confronting any difficulties, or sustain hope in the face of historical failures. In the socio-political mystical, utopia always exists as an action.
>
> (Boff 1993: 154, my translation)

Practices also follow Paulo Freire's *Pedagogy of the Oppressed*. For example, the schoolbooks of the MST portray how one stick breaks easily, whereas many sticks together do not break (see Cerioli and Broilo 2003). Through this politicizing, Brazilian *indivíduos* become *pessoas*. Many proclaimed to me how happy they were since becoming "conscious of concepts," "aware," "hungry for information." These are transformations in the symbolic space.

Of the transformations carried out, politicizing people into seeing themselves as citizens and land access as the natural right of all is arguably an even greater feat than its achievements in terms of settlement creation. The organizing and politicizing strategy encourages members to solve their problems together through very practical common sense. Especially important has been the investment in popular education, argues Carter (2009: 23): "the movement has placed a uniquely strong emphasis on providing an education to its participants and raising popular consciousness." MST's educational system offers channels for everybody to rise to the top of the organization, which is a striking difference from most Brazilians who face the inequitable private/public primary school system as a class-dividing relational mechanism. The United Nations Educational, Scientific and Cultural Organization (UNESCO) has rewarded the MST education system utilizing the pedagogy of the oppressed.

Territorial dispossession, discussed in the previous chapter and which most people in the camps and settlements have experienced, relates to symbolic violence inflicted in the social space and felt personally as very low self-esteem. This makes territorial dispossession of lands easier, because one does not conceive of one's own power or potential for agency. In such cases, land is not conceived as a right of all citizens, but rather a consequence of possible citizenship that the person with low self-esteem feels he/she can never attain. For example, in the extreme south region of Bahia, eucalyptus expansion has pushed those people who do not fit into the model of paper pulp production into landless movements and other agrarian reform schemes, or into the periphery of cities. "We feel like the rest, like we were the rest for Veracel,"

64 *The Brazilian landless movement*

an ex-construction worker of the company in the Rosa Luxemburgo MST camp said sadly (interview, MST Bahia, July 26, 2006). This type of territorial, symbolic and social exclusion and violence offers good breeding ground for Polanyian counter-movements to pop up – given that organizing and politicization and other strategies are used by activists.

The alternative relationship to nature

A land-centered and -based resistance movement such as the MST cuts pieces of the territory and builds movement structures in these spaces: settlements, camps, land occupations, roadblocks, marches and squats, the visible territorial space of the resistance. Indeed, space is a central element in the MST's trajectory: the movement focuses on territorializing a physical, social and symbolic space with an alternative organization and ideology.

By symbolizations, one can invoke ideology and relate it to objects. In the MST, land as a principal object becomes so richly imbued with key meaningful events and symbolizations that the landless are emotionally tied to land. The MST ideologists foster a conception of land as the result of everybody's struggle. Selling land would harm the very mobilization and efforts of the movement; indeed, one would destroy the prevailing ideology. Obtaining land is the biggest personal gain for those within the system of the MST: the transformation from a servant, from rural worker to farmer, from extreme poverty into self-determined subsistence or even prosperity is a huge step, bringing tears to movement members' eyes and creating a sacred tie to the land. Land is associated with work, production and subsistence in the MST – to its use-value – but also with other schemes. Land has a divine quality as it comes from God. Emotions typically bond one to the land: land is imbued with the personal and collective sorrows and joys of *Sem Terras*.

This is also a more common feature among many traditional rural populations. For example in Bolivia, Ley de Derechos de la Madre Tierra (the Law of the Rights of Mother Earth), was passed in 2010. In the law, Mother Earth is considered sacred. Seven specific rights, to which Mother Earth and her constituent life systems, including human communities, are entitled, are listed: life, diversity of life, water, air, equilibrium, restoration and life free of contamination. Such examples illustrate how there is not only a global race in capitalist land grabbing and resource extraction, but also in alternative holistic nature relations.

The relationship of a local actor like a peasant within a radical movement to place and land is typically holistic and personal, creating much more intensive and dedicated action in conflict situations than the less binding tie to a place a multinational actor like a corporation confers on its members. Expatriate directors and outsourced seasonal plantation workers are emblems of the less land-tied paper industry members and the underlying metaculture of dissemination. The MST's alternative symbolizations signify that members within the movement want autonomy to make decisions regarding their land

The Brazilian landless movement   65

use themselves and retain the control by replication. Thus, these decisions will probably not include selling or leasing the land. For example, the MST sees the small-scale outsourced plantation of eucalyptus by a farmer as negative, as this ties the eucalyptus grower into the company.

In the creation of a utopia – and making people strive for this utopia – simple politicization via object symbolization and other means is not enough. Leaders and militants need to direct the newly politicized participants into acting for a particular cause. By itself, organizing and politicizing creates rebels without a cause. Coupled with campaigning by heterodox framing, this strategy directs rebellion towards a certain goal. Together organizing, politicizing and campaigning create rebels with a cause.

Campaigning by heterodox framing

Campaigning by using heterodox framing is a prime strategy to gather, foster and direct grievances. Campaigns are composed of frames. Heterodox framing is an act of spreading contentious ideological contents within a movement. A mass social movement such as the MST can separate functions to ensure participants follow strategic shifts efficiently. Some focus on campaign and frame creation (leaders), others on spreading them to the camps and settlements (coordinators). Meaningful, directed campaigns can unite the many currents within a movement. They may also bring local populations closer to the heterodox framing, which helps to attain the campaign outcomes, even if people are not sympathetic to other aspects of a movement.

The MST has had a strategic shift from a narrow agrarian reform focus to a more general contestation of multinational and national elite capital and its allies in the conservative media. In 2007, reflecting this change in attitude in 2004, the movement vanguard Stédile argued that "Our enemies are the agribusiness, the transnational companies, the banks and the financial market" (*Letraviva*, August 2, 2007). Another MST leader, Ana Hanauer, explained why the movement started to campaign against large-scale eucalyptus plantations and pulp projects, without intentions to negotiate or end the conflicts: "you do not sit at the table of the enemy ... we have no other option than to fight" (interview, MST RS, May 2008). More recently, some of the movement's most successful campaigns have been based on more generally topical issues in society, particularly publicizing, criticizing the fact that Brazil uses the most agrotoxics in the world (which has been an easier issue to communicate than resist directly genetically modified crops, a topic not well understood by publics) largely because of the spread of Monsanto's RoundUp Ready in new industrial plantations including GM soybean.

Such campaign framings flow from the master ideologies movements adopt. In large-scale resistance campaigns focusing on corporate resource exploitation in Brazil, the master ideology was first liberation theology. After democracy, this expanded into a political ecology master ideology, as Rothman and Oliver (2002: 128) found by a case study of a south Brazilian dam

66   *The Brazilian landless movement*

resistance movement. Anti-monoculture campaigns are part of the political ecology ideology and later food sovereignty paradigms.

Effective framing should be based on ethical and moral grounds, and not only aims to bring the challengers to the table, but offers a good alternative proposal. The MST's campaign against the large-scale pulp model has followed a typical strategy of La Vía Campesina "to occupy and defend political space, and then rapidly move the debate out of the merely 'technical' realm onto a moral terrain of 'right and wrong'," which has proven an effective strategy (Martínez-Torres and Rosset 2010: 163). In the case of social movements, Tarrow (1998: 122) finds, "It is the combination of new frames embedded within a cultural matrix that produces explosive collective action frames. Combining them depends on the actors in the struggle, the opponents they face, and the opportunities for collective action."

When campaigns lead into active protesting, the heterodox frames become truly activated. Then they start a more meaningful, directly experienced journey across the movement and the impacted society. Organizing, politicizing, campaigning and protesting overlap and interlink. When protests are massive, disruptive, re-symbolizing and pioneering, they are more likely to generate attention, as the next section argues.

Protesting

Earlier social movement literature convincingly shows that there is a strong correlation between the use of disruptive tactics and contention outcomes (Gamson 1990). According to Piven and Cloward (1978), disruption is a more successful tactic than moderation for poor people's movements. This claim stands in contradiction to Robert Dahl's classic findings. Based on the Brazilian pulp conflicts, both Dahl, and Piven and Cloward were right and wrong. The MST's protests aim to dramatize a public demand and bring state authorities to the bargaining table in a situation where embedding in the state (strategy e) via electoral or institutional politics, or via private politics, does not reap results or is in need of political support via direct contentious politics pressure. Pulp conflicts suggest that moderation and disruption together lead to better outcomes from the movement viewpoint. Protesting has been a way to bring state authorities to the negotiations table, and to gain leverage in the routine political games around natural resource exploitation.

In view of the MST national coordination, the anti-eucalyptus monoculture and anti-large-scale pulp production campaign, and the promotion of food sovereignty, and varied and distributed rural industry as an alternative, has resulted in a "general debate on and attention to the green desert after April 2004: we have had actions against the large-scale pulp industry since 1994, but these have not managed to break the silence. These were acts without impact – which are the same thing as not to do them. It is important to do something to generate attention" (interview, MST São Paulo, September 2006). In the Veracel occupation, the *sem terra* activists cut down eucalyptus,

The Brazilian landless movement   67

a new symbol in an old struggle for land, and framed it as a threat to food sovereignty. This symbolization effectively led to some social re-appraisal, in Brazil and transnationally, of eucalyptus and land as symbols of widespread clashing phenomena, such as the land question of the global South, landlessness, dubious monoculture plantation expansion and contestable pulp investment. The territorial occupation linked to symbolic space in which the *sem terra* activists set the real world moving by symbolic reframing.

Re-symbolizing protests

The basis of a symbolization reframing is the displacement of an object to a different, unusual space. Symbolization puts people on the alert and thus heightens awareness. As an object moves from its familiar place to another domain, this dramatically increases our "awareness of the nature of the object, the characteristics of its original place, and the congruity of its new position. Such displacements, then, lead to a heightened awareness of all social processes, especially of the arbitrary nature of ideological constructs which sustain social life" (DaMatta 1992: 71). In re-symbolizing protests of land occupations, this mechanism is used, by changing the land use, wishing for society to become more aware of the current situation and the possibility of alternatives to it.

If perplexity and discussion of the objectified symbolic capital starts to take place on a socially significant scale, this will call the value of capital into question. The effectiveness of land holding and expansion thus depends on the framing of key objectified symbolic capital. Manifestations can unveil "the founding violence that is masked by the adjustment between the order of things and the order of bodies" (Bourdieu 2000: 188). Cultural capital transfer "enables the dominated to achieve a collective mobilization and subversive action against the established order" (ibid.). ITP resistance such as this attempts to transfer cultural capital by re-symbolizing land and eucalyptus. By symbolic actions, protests transfer cultural capital from the symbolically powerful multinational corporations to the needs of the political games involved in the land question.

I argue that visibility promotes contentious agency when protest acts engage in symbolic politics that displace an object from its traditional place, thus raising consciousness and arbitrary opinions in minds that were previously indifferent to the issue linked to the object. It is by the symbolic stability, public acceptance and legitimacy of land and eucalyptus, that the maintenance or fall of the pulp investment model depends. The protesting action has led to breaches, transformations in the value of the objectified symbolic capital in the investment areas. This signifies that the resistance has managed to transform the cultural stock by its symbolic politics, which is crucial, as "when and how movements add to or change the cultural stock are an important dimension for understanding social change in general" (Zald 1996: 274).

68 *The Brazilian landless movement*

Land occupations displace objects and bodies from one site to another. MST members put their bodies where they ought not to be as a fundamental part of their disruptive protests. *Sem Terra* bodies displace objects like eucalyptus from their circles of dissemination into circles of replication by turning the eucalyptus tree bound for paper production into a material for shelter building. In a re-symbolizing act that tries to shake the meanings and social position pulp investments enjoy, eucalyptus is replaced by food crops. At the analytical level, this signifies the contestation of established order, a claim of power, a demonstration of force and attitude by the movement. Charles Tilly (1999) would call this a WUNC display: participants' concerted public representation of worthiness, unity, numbers and commitment.

The effectiveness of the pulp companies' land expansion depends on the power or lack of power of the alternative approaches to organizing the social, symbolic and territorial space. When the alternatives thrive, new land symbolizations circulate in society. In such a situation, corporate land access becomes a mechanism not simply denominated as buying/selling, but something else. The commoditizing "buying" and "owning" activities acquire the tag of "grabbing" or "colonizing" the land. This type of symbolic political transformation took place in many areas where eucalyptus plantation was questioned by re-symbolizing protests. These dynamics of contention between companies and resistance can be illustrated by an example from southern Brazil.

Example of a pulpwood expansion protest in Rio Grande do Sul

In May 2008, more than 1,200 MST families camped next to Southall farm in Rio Grande do Sul. Aracruz Celulose had announced its intention to buy this massive property, but INCRA, the National Institute of Colonization and Agrarian Reform, had already marked the area as suitable for agrarian reform. The MST aimed to pressure the state government to expropriate the land and to protest against the eucalyptus plantation expansion. I was in the area during this event doing field research. My intention was to arrive at this massive camp and see the scene at the spot of contention. Alas, my plans changed, as the episode quickly evolved into a potentially bloody clash.

The governor of the state at the time, Yeda Crusius, ordered the Brigada Militar forces to surround the camp – an area of 16 ha officially bought by INCRA – and block the entrances and exits to the camp. More than 1,800 police with full riot gear surrounded the camp. The police started to check everybody and arrested all who had a police record – for example, if one had not voted in elections (it is compulsory to vote in Brazil). Six militants were arrested. As a supporting protest and pressure, the MST groups in Rio Grande do Sul organized roadblocks in fifteen municipalities. I was in the Nova Santa Rita settlement observing as the MST farmers blocked the federal highway next to their settlement.

In a very alarming and potentially violent subsequent decision, the governor declared a state of emergency in the fifteen municipalities where the MST had roadblocks. If the MST had continued the blocks, the local courts could have ordered the Brigada Militar to intervene and clear them violently. However, because of the pressure exerted by the MST around the state by simultaneous roadblocks and mobilization of progressive lawyers and high-level politicians, such as the Minister of Justice Tarso Genro (elected governor in 2010), Crusius ordered the Brigada Militar to withdrew. This kind of organized pressure would have been hard to create and maintain without the active ideological congruity and diffusion promoting strategies.

The MST activists demonstrated their lack of fear of the authorities during the roadblock. They shouted to police cars running by: "Go spend the state's gasoline, go." I wondered why the ordinary citizens did not just come and clear the roadblock. The settlers replied that the public, not to mention the *latifúndio*, are far too afraid of the movement to do anything.[7] The MST members used the roadblock to take hold of the territorial, symbolic and social space, demonstrating that they have just as much of a right to occupy it as the state or any other actor. Some people affected by the roadblock questioned the MST's rights to do what they were doing, saying, "There are no laws" or "no justice in this country," to which the settlers responded: "Yes we have justice in this country, justice for the rich." According to one settler active in the roadblock, the protest showed society that, "we are united and can occupy the road or whatever space." In this way, the movement activists demonstrate and attempt to diffuse contentious habitus to society, to other spaces for other to replicate, not only within its ranks.

Roadblocks and other almost daily politicizing practices are much more than struggles for reorganizing the social and territorial space. They are personal experiences around which power relations revolve; they are "empowerment medicine" for those dominated in the society up to the point of denying their own subjectivity, agency and political potential. They are struggles in the symbolic space. "This is a continuous fight," a young male settler explained, waving the MST flag on the roadblock. He wanted to emphasize that "protest acts are not individual episodes, but a continuum." Perhaps he was trying to say that protests are signs of underlying movement strategies being utilized and developed.

Pioneering protests

The first massive (3,500 activists), pioneering, nonviolent, symbolic protest aiming to reframe a pulp project was the 2004 Veracel occupation. Also the Aracruz act of 2006 was a pioneering protest: the women of Vía Campesina decided to mark March 8 as a particularly important day of struggle, and for this reason they "needed to utilize innovative and highly disruptive methods" (interview, Kelly, MST SP, December 14, 2009). The goal was to "cause damages to the company, to open a debate, and mark a difference." The act

70 *The Brazilian landless movement*

was a conscious experimentation of new methods (destruction that caused a direct loss of about 200 million reais to the company). It involved new elements in both its outer look and inner planning. The new protest methodology attempted to avoid the assimilation of protesting, the softening of the cutting edge of the disruptive strategy (interview, Kelly, December 2009). MST Women sector coordinator Kelly explained that the assimilation happens easily. In the 1980s, to occupy land was a radical act. In 1997, the National March was a novelty, whereas occupations had become a normalized, assimilated part of the political game – many saw them already as "routine politics," even though most landholding antagonists see them still as "illegal invasions." Two years later in 1999, a similar National March, a replication of the protest form, no longer received the same attention. In this line of contention, the April 2004 Veracel occupation was the first pioneering act, and it created enormous public interest.

In fact, novelty, the pioneering quality of the protest act, appears to be very important, at least in the cases observed here. A generalization, however, cannot yet be made based on these cases, because variety in issue salience, and targets' and third parties' cost calculation, also influences the effectiveness of movement strategies (Luders 2010). There can be big differences in protest functioning depending not only on the industry and resource investment type and model in question, but also on the relationships of resistance, state, third parties and targets in the other political games apart from contentious politics. The combination of strategies, used in different political games, is likely to explain outcomes and effectiveness of single strategies better than the quality of single strategies. Nevertheless, disruptive and pioneering protests have been found in general to work well for movements (Tarrow 2011). Movements test protests; successful movements have a repertoire of them to be used in particular contexts and times.

The general tendency until 2009 was for the MST protest acts to become progressively more contentious. The more pioneering the act, the greater the efforts required. Furthermore, a rise in the level of contention leads to higher risk for the movement and its members. In developing new protest types, leaders are closely following how different types of disruption influence the effectiveness of more conventional strategies (interview, Kelly, MST SP, December 14, 2009), such as state embedding whilst maintaining autonomy (strategy e) and networking (d). In October 2009, the MST staged a protest against Cutrale, an orange producer in São Paulo, destroying the orange harvest. Although Cutrale was producing on INCRA-identified agrarian reform land, illegally, and land appropriation was promised, this information was not passed on by the media, but the protest was framed in highly negative terms for the MST, bringing it much negative publicity. Later, the movement acknowledged it made a mistake there. Since then, acts have become less radical, and in 2012, the tendency was to focus more on convincing the public via emphasizing the productive work the MST does, instead of gaining attention via very radical protests. In this way, the degree of radicalism

The Brazilian landless movement 71

provoking still positive social feedback fluctuates, protesting giving leeway to campaigning, networking and embedding when deemed more suitable by movement leaders and society. Nonetheless, it should be noted that the opportunities are not external to a movement, but the movement is one part of the society building these, sometimes massively, especially when observing local and not national settings. The industry and issue in question also play a role: destroying oranges is very different to destroying eucalyptus, which is much hated by many. Also, the Brazilian food industry responds differently to negative publicity than the international paper industry, which is very concerned about its image.

The MST has many different types of protests, all of which have a particular meaning. The Red April protests have a different methodology than the March 8 Women's Day acts. The former focus on creating pressure and negotiation leverage (so these come coupled with the active use of embedding), whereas the latter are openly hostile and do not even seek negotiation. The March 8 protests "seek direct confrontation and are very important for the formation of the women" (interview, Kelly, December 2009). The acts involve a small leadership, secrecy, non-violence, but attempt to cause considerable economic losses and the loss of reputation (*desgaste, prejuizo*), business reliability and performance for corporations. However, all the different protest types aim for the same broad goals: to foster a contentious habitus; land reform; food sovereignty; agroecological, right livelihood-based rural development; and change the targeted industry's investment pace and style.

Protests must be understood relationally. Adding a new protest type into the strategic toolkit changes the rules of the interactive, dynamic political games around investment policy. In fact, pioneering protesting is a mechanism of contention based on periodical innovations in the types of collective action. If mechanisms are "delimited sorts of events that change relations among specified sets of elements in identical or closely similar ways over a variety of situations" (McAdam *et al.* 2001: 24), change in mechanism quality leads into changes in outcomes. In fact, protesting has indeed led into the slowing of plantation expansion over a variety of pulp projects. However, as the qualitative comparative analysis truth table will indicate, a slowing outcome occurred only if all the strategies a–e had been active simultaneously in the case in question. Besides land conflicts, the MST participates in conventional political games through networking and many forms of state embedding, to which I turn next.

Networking with allies

The ideal resistance model is expanded by the transmission of strategies and mechanisms creating it, by a networked replication. Zald (1996: 271) argues that this confers success on movements: "successful movements have their tactics and frames appropriated by other movements; they become exemplars providing training grounds and models. Failing movements are less likely to

72 The Brazilian landless movement

Figure 3.1 La Vía Campesina Women's Stora Enso plantation occupation, Santana do Livramento, Rio Grande do Sul, Brazil, 8 March 2008

provide ideological and symbolic models." The metaculture of replication often used within the MST explains how the movement has propagated its model to other movements, created a network of allies, and embedded with the state whilst maintaining autonomy. Resistance model transmission is an endeavor in which the MST has been especially active.

The movement is capable of fostering external coalitions and networks, but the most interesting and particular feature of the MST's networking work is its insistence on transmitting the metaculture of replication, and not merely brokering or diffusing to gain allies. Reitan (2007: 19) identified that different types of attribution among networked activists (such as worthiness, interconnectedness and similarity) produce solidarity of differing qualities, with distinct impacts on the cohesiveness of networks. A shared metaculture of replication can cut across all types of networks, be they constituted mostly by worthiness or similarity; it would be interesting to investigate whether networks where replication dominates show distinctive outcomes than those based on dissemination. I would hypothesize they do: that they produce distinctive types of subjectivity, action and power relations is obvious.

The MST has fostered cooperation within the pulp investment resistance network by the creation of regional forums and by widespread networking. Compromises, plurality and joint actions mark resistance networks like the

Network against the Green Desert (Rede Alerta Contra o Deserto Verde), established in 1998. The World Rainforest Movement (WRM), the Federation of Social and Educational Assistance (FASE) and the MST are the central actors in the network, which is most active in south-eastern Brazil. It has organized enormous meetings with over a hundred heterogeneous organizations varying from syndicates to social movements, research centers to all kinds of associations. The network has managed to embed itself into the state. The network has created Latin American and transnational ties by participating in the World Social Forum (WSF). It disseminates the negative experiences of the large-scale pulp investment model and replicates resistance in locales where the model is about to territorialize. Aracruz acknowledges the other side: "The Green Desert Network (led by NGO FASE) and the MST can be considered today the major opponents of the company" (Aracruz, Cf. MMA 2005: 91). The goal of the network is to reverse the advance of tree plantations, to require the rule of law and enhance the situation where tree plantations already exist.

Transnational networking is used also. The MST was one of the founding partners behind the WSF, which was actually found after the failure of earlier attempts to form a more radical and social movement-based space. According to Neuri Rossetto, who has been the representative of the MST in the WSF since its start, in the 1990s the Zapatistas (the Ejército Zapatista de Liberación Nacional, EZLN, or Zapatista Army of National Liberation) proposed for the MST that they could together form a new platform that would transnationalize their radical new movements to other parts of the world. The MST wanted to include also other Latin American social movements, with which it had been building up networks for years. It wanted to create a wide coalition. The Zapatistas agreed to this, and to a careful organization of the future event together with other movements. However, Neuri disclosed that the two representatives of the EZLN continued from São Paulo to Belem, and after talks with its mayor, pronounced that the future meeting would take place in Belem. The MST felt that the EZLN had betrayed their deal and called off the meeting, which they would never have organized in Belem. The relationship of the MST and the EZLN is still shadowed by this event. The MST sent several militants to join the campaign of EZLN in recent years, but these representatives were not given any serious attention; Subcomandante Marcos did not even receive them, Neuri lamented. As a substitute to the forum of radical social movements, the MST helped in forming a space for discussion, the WSF. After ten years, the MST sees little potential in the WSF: Neuri argued it has been dominated by NGOs that are not themselves creating real alternatives. For this reason, the MST aims to organize a new platform of social movements of the ALBA that would function as a real alternative globalization transmission base, as a decision-making and campaigning platform instead of simply a space of discussion. Since then, the MST has allied more clearly with ALBA. The reason for this, they argue, is to be able to resist imperialism in Latin America.

74 *The Brazilian landless movement*

Contentious agency replication: examples from eastern Brazil

MST leaders meet constantly with a plethora of Latin American, European, Asian and transnational social movements, putting great effort into building a transnational network of allies. MST militants and leaders have increasingly supported the indigenous people in their disputes, offering new heterodox frames and protest types correlating with the frames. This has resulted in a considerable transformation in the pulp project attitudes of the indigenous people. On February 19, 2005, following the MST networking, the indigenous people in Espírito Santo turned to radical acts as opposed to their earlier negotiating with Aracruz. According to Luciana Silvestre (interview, São Mateus, MST ES, June 16, 2008), the Regional Coordinator of MST in Espírito Santo, the movement and the indigenous people have had an extremely close relationship for years, their relations intensifying through purposive assemblies organized by the MST, co-operation and mutual help in various situations. The change in strategy happened after all routine political means had failed to address the problems.[8] In an assembly, the Tupinikim and Guarani leaders proclaimed: "We came to the conclusion that the Agreement with Aracruz did not manage to resolve our problems; on the contrary, it has caused us even more difficulty, generating economic dependency, division between *aldeias* and the weakening of our culture" (cf. MMA 2005: 68). The transformation of frame and agency was drastic: "The struggle for land, which is also the fight for the physical and cultural existence of Tupinikim and Guarani will, from now on, be our principal objective and we will not cease until we manage to totally recover our lands" (cf. MMA 2005: 69). They would no longer negotiate with Aracruz. The MST was there, and the strategies it offered were the best choice available. According to Winnie Overbeek (from the Federation for Social and Educational Assistance, interview, September 2007), the MST's solidarity with the indigenous movement was crucial: "In the decisive moments of struggle by the Indians, the *campesino* movements were there." It was a small step from the already established ties and sharing of similar territorial and social spaces with the MST (vis-à-vis a common enemy, Aracruz) for the two to organize joint occupations of export ports and eucalyptus plantations. This was a strategic and pioneering shift into campaigning by heterodox framing and protesting disruptively and symbolically, and brought the indigenous a victory in their land struggle, uniting the MST and indigenous people's symbolic systems by shared contentious agency.

The networking by the resistance is crucial, as all other constituencies that join the struggle against a commonly framed enemy strengthen the resistance network against exploitation expansion. In September 2006, the indigenous cut and burned several hundred acres of the eucalyptus plantation of Aracruz Celulose (AC), "and for two days the following December, they and about 500 MST members occupied the port through which AC and three other corporations export cellulose, costing them an estimated \$21 million," as

NACLA (2007) elucidates. Based on various key informant accounts, the reasons explaining the new contentious stance were multiple, including the greater pressure placed by growing corporate agency imposed on the indigenous people, the organizing help and heterodox framing offered by the MST, and the willingness of the larger indigenous movement to change their strategies, as well as their allegiances. In 2010, President Lula da Silva approved the demarcation of over 18,000 ha of land into Indigenous Lands in the municipality of Aracruz (*Diário Oficial da União*, November 11, 2010). The unlikely outcome turned the case into one of the most important victories of the indigenous movement in Brazil.

A similar case in Bahia suggests that the replication of contentious agency across movements may increase the possibility that state actors take the side of the movement. By 2008, the homeless of the region had organized into a homeless *sem-teto* (homeless – literally, "roofless") movement integrated with the MST. I observed how their relationship grew closer between 2004 and 2008. One night in July 2006, the military police came and torched a homeless people's camp in Porto Seguro. The next day was a day of rallying: the MST came to support these people, and I went along with the folks of the Lulão camp in southern Bahia, next to Veracel, where I was doing field research. The eviction was illegal, said demonstrators, as according to the law the police must give prior notice and make the expulsion during the day. The police act signified for the camp members that people who embrace power might burn down dwellings in the middle of a city without any threat of punishment. What is certain – I witnessed this all – is that such actions bring the historically distanced city dwellers closer to contentious agency, encouraging the strategies of resistance to expand and integrate passive people. City workers with almost no previous contact with the kind of ideological and cultural elements incorporated by the *sem terras* very quickly became interested in conversations and joined action with the MST. The relative grievances were the mechanism-as-cause launching the willingness for mobilization – engaging in networking with such a powerful and experienced movement as the MST was the best way for the homeless people to increase their contention capacity.

The transformation within this group shared same characteristics as the Espírito Santo case. First, people are displaced due to plantation expansion and inadequate housing policies by municipalities. Second, routine political means are found inadequate to address problems, and people face repression significantly worsening their land position. Third, purposeful help and networking attempt by the MST in crucial moments puts the people whose social and territorial positioning is already close to that of the landless, but who do not practice contentious agency, into contact with heterodox strategies of protesting and framing, which will end up changing their habitus into fully fledged contention. From September to October, one part of the *sem-teto* movement in Eunápolis occupied an area of Veracel. "We will not leave before rules are established for the use of soil for this company. We want homes and not eucalyptus plantations," said Wedson Souza Santos, the president of the movement's Eunápolis association. The public prosecutor in the area, João Alves da Silva Neto, followed the occupation closely. Instead of the usual condemnation of occupations as invasions, the Brazilian state actor entered into legal action against Veracel, accusing the company of predatory expansion: "I will denounce the expansion this company has carried out by irregular licensing and false documents," the public prosecutor affirmed (*A Tarde*, October 14, 2008). Both the Espírito Santo and Bahia replication cases suggest that the wave of contention has spread from the MST to other social movements and state actors, to which I finally turn.

The embedded autonomy with the state

In this section, I assess the relationship between the MST and the state, and the general importance of embedding in the state whilst maintaining movement autonomy in promoting contentious agency. Classic social movement studies, for example the civil rights movement research in the USA, have argued that movements normally have to choose between state support and autonomy (Meyer 2004). It is impressive that state embedding has not jeopardized the movement's critical ideology and relative autonomy. I see this character of movements as a type of embedded autonomy, developing and flipping the classic conceptualization of embedded autonomy by Peter Evans (1995). This is an addition to the literature on social movements. I argue that successful movements, such as the MST, manage to utilize embedded autonomy as a technique to achieve both state support and autonomy.

Figure 3.2 illustrates how the strategy (e) functions in general. Once the movement has secured a set of state institutions driving its agenda, laws governing these institutions and sympathetic state actors to staff them, it has used an important extra mechanism of resistance (e), besides protests. The

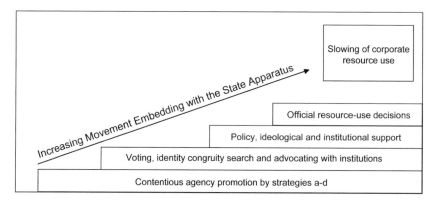

Figure 3.2 Steps of state embedding by a movement: the influence of movement embedding with the state apparatus on resource use

government has had to give in to the demands of the movement, for example, by granting state actor positions to movement sympathizers or more resources to the pro-resistance institutions, or allowing greater legitimacy to contention. This shows that a movement has had an important role in resistance outcomes, even where state institutions have made the final decisions. The MST has always targeted state actors, especially state and federal-level executives and land reform institutions, trying to press for "higher" political presence for its agenda whilst maintaining autonomy. Continuing to utilize and develop strategy (e) signifies advancing up the steps of embedded autonomy by the movement, as Figure 3.2 implies. Figure 3.2 demonstrates how social movements can utilize the strategy of embedded autonomy, how the rise up the steps of embedded autonomy brings benefits in the process of struggling for the state apparatus support.

The MST has secured a pool of state resources by demanding, as citizens with rights in Brazil, access to schools, health care, agrarian technicians and other state and legally guaranteed institutions. However, MST groups implant the state support within and by their own ways and spaces: there are strong regional variations in implementation. In general, the MST is relatively autonomous as it can determine or negotiate the type of external intervention in its communities (Vergara-Camus 2007: 114).

The fact that the movement has been an active contester of the Lula da Silva and Dilma governments' economic policies, whilst simultaneously embedding with these Workers' Party governments (by support in electoral politics, ideologically as an ally in the broader leftist block in Latin America, and institutionally and structurally by many MST militants positioned as Workers' Party members and/or state actors) illustrates how the MST has not fallen (at least too deeply) into the role of a clientelist underling that is integrated as a political movement into a coalition or alliance with the government or the state, in spite of embedding. The ideological work in politicizing and heterodox framing are central in ensuring spatial autonomy, as this creates a particular symbolic system based on contentious agency. By this, a movement can limit incoming cultural traffic but extend its impact on state policies and public opinion.

The embedded autonomy of a movement relies on a fine balance between autonomy and embedding. The general MST embedding within the state is currently quite deep. According to a member of the movement leadership, Neuri Rossetto (interview, December 15, 2009), the situation is such that a further embedding would make it difficult to foster and maintain a good network of allies. A further state embedding would result in fewer struggles and protests and in a higher importance given to negotiation instead of confrontation. This would compromise the other strategies, such as protesting. Thus, the national leadership does not encourage participants to strive for political power with the cost of losing autonomy.

However, autonomy also does not mean isolation. Many movement members have become experts embedded in the state. Professionalization has

78 *The Brazilian landless movement*

generated movement power by tying members into professional habitus categories and fields within the state – the movement has its own teachers, agronomists, technicians, cooperative bankers, nurses, accountants, administrators, politicians and state officials – while retaining them within the movement ideologically and in practice, if not always pronouncedly. The increase in roles taken by movement members and increased access to the most varied fields allows resistance to enhance its embedded autonomy, and thus gain power. Building on Bourdieu's (1991) concepts of field and capital, in both theory and practice a movement can trade and create capital in more areas as its members gain a habitus accepted and proficient in those fields. This ensures embedded autonomy in practice. The MST has managed to spread its model and exert influence while keeping an eye on and control over incoming impacts and attempts at co-option. Professionalization of the activists does not mean that the movement will turn into a formal or official organization. In fact, professionalization allows them to embed better with the official spheres of the state and society, whilst maintaining the flexibility of a non-registered movement. State embedding is a tool for the MST, not a goal per se, but a strategy in the broader conflict with globally operating corporations, in which the state is just one, albeit important, dimension. In general, movement-state interaction should be always studied within the dynamics of movements, corporate (or other target actor) agency, and the state, as the next section illustrates by a case study of INCRA-MST-pulp company relations.

MST-INCRA-agribusiness dynamics

Wolford (2010b) suggests that the way the MST interacts with the state land reform agency INCRA is participatory democracy by default. I complement her findings by discussing the influence of third parties, such as the powerful large landholders or agribusiness, and approaching the state dynamics as formed by political games where members, challengers and subjects interact (following the dynamics of contention approach of McAdam *et al.* 2001). I contest Wolford's assessment on two issues. First, civil society in Brazil, where the MST is the most well-known continuing contentious actor, has not risen to a prominent position only due to the weakness of the state; this process has been much more interactive. Contentious agency promotion by the MST has been even more important than the weakness of INCRA: the MST brigade-level variations in the activeness of strategies, the implementation of the ideal MST model, helps to explain in detail how particular MST-INCRA relations have formed.[9] Second, my comparison across seven states (Rio Grande do Sul, São Paulo, Rio de Janeiro, Bahia, Espírito Santo, Pará and Maranhão) suggests that INCRA is not as weak and its role regarding the MST is not as simple as the assessment of the Paraíba state and the MST-INCRA interaction in Wolford (2010b) suggests. Both of these issues can be addressed by moving from a state-social movement analysis towards a study of the dynamics between movements and corporations/landowners remediated by

The Brazilian landless movement 79

the state. An example from the eucalyptus plantation disputes in Rio Grande do Sul can illustrate the point.

In Rio Grande do Sul, under the label of Poupança florestal, Votorantim Celulose e Papel (VCP; currently merged with Aracruz as Fibria, see Kröger 2012b for analysis of this merger) approached small farmers to gain access to their lands in a eucalyptus plantation outsourcing scheme for a possible future pulp mill. Some settlers within the MST started planting eucalyptus for pulp companies in 2003, but this process stopped in 2007. According to INCRA, in the contracts the farmer plants eucalyptus and cultivates it, and then the company hypothetically buys the production. Since 2006, VCP signed 160 contracts with farmers from the MST's agrarian reform settlements, totaling 1,000 ha. As INCRA discovered the existence of these contracts, the institute notified the farmers that they would withdraw the agrarian reform lots from those settlers who planted trees in the VCP scheme. According to the law, agrarian reform lands belong to the state for at least ten years, after which the state might theoretically privatize land for farmers as private property, for which the farmer would have to pay (interview, Dietrich, INCRA RS, May 14, 2008).[10] Mozar Dietrich, the superintendent of INCRA in Rio Grande do Sul, said that the institute followed Brazilian law in this case. When Votorantim found out that INCRA was charging them and their contracts as being illegal, the company lawyers visited the institute. After talks, VCP discontinued the illegal outsourcing program, explained Dietrich. INCRA also contacted the MST, asking them to discontinue tree planting for VCP. About 120 farmers cut down their eucalyptus plantations, many of which covered the whole area designated for the settler family to produce food. Under the illegal scheme, the families were becoming dependent on the corporation, had discontinued the planting of food crops and were buying basic food from the markets, which was in complete contradiction to the ideas and laws of agrarian reform – for which reason INCRA had to act.

I visited many farms where the MST farmers had cut eucalyptus and were now using the land for agricultural purposes. Eucalyptus was still growing in some parts. "It is a real nuisance and hard to get rid of, like a pest. After you have planted it, it grows again and again even if you cut it down and even if you turn the soil many times," said one farmer – the same story was repeated various times by others. However, the story was not unanimous: forty of the original 160 MST farmers under Votorantim's outsourcing scheme resisted INCRA's notification. As a movement, the MST did not interfere by demanding that these farmers cut down eucalyptus. This is a sign that the movement, at least in this area, gives a high degree of freedom to members and settlements to decide what to do. If they will, they can engage in private politics with companies. Indeed, the MST does not have any legal means to force its members to do this or that, or a hierarchical coercive system to impose such measures.

It is the state, in the form of INCRA, that has a legal role as a state institute to regulate and order settlements and take disciplinary measures under

Figure 3.3 MST camp in Pinheiro Machado, Rio Grande do Sul, May 2008. The MST is pushing for the expropriation of the surrounding land areas, whereas VCP, a pulp company, tried to buy the land for eucalyptus and to extend eucalyptus by outgrowing schemes even within the nearby MST settlements
Source: Photograph © the author

the rule of law. Institutional politics can overrule private politics where the latter violates state laws and power holders seek to defend these – a healthy reminder of the relational position of power of the field of private politics in relation to state-remediated games where resource exploitation pace and style are determined.

In the pulp company-movement-state interaction case, INCRA was defending the MST – in most other cases I have observed around Brazil it has been the other way around. For example, in the 2004 Veracel protest, the MST demanded and assured more resources for INCRA. Companies and land grabbers acting on the verge of legality can penetrate movements and gain the allegiance of peasants via private politics; state embedding comes in handy to both prevent and solve such problems. This suggests that movements should in any case embed the state, even if, and particularly if, they would engage more with private politics to gain influence over investments. Embedding with state institutions presents the contentious agency formation with both challenges, as well as opportunities and situations in which state actors that enforce laws may defend movements vis-à-vis the society (for example, against corporate intrusion). Furthermore, state embedding is essential in the struggle over the setting of institutions, laws governing them, state actor positions, policies and grand government strategies, which are all essential regarding investment policy. Well-equipped resistance embeds in all of these political games.

However, the other strategies (organizing and politicizing, framing, protesting and networking) besides the embedded autonomy are also important: they concatenate and are all needed for contentious agency promotion. If the ideological congruity within the movement in relation to a critical issue is not assured by organizing, politicizing and campaigning, or if there are no significant protest acts, embedding is of less importance. Indeed, without protesting, the more likely outcome is unchecked and rapid agribusiness expansion (in the territorial, symbolic and social space) that can even penetrate a movement aiming for agrarian reform. At least this is what the empirical evidence across thirteen pulp conflicts presented next suggests. The movement gains from its positioning between "law and disorder," as Hammond (1999) has brilliantly remarked. The MST can put a lot of pressure on state actors, as state actors are afraid of the potential proliferation of disorder; at the same time, the movement can argue for the rule of law due to conventional state embedding and networking.

Findings: relation of strategies and economic outcomes

This chapter has offered detailed descriptions of Brazilian pulp conflicts and the strategies MST and other movements used in their political dynamics. I outlined a few illustrative cases from the dataset on all pulp projects to highlight how the promotion of contentious agency works as a rewarding movement strategy. The qualities of the truth Table 3.1 summarize the larger QCA on thirteen pulp conflicts, on which this chapter's evidence is based. At the top of Table 3.1 are the slowed or discontinued cases, while at the bottom are those in which plantation expansion has continued unchecked. The dependent variable (Y) measures the reversal, discontinuation, slowing or unchecked continuation of plantation land expansion by paper companies.

The following empirical indicators (condensed also in Table 1.1) were observed (by participant observation and interviews) to decree whether strategies a–e were active in a given conflict, movement and period: a) for the organizing and politicizing strategy to be deemed as having been active, the movement in question had to have a visible territorial space in the form of camps or settlements AND a revolutionary attitude amongst the participants; b) for campaigning against pulp projects to be active, the participants had to voice heterodox eucalyptus discourses; c) for a protesting strategy to be active, I observed the number of directed, pioneering, re-symbolizing, disruptive and massive (over three hundred people) and mass media-reported land occupations and other protests – even one protest counted; d) for networking activeness, one of the following instances had to have happened: existence of a strong local coalition network directed against eucalyptus monoculture OR replication of the MST model by other social actors in the area OR case-specific transnational networking (for example advocating with NGOs from

82   The Brazilian landless movement

Table 3.1 Contentious agency promoting strategies and plantation expansion in 13 pulp holding cases, 2004–08 (active = 1; inactive = 0; c = number of protests)

Holding (and Brazilian state)	A	B	C	D	E	Y plantation expansion (indicator: empirical proofs)
Aracruz (ES)	1	1	3[1]	1	1	Reversed (government gave the indigenous groups 18,000 ha that Aracruz had planted with eucalyptus)
Veracel (BA)	1	1	1[2]	1	1	Slowed (MST gained 30,000 ha of settlement promises; Veracel was ordered to uproot 47,000 ha)
VCP (SP)	1	1	1[3]	1	1	Slowed (the resistance obtained a court decision to stop eucalyptus expansion in São Luiz do Paraitinga municipality; a municipal law restricted plantation at Capão Bonito municipality)[4]
Stora Enso (RS)	1	1	1[5]	1	1	Discontinued (the MST protests made the company decide to leave the state; INCRA did not concede license for the expansion of plantations)
Aracruz (RS)	1	1	2[6]	1	1	Slowed (MST gained over 13,000 ha – destined for pulp plantations – for landless families)
Suzano (BA)	1	1	0[7]	1	1	Continued
VCP (RS)	1	1	0	1	1	Continued[8]
IP (SP)	1	1	0	1	1	Continued
Suzano (SP)	1	1	0	1	1	Continued
Ripasa (SP)	1	1	0	1	1	Continued
VCP/IP (MS)	0	1	0	1	0	Continued
Cenibra (MG)	1	1	0	1	1	Continued
Jarí (PA)	0	0	0	0	0	Continued

Notes: 1 The MST-supported indigenous peoples and quilombola occupations and uprooting of large eucalyptus land areas 24/07/2007; Aracruz export port (Portocel) occupation by the MST and the Indigenous peoples 12/12/2006; the MST-supported eucalyptus land occupation by the indigenous peoples in Aracruz, burning and uprooting of eucalyptus 07/09/2006. There was also a eucalyptus land occupation in Teixeira de Freitas on an Aracruz farm 07/04/2008, but this did not have a pioneering quality but followed the 2004 Veracel occupation type, and was thus not counted.
2 Eucalyptus occupation and uprooting on 25 ha in Porto Seguro 04/04/2004.
3 Occupation of VCP eucalyptus farm Fazenda Una in Taubaté 17/05/2004.
4 Defensoria Pública do Estado de São Paulo (2009).
5 Women's day occupation of Tarumã farm and roadblocks 04/03/2008.
6 Southall farm protest and roadblocks around the state 22/05/2008; Aracruz eucalyptus breeding site destruction in Barra do Ribeiro 08/03/2006. Both of these were pioneering, new-type protests.
7 The local MST did a large eucalyptus land occupation in Teixeira de Freitas on Suzano farm (16/04/2006). However, this protest act was not of a pioneering quality, but closely resembled the April 2004 Veracel occupation. Thus, it did not qualify as a pioneering protest.
8 This project was also stopped after the 2008 analysis period, following a combination of changing market and corporate arrangements, and growing resistance strength in the state, which managed to block laws and regulation permitting unchecked eucalyptus expansion.

the home country about the corporations in question); and e) for embedding to have occurred in the given period, I observed for targeted voting and the congruity of state actor discourses and decisions with the MST, and for autonomy, I observed movement-controlled decision making and utilization of external resources.

The Brazilian landless movement   83

Based on the truth table, the most important factor for movement success is to utilize strategies a–e simultaneously. The table indicates that when a–e are active simultaneously, the economic outcome has been at least plantation slowing. From this, it can be deduced that the main process of contentious agency promotion will not produce its results if, for example, protest actions are taken away. The two Bahian cases, Veracel and Suzano, are interesting: in both, protests were utilized, but only in one case did this challenge slow the expansion of plantations. This anomaly can be explained by the difference in the quality of the protests: in the Veracel case, the protesting was pioneering; the Suzano act merely replicated the earlier protest.

A comparison between outcomes and active strategies suggests that embedding with the state apparatus, filing lawsuits and utilizing a variety of official channels to file class actions denouncing pulp companies' illegal activities, was active in all the cases where plantation expansion was slowed. Indeed, in almost all of the cases where plantation expansion has been slowed, discontinued or reversed, this change was derived in the last instance from a sustained legal process in which movement strategies support the official process wherein corporate actions are being investigated by officials in the state apparatus. However, legal decisions alone have not been able to curb plantation expansion. For example, Stora Enso decided to withdraw from Rio Grande do Sul mostly due to the contentious episodes, considering the state impossible to operate due to the resistance (based on several interviews with company executives, 2005–10). Judges, courts, attorneys, police, ministers, politicians and other authorities have made decisions, new laws, given judgments, or left the companies without proper authorization, for which reason the expansion of plantations has been slowed. In all such cases, however, the initial investigator and framer of the pulp question has been the local resistance front, in which the MST has been crucial.

Observing temporal changes (I covered the dynamics of paper, pulp and other industrial forestry investment since the 1930s, particularly since the 1990s), embedded autonomy by a movement requires the prior construction of strategies a–d. To be able to embed with the state can be a goal of a movement, but it may also be that the movement gains sympathetic state actors even without conscious effort, when judges, prosecutors and other officials adopt the movement's alternative framing and start to promote the goals of the movement as their own. If a powerful state actor in a given episode of contention adheres to the movement's framing, this is sufficient for success. For example, in the cases of Aracruz (Espírito Santo and Rio Grande do Sul), the minister of justice was the right person with whom to embed. In the case of Veracel (Bahia), some judicial power (judges and prosecutors) turned increasingly to the side of the MST, even though most executive and legislative powers did not. It is interesting to note how routine and private politics need to be supported by contentious strategies for movements to gain leverage and their desired outcomes in the political games of natural resource exploitation.

Concluding remarks

A qualitative comparative analysis comparing the land expansion of pulp holdings in different regional contexts shows that resistance movement strategies can explain the variation in plantation expansion outcomes to a great degree. During the research period, in Brazil there was growing government interest in pulp investment and a simultaneous spur in available state financing, which increased corporate agency. Against this backdrop of a worsening configuration of political opportunities to slow plantation expansion, the fact that there was more widespread slowing of plantation expansion in 2004–08 compared to the pre-2003 period is an interesting and vexing empirical finding. This anomaly can be explained by a simultaneous spread in contentious agency promotion, primarily following an "ideal resistance model," across some pulp holding areas.

I assessed the MST's resistance model as an example of a contentious agency-endowing set of strategies. The model has not been fully operational everywhere, since the model is an ideal, and only sometimes have activists been able to construct it. Strategies support each other and overlap. Strategies concatenate: when organizing and campaigning are simultaneously active, then a movement is forming rebels with a cause. Campaigning supports organizing and politicizing (base construction), they overlap, come hand in hand and form the core of contention; in the case of the MST's (contextually defined) struggle they are necessary but not sufficient conditions for the promotion of contentious agency. If these are active, a movement can further boost its potential by conventional strategies such as networking. It can also embed directly in political games, aiming to influence outcomes via dynamic interactions within the state.

If the resistance has visibly protested against pulp projects, maintaining an active contentious agency, the expansion of eucalyptus plantations has been slowed or even reversed. In comparison, if the locals have not organized resistance, plantation expansion has not been slowed to even the slightest degree. Therefore, there is a causal relation between conflict outcomes and contentious agency. In conflict cases where strategies a–e have not operated simultaneously, plantation expansion has continued unchecked.

The comparison of large-scale pulp project conflicts demonstrated clearly the complexity of the relationships between land owners, state representatives, movement leaders, settlers and encampment members, particularly by conveying concrete empirical examples. Regarding the state land institute INCRA, the MST and the pulp industry, the analysis showed the contextual and dynamic relationship between them, as it happens in practice. If contentious agency falters, the main process resisting agribusiness expansion is routine politics. However, I am not aware of any case where state actors have curbed the expansion of pulp plantations independently of social movement pressure.

Resistance and the efficiency of its strategies depend on the temporal-spatial transformations, the incorporated comparative analysis of which

The Brazilian landless movement 85

should be spread into local units and across a set of overlapping, complementary and mutually influencing political games of state-movement-target interaction. The next chapter continues studying how contentious and corporate agency engage in different political games to influence economic policy and outcomes.

Notes

1 Parts of this chapter were adapted and developed from Kröger (2011).
2 For a sociogenesis of protest mechanisms employed by MST, as well as its replication in several states of Brazil, see, for example, Fernandes (1996) and Sigaud *et al.* (2008).
3 Sigaud (2005) questions the presupposition that the people within the MST would be MST members, calling for self-criticism, so that scholars would not reproduce movement leaders' worldviews where movement participants are labeled automatically as members. Rangel (2010) argues that the majority of the participants of mobilizations organized by landless leadership do not perceive themselves as members of the movement, but as being (momentarily) with the movements and maintaining a series of reciprocal obligations. The relational approach utilized here supports these claims in not placing central explanatory force on assumed table organization structures, but on the strategies of changing social relations, such as organizing and politicizing. However, my participant observation in 2004–11 does not support generalizing Rangel's empirical findings.
4 See Polletta (2002) for an explanation of why these two are not actually contradictory, but mutually supportive. For Wolford (2003: 507), "Leadership in the movement is carefully structured to be as horizontal as possible and all offices are, in principle, occupied temporarily." See also critical studies on the MST's internal hierarchy and problems (e.g. Martins 2003; Caldeira 2008; Graziano 2004).
5 See Fernandes (1996) for extensive geographic research on the spatial dimensions of the MST.
6 If I had not met Simula, my access to the MST would have been much harder and the research results less encompassing and deep. Simula is a psychoanalyst working for the MST, especially the movement's social companies and helping in crisis reduction. He has worked for the MST for a long time, especially in the south of the country and in São Paulo. He helped me to access the MST.
7 The fear is a product of the often demonizing image the Brazilian media creates of the MST (see Hammond 2004), lack of contact and knowledge with settlers and campers, and dominant class-based judgments people make on the landless people and echoes of disruptive and sometimes destructive protest activities of the movement (Macedo 2005).
8 For example, state-level laws banning further plantations which were overruled by the Supreme Federal Court and Parliamentary Investigations that were never concluded. See the Ministry of the Environment report (MMA 2005) for a detailed description on the failed conventional political attempts.
9 In studies of the MST, it is highly problematic but common to talk about "the MST" based on limited field research and comparison across the hugely diverse Brazilian rural mosaic. After intense participant observation across many Brazilian states, I suggest that not even the state level is a sufficient level of observation. One has to go even deeper, to the brigade level (the MST divides its state operations across different territorially bounded "brigades"), and see whether the strategies were active there. There is huge variation in the way the local groups implement the ideal MST model. The same rule applies to the study of all resistance

movements: the more local the level of comparison, the more accurate the yielding analysis.

10 The MST is against the privatization of land, seeking collectivity and a scheme in which lands will remain state property, under the guidance and control of those who cultivate and live on the land. This way the movement avoids selling the land, speculation, and maintains the goals of sustained agrarian reform.

4 Political games determining resource exploitation pace and style

An analysis of the contemporary Brazilian natural resource politics is used in this chapter to demonstrate further how the theoretical framework outlined in Chapter 1 can be applied. Most focus is placed on the national level, but also state- and municipal level interactions between companies and resistance will be discussed. In ideal research, data should be gathered to analyze the political games in all levels of governance (global, national, sub-national, local and private); the analysis here suggests how to do this, illustrating what interactive mechanisms and strategies should be studied in a thick description of resource politics. Considering the assessment of the hypothesis, this chapter is important in demonstrating that the slowing outcomes in resource exploitation influenced by resistance can come *in spite of*, or in the middle of, rising and different types of corporate agency. As resource politics is a zero-sum game between resistance and corporations, the existence of slowing outcomes lead to the logical conclusion that contentious agency has risen relatively (but not absolutely) even more than corporate agency in some cases. The analysis of political games is central in explaining this.

The chapter divides the analysis of dynamics of contention into four political games where the resistance and the industry meet: contentious, electoral, institutional and structural, and private politics. Emphasis is on the last three of these, as contentious politics were dealt with in the previous chapter. This chapter shows how the state alliance enjoyed by the paper industry has simultaneously gained strength, but also been more contested, as the resistance has gained the sympathy of some state actors. The issues that the resistance network, principally the MST, by its disruptive protest acts has framed as problems, have gained increasing attention. I argue this is due to a simultaneous embedding of the resistance with the sub-national and municipal legislatures, and some parts of the state apparatus: Ministério Público, Instituto Nacional de Colonização e Reforma Agrária (INCRA), Fundação Nacional do Índio (FUNAI) and the Ministries of Justice and the Environment.

The state plays a brokerage role, mediating between the interests of the corporations and the pressure from the resistance and its allies. By the strategies of embedded autonomy for movements and corporations, the two actors attempt to gain greater leverage on the different spaces and platforms

88   *Political games*

of the state. In this game, the industry is in a far more beneficial position; it enjoys of the already active institutional mechanism of state corporatism that offers a preferential channel for corporations to receive subsidies via such executive-controlled institutions as the National Development Bank. The continuity of this institutional mechanism, alongside the introduction of another pro-corporation institutional mechanism since 1990, neoliberal policies, accrues the paper corporations a very comfortable interaction with the government, which can be characterized as an alliance. This is true even more so because of the ideological congruity of high-modernist developmentalism that currently connects most parts of the Brazilian state with the resource exploiting corporations. Thereafter, before I explain each of the political games where corporate and movement embedding meets (electoral, institutional and structural, and private politics) separately, I will discuss the central role of ideology in all the political games where natural resource policy is determined.

Policy, ideology, space and political games

Ideas, visions, ideological discourses and framing are used by the actors in all political games. The activeness of corporate and movement embedding can be measured by analyzing the congruity and difference between state and company discourses framing investments and those resisting them. The Brazilian government supports pulp production by structural and institutional means in a circle of favors with the widespread election financing of politicians by the paper industry, sharing with corporations the developmentalist vision of large-scale investment as the key to economic development.

Typically, the government actors have shared the orthodox corporate framing of pulp investments as "good" and the resistance to them as "bad." Export-pulp promotion is understandable as it provides quick and plentiful foreign currency to balance the trade and foreign debt deficits of Brazil, helping to maintain an orthodox monetary policy and keep the transnational financial regime supportive of Brazil. This policy is dictated not only by the prevailing financial and technocratic order of the capitalist world system, but also by the legacy of Brazilian ideological currents, namely Brazilian positivism. This influences the symbolic, social and territorial spaces in the country, and the rules of interactive political games by which continuity and change in those spaces are battled over.

Eucalyptus plantations, trees in ordered lines extensively utilizing pesticides, fertilization and machinery, are a visible symbol of positivist decision making. High-modernist positivism denies that the technology selection is political, and is based on the idea that progress is best promoted and defined by technocratic elites and experts, and that the society and the economy should be hierarchically ordered. As lately as 2012, President Dilma Roussef demanded a "non-politicized" agrarian policy, without land occupations, where focus would be set on "peaceful and technical" development of existing settlements.

Political games 89

This vision of development is a shared quality in the epistemic community between the government and the paper industry. Anthony P. Mueller (2000) has analyzed the Brazilian positivism, from which the Brazilian type of expert-led, high-modernist developmentalism draws, in the following way:

> Positivism says that scientism is the trademark of modernity and that in order to accomplish progress, a special technocratic or military class of people is needed who are cognizant of the laws of society and who establish order and promote this progress. The prevalent ideology of a large part of the ruling elite [of Brazil] stands in sharp contrast to the traditions held by the common people.

The country's forest industry is built within this historical legacy, activating the cultural stock of positivism by discourses that refer to such key concepts as "order and progress" and "property right," framing themselves as promoting these, and their opponents as attempting to destroy them. Thus, the industry encounters a National Development Bank (BNDES) – a federal public company associated with the government through the Ministry of Development, Industry and Foreign Trade – at ease with supporting developmentalist investments.

A look into the "other," those outside the circle benefiting from corporate power, can reveal the qualities of the mechanisms promoting corporate agency even better than an analysis of them per se. When the resistance questions corporate resource exploitation, the powerful have to respond by protecting their innocence and rightfulness, use discourses to retain the epistemic community alive and show what is not allowed. In an illustrative contentious politics-based interaction, as 150 MST families occupied a VCP eucalyptus plantation in Taubaté (São Paulo) in May 2005, the main owner and President of the Votorantim Group, Antônio Ermírio de Moraes, argued that Brazil was moving towards "total anarchy" (Barros 2005). Moraes strongly condemned the new protesting strategy of the MST of targeting productive plantations, seeing that "Instead of order and progress, now the motto is disorder and dereliction" (ibid.).

The passage aptly depicts the battle lines where technocratic discourses can be utilized as a framing strategy of corporate agency promotion, and against anyone who attempts to question the orthodoxy of developmentalist industrial policy. Osmar Zogbi, the president of Bracelpa, presented the viewpoint of the paper industry after the MST had targeted pulp investments in Bahia and São Paulo: "To invade productive areas is a political question. We want the government to secure property rights, because the national and transnational companies are fearful in relation to this" (Barros 2005). Such orthodox framing discourses activate the class-structural (that is, relational) embedding of the state by corporations, by which an epistemic community, ideological congruity and shared symbolic-social-territorial space is created and maintained between the government and the industry. It is clear that the acts of the

90 *Political games*

MST questioned the validity of this link, and the functioning of this embedding, since Zogbi refers first to the occupation as a "political question." Occupations surely politicize investments, taking them out of the realm of the economy into the broader field of politics. Meanwhile, Bracelpa's discourses attempt to maintain the alliance of state, national and multinational capital in Brazil, even in the face of contentious agency attempts to include also the social movements and the larger civil society in the decision making directly affecting their lives.

The developmentalist discourse attempts to conceal its own political nature, the power relations it envisions, the embedding it uses, and the political games with which it is linked. The passage also demonstrates another fundamental point: those utilizing corporate embedding, relying on developmentalist visions of industrial policy and an orthodox conceptualization of property rights that forgets the process by which "property" was forged in the first instance, are "fearful" before the rise of contentious agency. An efficient state embedding by resistance will require ardent political work using ideological and identity creation tools in all the political games and strategies. This means that movements will have to try to transform the dominant symbolic system, to contest the prevailing ideological orthodoxies. This requires efficient bridge-building accompanied by communication, for example via countering the clout of corporate election financing via targeted voting by member masses and framing of key politicians as friends.

Electoral politics: contributions to state actors

Because control over state institutions and laws is crucial in the dispute, it is no wonder that the struggle over access to the state has increased dramatically as the dispute has been exacerbated. Political party and candidate election financing by pulp companies has continually increased, as an analysis into the publicly accessible website of the Supremo Tribunal Federal demonstrates.[1] I have studied the activeness of the potentially resistance- and corporate-used embedding sub-strategy "contributions to state actors" in electoral politics by analyzing corporate election financing and targeted voting by the MST.

All pulp companies have given money to candidates in the Brazilian elections. Stora Enso gave 24,000 reais to Yeda Crusius, the then-winner of the 2006 gubernatorial race in Rio Grande do Sul state, a paltry sum in comparison to Aracruz that gave 281,556 reais, or Votorantim that gave Crusius 200,000 reais.[2] It is notable that Crusius is just one political candidate that the paper companies are financing. In the Rio Grande do Sul state alone, Aracruz financed 70 candidates to the tune of 1,217,346 reais. Aracruz gave more than US$200,000 for Lula's two presidential campaigns (NACLA 2007). In 2006, Stora Enso financed candidates from all parties to the tune of 1,006,604 reais. In a letter dated August 29, 2008, Stora Enso claimed it financed "the election campaigns of Brazil's President, governors, federal and state representatives, and senators."[3] Veracel gave 1,170,000 reais in the 2006 elections,

Political games 91

focusing its support on Bahian governor Jaques Wagner (PT, 100,000 reais) and Paulo Souto (PFL, 200,000 reais).[4] Where Veracel bet on two candidates, Aracruz and Votorantim spread their largesse more widely. After counting together the sums from the official Supreme Electoral Court statistics, Aracruz gave in total 5,523,353 reais to political representatives in the 2006 elections and Votorantim Celulose e Papel S/A gave 1,657,379 reais.[5] Aracruz is clearly leading this table of figures.

Private contributions to state actors such as these influence strongly the opportunities the state presents to different socio-economic actors. Claessens, Feijen and Laeven (2007: 1) from the International Monetary Fund (IMF), the University of Amsterdam and the World Bank, respectively, have studied election contributions by companies in Brazil. They find that election "contributions help shape policy on a corporate-specific basis ... contributing corporations substantially increased their bank financing" (ibid.). Preferential financing decisions by politicians conferred on the election campaign-contributing companies are common in Brazil (ibid.). Politicians have power both in state-controlled funds like BNDES and pension funds, and in many public and private banks as board members.

The circle of money between powerful state and corporate actors is the principal political tie of favors between companies and politicians, Claessens *et al.* (2007) argue. In addition, the development theorists Drèze and Sen (2002: 9) point to the negative influence of electoral campaign financing:

> Economic inequality can seriously compromise the quality of democracy, for example through the influence of money on electoral processes, on public decision-making, and on the content of the media. Overcoming the inequalities of power associated with economic privilege is an important aspect of democracy in the full sense of the term.

This is not big news. What is interesting is that in spite of extensive electoral campaign support, the Brazilian state is not totally in favor of monocultures or pulp mills. Especially when it comes to certain ministries and personalities, and especially at state and municipal levels, the unanimity of the state-paper industry alliance declines. For example, in São Paulo "the acceptance of monocultures is not so generalized and municipal and state-level parliamentarians have already expressed their concern with the level of territory occupation ... trying to regulate these practices" (MMA 2005: 179).

My field research around Brazil suggests that the acceptance by municipal politicians of a particular resource exploitation practice, like eucalyptus monocultures, depends greatly on the location and the existence and the quality of organized resistance. If the value-adding parcels of the commodity chain are all situated outside the municipality, the municipality does not gain so much tax revenue and social movements can publicize this fact. One can see that in southern Bahia, the municipalities of Porto Seguro, Belmonte and others not possessing a pulp plant have made laws prohibiting eucalyptus

92 Political games

plantations. In such situations, following negative public opinion on pulp projects, the politicians correctly calculate that it is economically better to use the land for agriculture that produces food and jobs for the local markets. These produce many more jobs and tax reais per hectare than mechanized monocultures without a processing plant in the municipality.

Pulp project disputes demonstrate how certain politicians are "owned" by either companies or social movements, trying to pass legislation in their favor. What happens when a politician gains support and receives attention claims from opposing political fronts is an interesting question. The MST calculated that in 1998–2002 it had seventeen PT deputies and four others as its supporters, whereas the *Bancada ruralista* had 83 deputies and a large majority of senators compared to the five senators supporting the MST (Vergara-Camus 2007: 305). The MST's João Pedro Stédile argues that companies specifically tied up deputies in the parliament. He calculated that, for example, in 2007, Vale do Rio Doce, the world's largest mining company, had 47 *deputados* in the parliament, Aracruz had 16, Banco Itaú had 27 and Grupo Gerdau had 27 (*Letraviva*, February 8, 2007). The MST attempts to counter company financing by supporting particular candidates by electoral mobilization. Carter (2009: 9) comments on the electoral politics centering on the MST and its adversaries:

> Between 1995 and 2005, landless peasants had an average of one federal deputy for every 612,000 families, while the large landlords had one deputy for every 236 families. The political representation of landlords was therefore 2,587 times greater than that of landless peasants. As a result of these disparities, each of Brazil's largest landlords had access to U.S. $1,587 from public coffers for every dollar made available to a landless family. The numbers speak eloquently for themselves.

The MST and the paper industry support the same individuals, like Jaques Wagner (PT), now governor of Bahia. The ambiguity felt by an individual politician encapsulates the dilemma faced by the politicians in power. Most state actors have not been worried in resolving problems as this would eventually discomfort some of their supporters. What ensues is politics as usual: resource exploitation investments harming agrarian reform continue even though the MST has its politician in the number one post in the country. However, Lula and Wagner are at the same time the number one politicians of the industry as well. Pulp investments like Veracel are the "face of the Lula government," Wagner said at the mill's inauguration.

For the MST, "Lula is more a friend of the enemies [than of the MST]. Lula is not our enemy, but the current economic model is. One person does not make a difference, only the combination of people can make the transformation" (interview, Santos, MST São Paulo, 2008). The MST sees the grassroots mass organization as the only way to bring transformation about.

Parliament is only a reflection of the society, "a space to be occupied" but not a priority, João Pedro Stédile from the MST said. This reflects the embedded autonomy strategy the movement has adopted. The movement does not want to become integrated into the state, but wants to remain autonomous. Yet it also wants to embed it, occupy it spreading contentious habitus to state actors and elected politicians and pushing for institutional and structural reforms. Occupying a space signifies using it in a different way than the space was previously used. Embedding means that resistance ideas and practices are spread into the occupied space.

This is a rocky path. To begin with, the resistance has no way to ensure support from elected politicians as long as they receive electoral campaign funding from companies bent on expansion. This can often mean it is more fruitful to use institutional than electoral politics; state institutions are more secure from politician steering than legislative bodies. Active election financing by paper corporations has made it essential for the MST to embed also, by greater effort, with the state institutions, besides offering votes to politicians. This shows how the main pathway of embedding depends on the dynamics, the activeness, quality and combination of strategies utilized by resistance and targets in different games available.

After getting to power, helped also by his long-term ally the MST, many expected Lula to utilize his new power as the most influential state actor to form a radical partnership with the MST. Meszaros (2007: 16) argues that the Lula presidency could have supported the agrarian reform agenda by several legal measures, including clearing cultural and legislative obstacles and making senior judicial and other appointments. In fact, the Lula governments did not engage in violence and direct oppression of the movement, as all the earlier governments had done. Yet its legal discourse towards the MST oscillated between brinkmanship and conciliation and thus sent out mixed messages, perhaps on purpose. Some of these the MST could utilize. Lula appointed Claudio Fontelles as the new Attorney-General. In 2003, he publicly endorsed a key argument advanced by the MST: "that property was not absolute and could, under certain circumstances, be occupied" (ibid.). Meszaros points out how this strengthened the MST's wider claims and emboldened prosecutors to question land ownership.

Lula was too timid in appointing judges to the Supreme Federal Court and this backfired, as the court rejected on procedural grounds the first major expropriation order signed by Lula (Meszaros 2007: 17). The Supreme Federal Court has been systematically on the side of the dominant legal orthodoxy, the power elite and corporate interests, and acted in such manner also in the pulp conflict cases. This should not be seen as a defeat of the MST within the institutional game, but as a defeat within electoral politics, as Lula had the chance to appoint more progressive judges, but decided not to do this. The reasons can be seen as an amalgam of Lula's campaign financing by corporations, need to form a broad coalition, and ideological congruity with the agribusiness and other technocratic developmentalists. The support given

94 *Political games*

by Lula to large-scale resource projects has trumped support for their resistance; this has been even more the case during the Dilma Roussef presidency.

However, the government restricted foreign land ownership in August 2010. According to the Associação Brasileira de Produtores de Florestas Plantadas (ABRAF), the country's tree plantation lobby group, this led to the suspension of foreign investment in the sector of at least 14 billion reais in 2010. Many foreign projects in the pipeline or planned were discontinued. The industry lobby sought to convince the government to remove the restrictions to attract more foreign investment (*Folha de São Paulo*, "Restrições a estrangeiros reduzem plantio," October 20, 2011). Although this government decision was helpful from the resistance viewpoint, this resource nationalism benefits mostly national capitalists.

Electoral politics have given some advancement towards the goals of the resistance seeking more democratic decision-making over natural resource policy, but mostly curbed these. In comparison, the recent changes in the institutional game have been far more beneficial to the resistance.

Institutional game: structural and institutional embedding

Besides election financing, institutional and structural legacies play a role in the actual support enjoyed by corporate resource exploitation. First, I open the structural game in Brazil, which still strongly favors corporate agency due to the existence of a power elite, but which has started also to even out by the society-wide expansion of contentious agency and the advance of a social movement society that follows this process. After this, I assess the historically built-in institutional mechanisms that favor corporate agency and that the resistance has started to challenge.

Power elite: structural embedding by corporations

There's a structural setting of relations largely benefiting corporate resource exploitation in Brazil. A political-economic-social class elite still exists in Brazil and keeps on accumulating power. These elites hold most of the high salary-earning positions, which offer their holders "a privileged position from which to influence in the legislative and legal process, the administration of the public machine, the hiring of large quantities of workforce or even in the formation of public opinion" (Medeiros 2005: 251). Eakin (2001: 173–74) writes that "In the 1990s, 287 of Brazil's 300 largest corporations were controlled by families ... the continuity of elite families and their networks is impressive." After waves of corporate mergers in the past decade, the figure is even more concentrated (Berterretche 2010): 1% of the population controls more wealth than the poor half (Medeiros 2005); five thousand Brazilian families, 0.001% of the population, control 40% of the country's gross domestic product (GDP) (Pochmann *et al.* 2006).

Political games 95

For Medeiros (2005: 251), as "wealth and political power are associated," economic growth under the current economic policy trajectory cannot resolve the dilemma of under-development and corresponding inequality. By contrast, Bresser-Pereira (2010) sees that the current developmentalism will resolve the problems. For Lazzarini (2011: 111), too, the institutional and structural characteristics of the Brazilian "capitalism of ties" are not wholly negative, but also allow synergy benefits by summing resources and limiting investment risks. Even via modest changes in the trajectory, much has also improved in Brazilian society in the past decade (Neri 2008; Santana 2011). For example, during the terms of Lula, incomes have risen dramatically, for the lower classes mostly through the 60% rise in minimum wages and less so by the much-lauded *Bolsa Familia* program (*The Economist,* "Brazil's Northeast: Catching up in a Hurry," May 19, 2011). Brazil's neomercantilist capitalism has led to increases in the incomes of lower classes, because it has been applied to schemes eradicating extreme poverty and offering more job opportunities for the lower and new middle classes to rise, but mostly reinforced class cleavages in economic decision making by corporate, national elite capital favoring, for example by bailout schemes. It is interesting that the resistance has still managed to gain some success within this setting.

Social equity and social movement society: structural embedding by movements

Some contextual, societal transformations in which the MST is now a significant agent favor the resistance in the structural game. In a volume edited by David Meyer and Sidney Tarrow (1998) movement scholars argue that since 1964 we have seen the rise of a new order, which they call the social movement society. According to Marco Giugni (2004: 10), a new social movement family emerged in the West through the cycle of student and New Left protests, peaking in 1968. Immanuel Wallerstein (2001) goes even further, arguing that 1968 was a turning point in the whole world system. Brazil and Latin America have also created a rapidly consolidating social movement society since the 1980s, based on grassroots mobilization, of which the MST is a crucial builder. Even though social movements have not had absolute success, their role, strength and breadth have definitely increased in Brazil. The MST has tapped into this phenomenon – and is its prime mover – by fostering a network of allies. This is a distinctive argument in comparison to most research, which sees the general political opportunities as external to movements, or the Brazilian societal context as depressing, crushing and immutable. A social movement society as envisioned by the scholars in Meyer and Tarrow (1998) has taken hold of Latin America, a society extending in breadth and depth rapidly (see Collier and Handlin 2009; Silva 2009). It is crucial to link one's organization with this major structural factor and, in the case of a social movement, do this through replicated diffusion of contentious agency throughout a heterogeneous network.

96 Political games

State corporatism and neoliberalism: institutional embedding by corporations

Even though some important changes have taken place, the state still has corporatist ties with both labor unions and corporations, and this state corporatism (tending to favor corporations) continues to influence the Brazilian economy, politics and society (Diniz and Boschi 2004; Boito 2007; Mancuso 2007). President Getulio Vargas's authoritarian regime implanted state corporatism in Brazilian society in the 1930s. In state corporatism, following the strategy lined by Oliveira Viana, the state would actively promote links between its own structures and the leaders of both companies and labor (Viana 1922; Carvalho 1997). This change in the governmental strategy of ordering power relations between economic actors had long-lasting impacts. For example, since 1930, when the entrance of new entrepreneurs and owners into companies was made more difficult, traditional family enterprises with capital have expanded in an environment of limited competition and a strong government distributing most of the available credit (Lazzarini 2011). State corporatist structures have also meant that trade unions and industries do not organize horizontally over industry or profession specific lines, but hierarchically (Power and Doctor 2004). Not surprisingly, capitalism in Brazil has been called hierarchical (Schneider 2009), despite attempts to dismantle the legacy and power of state corporatist institutions, and transform them into neo-corporatism in which civil society associations and autonomous workers would gain deliberative power (see Doctor 2007).

Although councils and other participatory democracy institutions have also been developed, the institutional arrangements initiated in 1930 are largely still in place. For example, the state corporatist legacy negatively influenced the long-term and hard-fought, though ultimately failed, attempt to create an autonomous central trade union in 2010 (Berterretche 2010). On May 11, 2011, President Roussef installed a new state corporatist institution, the Chamber of Management Policies, Performance and Competitiveness, formed by four ministries and four large-scale entrepreneurs (*O Globo*, May 12, 2011: 11). The goal in creating the institution, according to Roussef, is to maintain good relations with the private sector, without conflicts of interest, and to optimize the performance of the Executive power in serving society, reducing costs, and rationalizing processes and policies. According to Director of the Chamber Jorge Gerdau, owner of a large globalized Brazilian steel company, the priority is to guarantee that the country keeps on growing and controls inflation. Yet, this institutional opening also gave Brazil's biggest capitalists one more channel of direct access to state bureaucracies. Thus there are clear signs of state corporatism in the country.

A study on Brazil's "capitalism of ties" (Lazzarini 2011: 119) argues that neoliberal reforms such as privatization, in the way they were introduced under Fernando Henrique Cardoso's presidency (1995–2002), created a context of fostering interdependent association between foreign and national

Political games 97

capital, along the lines outlined by Cardoso and Faletto (1979) in the 1960s. This type of privatization ended up strengthening the power of state institutions in economic decision making, which is why Lazzarini rebuts the commonly held view that neoliberalism has diminished state coordination of the economy. In Lazzarini's (2011: 14) words, "Fernando Henrique, long from 'forgetting what he wrote,' in reality helped in sowing the capitalism of ties in Brazil. And created bases for its reinforcement in the subsequent government (Lula)." Similarly, Gomes (2004) sees that neoliberalism actually fortified the state corporatist system in Brazil. Abu-El-Haj argues that intentional government policies during Cardoso's time led to an inversion of the hierarchy within the ruling classes in favor of local capital. At the end of Cardoso's period, his inner circle of developmentalist economists pushed for adopting neomercantilism. According to Abu-El-Haj (2007: 110), after Cardoso, a neomercantilist consensus has been adopted among the most important politicians, industry groups, banks and economic think tanks: this has led to "underdeveloped capitalism and inequality" and ended the relatively autonomous policies of Cardoso "that advanced the interests of the entire bourgeoisie without degenerating into clientelistic support for particular firms."

These institutional arrangements, even after neoliberal privatization reforms, (both advanced to varying degrees by both Cardoso and Lula governments) give big local capital preferential institutional access to the state, unifying the objectives of government and big capital so that it is hard to distinguish between them. This alliance also supports developmentalist and neomercantilist interests and delimits the institutional access of contentious actors, such as trade unions criticizing investment policies.

These findings go against the overall belief and theory on the non-compatibility of neoliberalism and state corporatism. When these two institutional mechanisms are exercised simultaneously, the results appear to be devastating for competition and civil society, as companies can use state resources to buy off competitors and crucially shape the marketplace, society and environment, whereas social movements and associations lack direct state access. This signifies that corporate agency is supported by institutional mechanisms. Commodity corporations operate with the Brazilian state through a relationship that could be characterized as embedded autonomy by corporations or, in many cases, even state capture by crony capitalism. In this institutional interaction setting, it is easy for the industry to utilize lobbying to reach its goals.

Activists, prosecutors, meritocracy and rule of law: institutional embedding by the resistance

Besides the inclusion of neoliberal support in the set of state-industry alliance fortifying institutional mechanisms, other changes have also taken place since 1990. Some non-corporate agents, such as the MST, have achieved closer relations with some parts of the state. Legal practitioners and the MST are in an increasingly rich interplay, and the movement has created a sophisticated

98 Political games

legal discourse and strategy (Meszaros 2007). In spite of remarkable continuity, the latest research on the Brazilian political system and activism has found that some changes have been taking place recently (Ondetti 2008; Hochstetler and Keck 2007; Kingstone and Ponce 2010). New generations of young, meritocratically selected state bureaucrats, in innovative institutions like the Ministério Público, alongside the social movements with which more of them sympathize and from which they gain new frames by which to interpret the old reality, have started to undermine the stronghold of the institutional and structural mechanisms promoting corporate agency.

The Public Ministry is a key state institution explaining contemporary democratic transformation in Brazil. The role of this institution is extensive and specific to Brazil: you could translate it roughly as the public prosecutor's office, but it covers more than that (Hochstetler and Keck 2007). Even though state institutions with the same name exist in other Latin American countries, these are not as powerful as in Brazil (ibid.). Besides companies and other civil society entities, it can inspect and prosecute public officials and institutions. However, its actuation and role depend heavily on the state actors. In Rio Grande do Sul, the Ministry's prosecutor has led an attack on the MST. In Bahia, the Ministry has been a vanguard of the MST agenda in the public spheres. The Ministério Público can be seen as the result of Brazilian society's Polanyian double-movement sectors that seek to regulate the economy and society. It is a sign of a strengthening state, making institutions more autonomous and meritocratically bureaucratic instead of being steered overtly by the government.[6]

The truth table produced by the qualitative comparative analysis technique (see the previous chapter) indicates that only the concatenation, simultaneous utilization of contentious and routine embedding strategies produces the economic outcome a movement seeks in pulp politics in Brazil. This becomes understandable by the slow and abrupt Brazilian policy process that requires frequent outside reminding by contention (Hochstetler and Keck 2007) and by the features of Brazil's justice system, composed by a very strong complex of formal and informal mechanisms that turn the system unjust, slow and saturated with class bias (Meszaros 2007).

In the 1980s, the MST did not yet have experience of or interest in occupying the arena of institutional politics. The initiative to start embedding this game seems to have come from progressive legal practitioners who were touched by the movement's contentious agency and became allies. Meszaros (2007: 10) narrates how "sympathetic lawyers scurried hundreds of kilometers from one occupation to the next and then back to the courts, improvising the best defence they could to legal counter attacks." Understanding the importance of such support, the movement started a "painstaking construction of legal personnel networks and arguments," which resulted in a slight but relatively important leveling of the battlefield (ibid.). In general terms, the legal enfranchisement is still very unequal (Taylor 2008). Only the established political actor groups, such as political parties, the Brazilian bar association, the Ordem dos Advogados do Brasil (OAB), and the Confederation of Agricultural Workers CONTAG, have direct access to the Supreme Federal Court, being able to veto or file complaints about legal changes directly at the last instance, without having to resolve to the painstakingly slow lower court processes before this (ibid.). Thus, it has been essential for the MST to embed the state via the help of allies, such as the Workers' Party, and progressive prosecutors. The prosecutors were active and powerful when the new 1988 constitution was being drafted, thus attaining so much power to themselves that prosecutors have become an autonomous "fourth" branch of government in Brazil (Taylor 2008: 161).

In the early 1990s, the MST developed both in-house legal services as a part of its organizing and politicizing mechanism, as well as networked increasingly with the National Network of Popular Independent Lawyers (Rede Nacional de Advogados e Advogadas Populares, RENAP), officially created in 1996. Exchanges between the radical legal profession and the MST have become continuous and deeply influenced both. Interaction with leading lawmakers, such as Plinio Sampaio (PT) led into the MST ideals being included in the 1988 Constitution and the National Agrarian Reform Program, besides developing a more mature and nuanced legal conception within the MST (Meszaros 2007). Leading leftist lawyers sought actively to incorporate the institutional legal game as a pillar of the strategy of the movement they saw carrying great potential for social transformation in Brazil. This points to a very interactive process between resistance, the state, targets and third parties.

In negotiations with centrist and conservative politicians and other state actors, law exercises a bridge-building capacity for the MST. The movement has started to use law as a way to put others on the defensive, not just to defend itself (Meszaros 2007). This is highly visible also in the increasingly proactive heterodox framing and exposing of irregularities of corporate resource exploitation. In the case of pulp conflicts, the resistance network has systematically been a primary investigator that brings forth illegalities of investment projects, which state actors such as public prosecutors then take under a systematic and official examination, to be passed to tribunals for legal proceedings.

Suits and legal proceedings are important: lawsuits targeting companies because of environmental infringements were found to be the most effective means to influence corporate behavior in the USA in 1971–2003, in comparison to protest, boycotts, letter-writing campaigns, or proxy votes (Lenox and Eesley 2006, cf. Soule 2009: 17). However, the specific quality of lawsuit importance has to be studied contextually. In the Brazilian context, being able to utilize lawsuits as a means of resistance to corporate resource exploitation has signified typically the utilization of all strategies a–e, including protesting, embedded autonomy and networking. The type of justice delivered has impacted lawsuit importance; to be able to impact justice, courts have had to be pushed by strategies a–e.

100 *Political games*

When courts have emphasized the importance of a contextual approach and substantively oriented legal reasoning, rather than the purely formal characteristic of the dominant legal orthodoxy, this has played in the favor of the resistance that faces extremely unequal structural mechanisms. In the pulp conflict cases, the MST initiated the legal offensive by utilizing contextual and substantive legal reasoning. It argued that the large areas required by eucalyptus plantations, and their negative socio-economic and environmental damage, have to be considered as the motivation behind the symbolic destruction of eucalyptus. Since 2007, the counter-movement has furthered, as progressive public prosecutors and judges have officially documented even direct and clear breaches of the purely formal legal codes by pulp companies. According to my temporal-spatial comparison across all investment areas, the legal interaction between companies and resistance turns increasingly to the side of the resistance where the resistance uses strategies a–e.

Thereafter, if the political games would take place only on the legal front, the economic outcomes in resource conflicts would be much more beneficial for the resistance. However, the institutional legal game alone contains much more than the law; state corporatism and neoliberal policies give the corporation preferential institutional access to the state. Besides this, institutional politics interacts with electoral politics and private politics, as well as contentious politics, which all are strongly determined by the burden of the structural game that favors corporate land access. The executive powers, such as Governor Wagner (PT) in Bahia, have undermined the work of public prosecutors and even judges, giving special rights to Veracel and other pulp companies operating in the state. The higher up the battle goes within Brazil (from the municipal to the state and federal levels), the more influence the electoral politics and the structural embedding by corporations has.

In all the pulp holding cases where the economic outcome was plantation slowing, discontinuation or reversal, prosecutors and other state officials issued open letters dealing with the social function of pulp projects in much the same terms as those advanced by the MST. These have not been just coincidental acts, but clearly a product of deeply embedded interactions between the MST's in-house legal sector and the state institutions' actors.

The institutional embedding operates by interactions between the MST's legal specialists, activist prosecutors, and judges. It is no surprise that the Ministério Público has given a big part of the support. The institution is one of the most independent sectors of the state (Sadek and Cavalcanti 2003: 220). Independent prosecutors do not have to obey the structural embedding by corporations or the pressures by executives influenced by the electoral politics. Autonomy positions them outside the dominant ideologies, including the legal orthodoxy intermeshed with class interests of the haves. This shows how, in the end, the best solution for all would not be the dominant advancement of solely this or that view, but the advancement of embedded autonomy by the state that managed to avoid capture, while embedding in society better to understand, influence and hear it, as Peter

Evans (1995) argued. This would boost space for agency. For this to happen, the judiciary, prosecutors and state institutions in Brazil should gain more autonomy vis-à-vis the power elite and the corporations.

When both prosecutors and the judiciary side with the resistance framing, the embedded autonomy by the movement has succeeded in creating a strategy, which together with the other strategies also in other interactive processes brings the economic outcomes sought by the activists. As Meszaros (2007: 18) points out, the Rule of Law depends greatly upon "correlations of force at a given moment in time, micropolitical arrangements and the willingness of operators of the legal system to use their powers in a particular way." For this reason, embedding is so important in defining the economic outcomes; movements and corporations can exert great influence as the autonomy and embedding by the state is still wanting. Furthermore, in absent, failed or captured state contexts, private politics seems to be important in determining investment pace and style, as is discussed next.

Private politics

The concept of private politics highlights the fact that negotiation takes place principally between private entities such as movements and companies, and the state is absent (Soule 2009). The state's absence has contributed to the "private" quality of conflicts in the most peripheral regions of Brazil, where state institutions are very weakly present and do not function well enough according to the MST, even some judges are traditional large landholders that have had slaves in the past in Maranhão, and react to invasions of large estates with strong violence (interview, Divina, Maranhão's state leader for the MST, Açailândia, March 2011). The state is captured by corporate agency.

It is a much more dangerous act to use contentious politics in such a setting than in settings with more modern and impartial institutional politics available. Yet, there's a paradox, as direct land occupations are one of the only effective, media attention-bringing political tools available to movements in settings where state embedding is rendered less efficient due to corporate capture. According to the MST, the conservative Sarney family, "connected to all large landholders," has been in power for over 50 years in Maranhão, "which turns action in all other [political] fields difficult (justice, naming of key bureaucrats, resources, and local media)" (interview, Divina, Açailândia, 2011). Better to understand the institutional game, and the lack of state involvement in the corporate-driven, private politics-steered expansion dynamics, I will present interview data enlightening the local land and environmental authorities' role and viewpoints on Suzano Papel e Celulose, building a massive new pulp mill in Imperatriz in Maranhão. The interviews reveal that the de facto governance of pulp expansion in these new resource frontiers is private.

102 *Political games*

Private politics in a pulp expansion frontier

At INCRA, which has knowledge about the state of agrarian change taking place, the directors were quite concerned about the entrance of Suzano in the Imperatriz region. José Duarte, an agronomist with state actor experience in the region since 1977 as an INCRA bureaucrat responsible for appropriation of land for settlements, said in an interview (Imperatriz, March 14, 2011) that Suzano is constantly acquiring more land. Most of the forests were cut from 1975 onwards, and a state of illegality prevails regarding environmental legislation (Franklin 2008), with 90% of the region's dominant land users, the cattle farmers, not observing the Legal Reserve conservation requirements: "there are people who cut everything" (interview, Duarte, INCRA). According to Duarte, also Suzano "does deforest." Deforestation is used as a tool to regularize land access, to create a claim on a (public) land, and to gain good land for production (Asselin 2009) – (tree plantation establishment serves the same purposes). A contradictory environmental and land tenure legislation in Brazil makes this possible (Puppim de Oliveira 2008). "In 1975, the more you cut, the more rights of registration you gained vis-à-vis the government" (interview, Duarte, 2011).

When asked about the INCRA-Suzano relationship, the official replied that "Suzano visits us to know if a land is designated for agrarian reform, in which case they cannot buy. If they do buy, INCRA will block the Registry Certificate, which is required for registering the land at a land office." However, the general impact was "strong" for Duarte. "They have bought prime lands all around, which could be given for food production. The government should earmark areas for the production of food ... Zoning must be done [to make the expansion more sound]." As in other regions of the country, INCRA officials also lamented that they do not have the resources of corporations to buy land for the landless. Peripheral investment regions typically have a deficiency of state capacity and thus state actors are not able to curb unchecked expansion in such settings. The state is often weak, non-autonomous and lacking bureaucratic capacity (see Evans 1995 for a discussion on state capacity).

For the superintendent of INCRA in Imperatriz region, José Redondo (interview, March 16, 2011), the land problem is serious, "as no one is interested in selling lands to INCRA ... only farmers who are in debts with the state. We do not buy farms here, we are not in the land market [as Suzano], but appropriate lands via legislation, paying farmers during 20–30 years." He also emphasized the weakness of their institute in instigating agrarian reform or influencing forest land policy or agrarian change. Social movements were seen by him as more important than INCRA: "Here we work depending on the pressure of social movements. We do not have land registries [on who owns what]." He argued that movements have better knowledge on the rural situation, and INCRA appropriates only unproductive farms and even these only if "the movements ask us." According to the superintendent, Suzano is taking over large land areas. In the region, there is also a lot of state land illegally held by land grabbers, which is now passing a process of regularization by a new federal program called *Terra Legal*. The grabbed land (*terra devoluta*) not regularized as part of large farms via the *Terra Legal* program could be used in agrarian reform: the new program has "more say than the institute's land appropriation division." The superintendent emphasized that according to his knowledge "eucalyptus is not entering on *terra devoluta*," and that communal lands of traditional Afro-Brazilian rural communities are also protected from eucalyptus intrusion (however, according to Barros 2008 and other stakeholders interviewed by the author this has also happened).

In another central institution regarding the steering of investment style, the federal environmental office IBAMA (the Brazilian Institute of Environment and Renewable Natural Resources, which the regional socio-environmental director of Suzano headed before joining the company), and its Director Orlan Ascenção (interview, Imperatriz, March 16, 2011), said that eucalyptus planting for charcoal and pulp is "reforestation," in line with Suzano framing. IBAMA is a state actor that verifies environmental laws are obeyed. Ascenção said that "we are not observing much the environmental impacts [of Suzano], as these are explained in the EIA [Environmental Impact Assessment presented by the company and approved by the state]." He continued that for the most part, the impact of the investment will be positive in terms of jobs and commerce in the area. Regarding environmental impacts and stakeholder relations, Ascenção claimed that "we do not have yet much information on this, or a clear opinion. Suzano shows preoccupation with its image, international markets, is afraid of negative impacts. All the NGOs have a critical vision [of Suzano and eucalyptus]."

When assessing the IBAMA-Suzano relationship, it is worth noting that Adriana Carvalho, the director of environmental issues at the Suzano project, was previously a high-ranking IBAMA and state environmental officer in Imperatriz, state of Maranhão, and the federal level in Brasília, with close ties to the governing party, the Partido dos Trabalhadores (PT). This might partly explain the markedly cautionary tone of the IBAMA director. Another IBAMA officer, an analyst in the area of environmental education, Elisangela Ambé (interview, March 16 and 18, 2011), had a slightly different and broader view, and more time to explain the changes in the region's rural mosaic of traditional communities. "Since 1970s, monocultures have expanded a lot. Small farmers were pressured to sell lands. They moved to urban centers, which was very bad particularly for the coconut breakers, who had access before to palm forests. Today they do not manage anymore to cope by. Traditional populations lost a lot, now areas are controlled by large companies." The reasons for planting eucalyptus in the Imperatriz region were clear for her as well: "favorable environmental conditions to plant eucalyptus, cheap labor, land, transportation, and water in abundance." According to her, the mining company Vale might have bought eucalyptus plantations that did not necessarily have land titles, and then passed these areas to Suzano.

104 *Political games*

On stakeholder relations, Elisangela noted that the strongest critiques of Suzano are the traditional coconut breakers, who have a large yet ideologically disperse movement (see Santos 2011). "Most of the locals support Vale and Suzano," but those who resist, "do this by forums, and networking with other movements such as MAB, of those impacted by large dams" (for MAB, see Rothman and Oliver 2002). According to Elisangela, even though Suzano's impacts will have only small impact, "all monoculture projects end up being very bad environmentally. They leave also very few areas for small farmers to derive their livelihoods, and cause a lot of migratory flux to cities such as Imperatriz." Regarding the power relations and attitudes towards Suzano, she also mentioned that the local media is seeing the investment "very positively" and gives "little attention" to the work of movements.

The IBAMA interviews revealed also interesting relations between different state actors in the conflict: the Federal Public Prosecutor's Office at Imperatriz was "very active, constantly sending questions to IBAMA" regarding Suzano's environmental licensing. This was no exception, as the public prosecutors filing class action suits proposed by rural populations have spearheaded pulp conflict debates to new levels, such as judicial decisions barring pulp expansion, in several areas of Brazil. An interview with Franklin, a local economic historian and journalist, offered more information on this and other more critical and pressing dynamics state actors did not discuss.

The highly educated intellectuals in cities normally present more critical views on unchecked corporate land expansion. This was also the case in Imperatriz, where Adalberto Franklin (interview, March 18, 2011) argued that eucalyptus expansion has "reduced the area for family agriculture." He observed closely for decades the development. There were differences between pulp projects' land access strategies: Celmar (a prior pulp investment that was interrupted by the Vale company pursuing it and turned into a charcoal project) bought "basically from the small farmers"; Suzano "from big, but circling small farmers, thus passively forcing also those to sell land who cannot bare to stay isled." For Franklin, lawsuits were the most important channel via which the resistance had managed to influence investment style, for example, to gain better working conditions and lessen environmental impact. Also direct acts, principally by the MST, that are "strong and respected by the locals since Lula's government," had "had an impact."

This case shows how the judiciary might still be usable by resistance even if other sections of the institutional and structural game were rendered unusable, and electoral politics were captured by strong power elite. Protests could also be used in such a setting, though more carefully (by greater masses and accompanying media surveillance that give protection) due to a heightened fear of violence against activists. Yet, this case illustrates how private politics cannot exist solely in its more pure form; markets or corporations cannot exist without the presence of the state in one form or another.

José Luis, from the MST in this investment region (interview, coordinator of the California settlement, Açailândia, March 13, 2011), had a friendlier attitude towards Suzano than the local rural trade unions. The MST had attained large settlements for their landless members in the region in the past, which might partly explain the difference to trade union-linked farmers feeling the pressure of eucalyptus advance on their irregularly or conventionally registered small plots. However, there are also other reasons. José Luis lives and is active in an agrarian reform settlement of 15 years containing 183 families next to the charcoal plant and eucalyptus plantations of Vale that Suzano bought. Since March 2010, Suzano has been visiting the settlement, "attempting to win people to its side, to co-opt them, offering courses, jobs, [books for and help with establishing] a library, equipment." Relations are cordial and even friendly. For José Luis, Suzano wants to be the friend of the settlement in the middle of their eucalyptus lands, "getting government money and using it for our benefit." Importantly:

> They promised that the charcoal furnaces would be closed after this cycle of eucalyptus. For Vale our presence did not matter much when they installed the furnaces in 2004 next to us. They did not communicate with us. Suzano was different, but we know it is not different. They gave us instructions on how and equipment to put out fires in the eucalyptus woods, and assured us we would not have the health problems we had with Vale's use of herbicides next to us.

In the MST discourse, this discussion of Suzano as "different" was the most striking example of a private politics-type of conflict remediation in MST-Suzano relations and possibly a sign of corporate outreach success. Suzano's promise to shut down the polluting charcoal furnaces pleased the regionally important MST California settlement. Since routine legal/political means used since 2005 had not brought results, in 2008 the MST settlers started regular protests against the pollution caused by the furnaces, for example setting direct roadblocks that had national repercussions, and insisting on the installment of filters (interview with José Luis). This conflict added to the growing hostility between Vale and the MST. Besides ridding itself of the contentious charcoal furnaces next to the MST settlement, Vale promised to transport Suzano's pulp via the railroads it operates. This was a win-win situation for all the parties concerned, including the settlement, even though the preferred land use policy of the movement would be family agriculture, not ITPs.

Suzano's Adriana Carvalho (interview, Imperatriz, March 18, 2011), argued the company acts differently, by "establishing good practices with communities. The company has time to wait for the community. California [MST settlement] is an example of this. First, Suzano goes to talk to people, it does not set up anything as ready-made, but engages in dialogue. We have learned from problems in Bahia and São Paulo." Suzano's "different" outreach practices help to explain the absence of conflict: in comparison to other pulp projects, there was no physical plantation-based conflict, and much more

106 *Political games*

dialogue in Imperatriz. This shows how, in the end, conflicts come down to personal relations (or the lack thereof). Contextually, Suzano's approach was different in Imperatriz in comparison to the extreme south of Bahia, where the company has a big pulp mill in Mucuri. Interviews with the Bahian MST leaders (Porto Seguro, April 1–15, 2011) revealed that of the three pulp companies operating in southern Bahia (Veracel, Fibria and Suzano), Suzano had given the least to the movements, and was the most antagonistic in the movement's eyes. This highlights that project and region-based differences are more significant than company-specific lines: management guidelines are applied in a variety of ways in different contexts, and the personal trajectories imbued in the local social life of the executing company personnel matter a great deal. Carvalho, the director of socio-environmental issues at the Suzano Maranhão/Piauí projects, was considered by environmental authorities, movements and state actors linked to the PT as someone who comes from their ranks. This required at least accepting her calls for dialogue, and surely influenced the creation of a friendly, even cautionary, tone in company-movement-state institution negotiations.

Temporality figured even more prominently than corporate outreach in explaining the absence of major anti-Big Pulp mobilization. The Celmar episode in the 1990s, where a promised pulp venture turned into a polluting charcoal project against expectations, deepened the charcoal-specific grievances, accentuating the relative desirability of the unattained pulp project. This was a good time, grievance-wise, for implanting a real pulp project. Such a project would be considered a relative improvement in land use in the area by most stakeholders.

The weak state and, thus, limited steering capacity via any state-remediated political game, also partially explain the nonexistence of protests attempting to influence the Suzano investment. Eucalyptus occupations make much more sense if institutional or other state-remediated political games are open for the resistance. Not only state strength and usability but also the issue matters: targeting a global iron-ore behemoth such as Vale gave the local MST's cause national attention: the federal government subsequently pressured Vale as the incident became a high-profile issue. Suzano protests would not have received such attention. Investment politics varies by industry and targeted companies, as do the outcomes of movements in general (Luders 2010). Contentious politics (involving conflicts/protests) seems to be a particularly useful political game in the contexts and state-industry-movement dynamics where the state is most present: state embedding by movements is more likely when the state is present.

The situation in Imperatriz could change. For Franklin (interview, Imperatriz, March 2011), a local intellectual influential among movements, Suzano was causing a "massive rural exodus," which he has seen is "filling the city's slums," and the company was also "occupying and claiming ownership on communally or customarily held lands of squatters that would have a right to these lands by law via their existing use of the land for production." Land ownership lawsuits have already entered the justice system, and the public prosecutors were actively following the drastic rural changes, filing suits against Suzano.

In a peripheral political region, both the potential resistance and state capacities are relatively weak vis-à-vis corporate actors. Weak formal education and social organization causes citizens to be less aware of their rights to demand state institutions to delimit negative investment impacts. Institutions do not have the power to steer investment. The institutional arrangement in Brazil, particularly in the Amazon, is complex, with environmental and rural institutes having contradictory and unclear roles: overlapping land access claims are difficult to govern in such a state of perplexity (Puppim de Oliveira 2008). This renders contentious politics with direct land disputes, requiring at least partial state remediation of conflicting land claims, potentially less efficient than private politics. In such a setting, the rural trade unions of Imperatriz region, even though very angry at Suzano for its land use, as well as other movements have mostly used private dialogue for attempting to influence Suzano's investment style (see Kröger 2013 for a more detailed analysis of this case).

Concluding remarks

Both top-down processes, such as the ever more meritocratic selection of judges, public prosecutors and other state actors, as well as bottom-up processes such as contentious agency promotion, can support the construction of a social movement society, the rule of law, and stronger democracy. If this tendency were strengthened, corporate resource exploitation could be more rigorously criticized.

Stricter regulation and democratic revamping of mechanisms by which political power is concentrated at the top are required to change the pace and style of investment. However, this will not be easy, as most companies are very adverse to any real regulation. The perception of ITP-reliant companies in Brazil is that their sector is already excessively regulated (MMA 2005: 231), and thus they resist all attempts at and discourses of regulation. As long as corporate embedding of the state remains relatively stronger than movement embedding or the embedded autonomy by the state, it is unforeseeable that the economic outcomes would be broadly different.

Since 2000, the growth in the strategic importance of pulp-holding areas and the simultaneous spur in available state financing (achieved via corporate embedding) increased the power of corporations. Against this backdrop, worsening the configuration of political opportunities to slow plantation expansion by the resistance, the more widespread slowing of plantation expansion in 2004–08 in comparison to the pre-2003 era becomes an interesting and vexing empirical fact. This anomaly can be explained by a simultaneous rise in contentious agency promotion, directed principally by the Brazilian landless movement. This chapter's analysis considering the interaction

108 *Political games*

between resistance and corporate agency promotion in several political games where resource use is determined supports the hypothesis on the importance of contentious agency.

The next chapters will extend the discussion to a global scale, studying first the politics of tree plantation expansion, including resistance, around the world, and then the recent mobilization against corporate resource exploitation across the globe, in different industries. These chapters comparing an even greater number of cases in different political-environmental contexts help in further testing the hypothesis on contentious agency importance, illustrating cleavages and key issues in the contemporary phenomenon of global land grabbing, particularly in fast-growth tree plantation expansion.

Notes

1 Even though helpful for research, the official election campaign statistics should not be trusted too much, being based on the candidate's own explanations of their election financing, so that many do not even give full details and some give none at all. Furthermore, it is easy to falsify any receipt in Brazil or circulate money by *caixa dois* and other corruption measures. Quite certainly, the real figures for political support given by companies are much higher, and are not limited only to those candidates named in the database. However, it is harder to find evidence of this, as these would be criminal offenses. At times, these cases of more general exchanges of favors and election financing pop up in the Brazilian mass media, as someone leaks information in the mainly day-to-day internal battles of parties and politicians.

2 See the public election financing data offered online by the Supreme Electoral Tribunal (www.tse.gov.br), "ELEIÇÕES," "*prestação de contas*" section, 2006 elections, then click on "Consulta a prestação de contas final de candidatos e comitês financeiros," and type the name of Yeda Rorato Crusius, 45 (state: RS, governador) in the "candidato" and "receita" search criteria. You can see that, for example, just one paper company, Aracruz Celulose, has given her 281,556 reais according to these official statistics (which probably do not include all the support, as it is not obligatory to reveal all sources of financing), under different registration numbers. Furthermore, these figures might overlap, as, for example, Stora Enso owns half of Veracel and it is not clear from the data source how much it has contributed to the financing of elections by Veracel, or whether this is also calculated in the direct financing by Stora Enso.

3 The CEO of the company, Jouko Karvinen, explained the contributions to the Finnish NGO Maattomien ystävät ry, which demanded explanation from the company as well as its board, in which the Finnish state is the most powerful shareholder.

4 Besides Veracel support, Wagner and Souto also received 200,000 reais from Aracruz.

5 However, as the company is a conglomerate of various economic activities, including cement, construction and finance businesses, one would eventually have to total their efforts as well to weigh the political clout of Votorantim through the financing of elections in Brazil.

6 See McAllister (2008) for a book-length study on the Ministry's story of becoming a central player in environmental conflicts and crucial role in advancing the rule of law in Brazil.

5 Key characters in contemporary global expansion of resource exploitation, illustrated by conflicts over tree plantations

This chapter draws on the knowledge of the expansion of tree plantations (TPs) across the globe, to make global comparisons on the significance of resistance in contemporary "land grabbing." The covered material includes United Nations Food and Agriculture Organization (FAO) data on TPs, existing academic literature, the extensive writings by the World Rainforest Movement on the topic, many other international, regional and local NGOs' publications, movement material, official documents, interviews and discussions with specialists, foresters, company directors, officials and activists aware of the recent changes, field research observations from plantation areas, and quite extensive Google searches to locate articles from local and global newspapers, research institutions, and other bodies on the politics and economy of TP expansion. The literature on the topic in English and Brazilian Portuguese was surveyed; also many studies in Finnish and Spanish were covered. Not all the studies read are referenced here, the aim being a central issue enlightening rather than an exhaustive literature review. The limitation of review in four languages signifies that the breadth and depth of expansion and conflicts in many countries is not thoroughly presented here. Indeed, in some parts, the exclusion of evidence in local languages on TP conflicts results in drastic misrepresentation of the state of affairs. For example, India surely has many more ITP protests (according to interviews of the author with activists aware of the Indian situation, for example Ville-Veikko Hirvelä, Helsinki, November 10, 2012) than the existing English-language literature claims (e.g. Gerber 2010). In many contexts resistance acts are not even locally reported; the most accurate depiction of events requires thus extensive field research, ethnography, participant observation and interviews of people in TP expansion (or would-be, projected expansion) areas.

Nevertheless, even considering these research material shortcomings, applying not only to TP research, the investigation of expanding non-food resource exploitation carries significant importance in the academic and political debate on rapid agrarian change in past years caused particularly by large-scale land deals. Borras *et al.* (2012) found, for example, that in Latin America and the Caribbean land and capital (re)concentration occurred in two broad mega-sectors: "flex" crop (usable for food as well as other

110   *Contemporary global resource exploitation*

purposes, such as energy) complex/food sectors, and the broad non-food sector. The survey of industrial forestry expansion sheds light on the latter, less studied phenomenon.

Timber products are still mostly extracted from natural or modified natural forests, but the share of plantations is increasing. According to a 2001 publication by Sohngen *et al.*, cited by UNEP (2012), plantations provided in 2001 some 35% of the globally harvested wood. Since then the plantation share has increased as plantations have grown while the total forestry area has not (ibid.). Considering this global importance, discussion on TPs has been remarkably absent, although there is a growing literature.

This chapter investigates the political-economic expansion of non-edible tree species cultivated in either: 1 industrial, large-scale forestry plantations of tens of thousands of hectares contractually controlled or owned by corporations (ITPs); or 2 small plots of a few hectares maximum size by rural households (smallholder-based forestry plantations, STPs). The conceptual division into corporate- and smallholder-based forestry is necessary to explain why there are divergences in the existence of resistance. There are also publicly (by state) controlled and community TPs, but these are not studied in detail.

The conceptual separation between ITPs and STPs flows from the available data and the existing literature on TPs and agrarian political economy. To assess differences in STPs and ITPs, Barney (2004) urges the study of the history of legal and informal resource tenure, within an analysis of rural political-economic restructuring accompanying TP expansion. An incorporated comparative analysis (see McMichael 1992) is used as an underlying frame to organize the accounts of different but globally and temporally connected political games and actor dynamics where plantations expand or are discontinued. A comparison of studies of different political systems suggests STPs have been the main form of industrial forestry expansion in places such as post-1992 Thailand (Barney 2004), Vietnam (Sikor 2012) and Finland (Forest.fi, Facts, Ownership, accessed June 28, 2012), whereas ITPs have been the mainstay in countries such as Brazil, Chile, Indonesia and Mozambique. In the first group of countries a counter-movement steered investment from ITPs to STP establishment, while in the latter conflicts are more common and resistance is trying to build up. Differences in class and power relations are discussed together with other socio-environmental issues commonly given as explanations for the ITP–STP divergence. The chapter reviews the state of knowledge in the abovementioned material on expansion and resistance causality, comparing very different contexts. First, different explanations on why TPs are expanding are summed up, so as to understand the phenomenon (the symptoms of which are conflicts), at a broad level.

Why?

There are different explanations for the rapid expansion of tree plantations in the forest industry. At the visible level, for Dauvergne and Lister (2011), the

Contemporary global resource exploitation 111

global discount economy where big box retail companies squeeze producers down the commodity chains to produce timber products for them as the largest quantities and as cheaply and reliably as possible is the main explanation for problems in the felling areas. Rising consumerism and an expanding consumer base, e-commerce and global trade drive the rapid use of fast-wood timber products. Packaging forest products amongst others in cardboard or paper, typically thrown away as soon as the item is opened or used, further increases consumption (Dauvergne and Lister 2011). Thus, the corporate agency of bottom line fixation explains central growth. TPs typically allow both lower costs and stronger tenure security, fiber-supply control, an oligarchic position in local land markets and even in global pulp markets, and general land use determination power.

When this corporate agency is disaggregated, a typical North-South capitalist dynamic explaining expansion emerges. With ITPs, the accompanying pulp mill and other technology sales, the North has gained a new outlet for expanding its forest industry cluster. This cluster has been developed in the North since the 1920s via capitalization and internal capitalist innovation, creating capital-intensive forestry technology. As rates of return started to fall drastically below 10% at the start of the 1990s, a new fix was needed for the accumulation to continue. Socio-ecological transformations were needed to expand forestry capitalism: ITPs fencing large land areas was the solution. Global forestry capitalism experienced a cyclic change from its capitalization phase into material accumulation and territorial expansion. Arrighi's (1994) theory has illustrated in general how such cyclic change is inherent in global capitalist expansion. For example, smallholder-based agrarian capitalism led to the development of globally leading capital-intensive farming techniques in the American Midwest by the 1960s: when this emerging agribusiness/food complex globalized, it took the form of the Green Revolution in its land relations, particularly in the global South (Moore 2011). A similar type of cyclic change from capitalization to territorialization took place as the Northern forest industry cluster started to globalize in the 1970s. New tree plantations are thus linked to this deeper cyclic change in global capitalism. In this view, capitalism is a socio-ecological relation (Moore 2011): the now-globalizing forestry capitalism a plantation-based land use change project.

Over-development of production capacity, in part pushed by machinery producing cores, further explains plantation expansion. The establishment of woodworking industries is the strongest driver of plantation expansion in areas where the processing capacity surpasses timber supply, and natural forest logging is becoming ever harder, such as in Indonesia (Obidzinski and Dermawan 2010).

The emergent global "bio-economy" will explain an ever-greater part of future growth. The main reason for the prognosis of robust expansion is that plantations are becoming areas where "flex trees" are planted. Flex trees are the commodity consequence of merging inter-industry interests in the emerging green/bio-economy. Biomass in the same plantations can be used for

112 *Contemporary global resource exploitation*

pulp or energy, pulp prices largely determining the use of biomass until now in the case of Brazil (Fearnside 1998). Energywood and other timber uses become more prominent, while pulp will continue to be important. Pulp prices have soared in the past 15 years, and consequently there's a mill construction boom. Companies and governments are now setting up very fast-growth (two-year rotation) plantations in the global South to export pellets for growing wood-energy markets and plants in the North. New pulp mills are becoming also major energy producers (*Valor Econômico*, "Produtor de celulose cresce em geração," September 11, 2012). Wood-based second-generation biodiesel plants are also being erected, with high hopes in the industry that wood fuel could become the next oil. Carbon sequestering plantations may serve in the REDD+ schemes. Polluting industries and consumers such as air travelers seek to buy carbon credits or offset impacts by crediting tree plantation. Myriad GM and nanotechnology paper applications are being developed based on the capitalization of specially engineered trees. The machinery development is still largely controlled by Northern companies, but fast-growth and flex plantation techniques, including GM trees, are an area of innovation where Southern "National Champions," e.g. from Brazil, are gaining a strong foothold. It is likely these strands will unite even more tightly into a global flex forestry cluster. This industry consolidation will lead to further expansion – new conflicts will also arise. Tree plantations are becoming flex tree plantations, a "renewable" capitalist response to depletion of nonrenewable resources. Yet, the degree of renewability depends on the soil, water and other environmental impacts of TPs, as well as on the political acceptance of TPs.

The most robust answer to the why question is the endless pursuit of accumulation in capitalism. By flex trees and crops, globalizing industries will reap the benefits of both capitalization- and material expansion-type accumulation simultaneously, as noted by Arrighi (1994). When the natural spaces start to become exhausted, as has happened, flex crops and species arise. Global corporate agency values lands in the South, and forestry as a business, more than before. Nature is molded to ensure it does not limit growth of GDP and returns to investment. However, there are limits, caused by nature, capitalism and politics, in flex accumulation. The question of where and what TPs are expanded is now assessed.

Where and what?

Clear statistics on plantation coverage are difficult to come by, as different entities use different conceptualizations of forest and plantations, and the field is evolving rapidly and with unsatisfactory monitoring. The FAO's Forestry Division maintains one of the most extensive databases, which is nevertheless also problematic in many ways. The FAO itself admits that "consistent definitions and reliable data have proven problematic in quantifying plantation forests or planted forest resources in both industrialized and developing

Contemporary global resource exploitation 113

countries."[1] Conceptualization differences produce incomparability in databases. The FAO, UN Environment Programme (UNEP) and other UN bodies talk about "planted forests": according to the FAO (2010: 5), there were 264 million ha of these in the world in 2010. NGOs claim that the real extent of plantation expansion is higher than those presented by governments and thus also the FAO. Although the following FAO (2011) table on plantations should not be read as the final word considering the methodological-conceptual-political discrepancies, Table 5.1 clearly indicates that plantations have expanded dramatically between 1990 and 2010.

The table indicates that global plantations have expanded by 48.1% between 1990 and 2010. Mexico has seen a whopping 815% increase in tree plantations between 1990 and 2010 and has now 3.2 million ha (FAO 2011: 25).[2] Alongside North America, South America (67% increase) and Asia and the Pacific (61.6% increase) were the two main areas of dramatic, above-average plantation expansion increase. In the Near East TPs expanded by 49.5%. Europe was an exception: plantations were expanded by only 12.8%. The rest of the regions in the table experienced plantation expansion of 30–40% between 1990 and 2010.

Even considering the faults in this tree plantation data – which are the most extensive data available – the expansion trend is clear and pronounced. The bird's-eye view afforded by Table 5.1 shows that plantation expansion is a major issue and significant trend in the modern world. The official statistics on global forests illustrate how tree plantations expand while primary forests and other natural forests decrease or retain their size (FAO 2010, 2011).

According to FAO data, in the world outside East Asia expansion has been driven as much by smallholders as by corporations. If excluding the East Asian increase from the total global TP expansion (in del Lungo *et al.* 2006),

Table 5.1 Global "planted forest" expansion by regions, 1990–2010 (million ha)

	1990	2010	% change, 1990–2010
Africa	11.663	15.409	32.1
Asia and the Pacific	74.163	119.884	61.6
Russian Federation	12.651	16.991	34.3
Europe	46.395	52.327	12.8
Caribbean	0.391	0.547	39.9
Central America	0.445	0.584	31.2
South America	8.276	13.821	67.0
Near East (excluding North Africa)	4.677	6.991	49.5
Canada	1.357	8.963	560.5
Mexico	0.350	3.203	815.1
USA	17.938	25.363	41.4
World	178.307	264.084	48.1

Source: Author's elaboration based on FAO 2011 data.

114 *Contemporary global resource exploitation*

smallholder plantations rose from 15.18 million ha in 1990 to 20.99 million ha in 2005 – that is, by 5.81 million ha. Meanwhile, corporate plantations expanded by 6.14 million ha. There are, however, reasons to suspect that the de facto expansion has been driven lately even more clearly by corporations than by smallholders. For example, the latest and most large-scale pulp investment in the world, Eldorado's 1.5 megaton pulp mill in Mato Grosso do Sul, Brazil, owns only 20–30% of its plantation base; the rest of the euca-lyptus cultivation areas are being rented (Siqueira 2012). The FAO statistics do not take into consideration the contractual expansion of de facto corporate plantations, but rely on official tenure calculation.

Indeed, it seems that most expansion of TPs has taken place because of corporate expansion. This becomes even clearer if only exotic species are included – the composition of which per TPs across countries are given by the FAO (2010) – and completely clear if the "planted semi-natural forests" are left outside the definition of TP.

Main land use changes

Very different landscapes have been turned into similar tree plantations (Patterson and Hoalst-Pullen 2011). The best, most fertile lands close to rural cities have been appropriated first in most expansion contexts. A study in New Zealand found that because forestry is a more intensive and higher-demand land use than pasture, tree plantations expand first closer to the city, pushing the second priority pasture and agriculture use to peripheries (Nagashima *et al.* 2002). As the best lands become occupied by TPs, the focus turns increasingly to marginal lands. According to Fearnside (1998), the industry focus on territorializing ever more marginal lands leads to damaging expansion in peripheries, with the search for lower costs cutting the limited local economic benefits in large firm-controlled plantation areas. The industry focus is on the decreasing cost of extraction and transport instead of increas-ing yields, and genetic work not focusing on yield increase on best lands but on developing hybrids for marginal lands (Fearnside 1998). This can be explained by the practical limit soil quality places on increasing yields in commercial-scale plantations to $30m^3$ per hectare per year even in the world's best tropical climatic conditions of Brazil (ibid.). Nature places limits on expansion. With depletion of finite resources, and natural limits on increasing yields on good lands, but the technical capability to make cultivation pos-sible on cheaper, marginal lands, expansion takes place in more peripheral, difficult-to-reach areas.

The rapidity of land use change can also affect the countries of the global North. In Australia, dramatic tree plantation (mostly eucalyptus) growth between 1997 and 2009 (from 1.2 to 2 million ha) represents a radical change in rural landscape character and economic activity, with food-producing family farms turning into corporate ITPs (Stewart *et al.* 2011). Farmers have widely opposed this expansion (ibid.), but according to the reviewed

Global TPs are expanding quickly, with many consequences. In South America, the expansion pace is at 500,000 ha per year (Jobbágy *et al.* 2012) and this is increasing. In Africa, the rise may be even more dramatic than in South America: for example, Pöyry Forest Consulting – a leading expert on ITP expansion – suggests that within a decade Africa will be the center of TP expansion globally. Africa will see a wide spectrum of tree plantation types and uses, including: ecosystem services plantations such as "carbon sinks" operating on the REDD+ markets and under development cooperation agendas; energy plantations; pulp projects integrated with plantations and mills; and other biomass ventures. Africa is also likely to attract timberland investment by portfolio funds seeking diversification, both from the private and the state sectors. Western pension and Church funds, for example, are looking to land investments for more secure returns than are to be found in the equity markets. A case in point is the Chikweti investment in Mozambique by Dutch, Swedish and Norwegian funds (Seufert 2012). It is likely that in Africa land tenure will be controlled more tightly by foreign actors than in the neo-developmentalist countries of South America (such as Brazil) and Asia (such as China, Indonesia and India), where new laws curb foreign land ownership. Actors from China, the European Union (EU) nations and some others have secured and will continue to attempt to secure fifty- to one hundred-year leases from weaker governments, with ample investment guarantees.

There are severe limits to ITP expansion in China, since "feeding its enormous population puts so much pressure on land use that China has no real scope for a pulping industry based on plantation forests. Establishing plantations can be a slow and complex business as most of the suitable land is held by households and communities."[3] Instead, a growing number of timber manufacturing plants, including paper mills, are located in China, promising for this emerging power a very different position in global forestry capitalism's division of labor and revenues than for the more clearly commodity-producing nodes of Brazil or Uruguay, for example. Much biomass used in China is imported, mostly from South America, Southeast Asia and Africa. Still, China is a mixed case, as there is considerable TP expansion in China, with violent conflicts involving dramatic suppression of human rights and even deaths (Ping and Nielsen 2010). For example, Stora Enso was involved at least indirectly in the death and beatings of local resistance activists and lawyers while expanding eucalyptus plantations for its planned 900,000 million-ton pulp mill in Guangxi, southern China, which has already 90,000 ha of eucalyptus plantations. A report by *Rights and Resources* argued that Stora Enso's "limits to their legal due diligence ... [are] ... raising risks for local people to both their rights to land and livelihoods" (ibid.).

According to some estimates, India plans to establish about 10–30 million ha of new TPs by 2020 (Ghosh *et al.* 2011: 16).[4] The Indian case illustrates

116 *Contemporary global resource exploitation*

many features shared among TP-expanding government strategies. A new government policy, the Green India Mission, aims to increase radically the country's tree plantation cover. According to a government document, "The scope of greening is not limited to just trees and plantations ... [I]t will not only strive to restore degraded forests, but would also contribute in protection/enhancement of forests with relatively dense forest cover (in line with country strategy on REDD Plus)" (Government of India 2010: 5). In more specific terms, "According to Environment Minister Jairam Ramesh, the overarching objective is to increase forest cover in 5 million hectares and improve the quality of forest cover in an area of corresponding size" (*The Hindu* 2010). Based on similar preceding policy lines and wordings around TP expansion in the global South, including India, one could read the government information as signifying that the 5 million ha "increase" will use TPs and a significant part, if not most, of the other 5 million ha "improving the quality of forests" will signify cutting "secondary" or "degraded" forest areas and planting them with TPs. For forest peoples and activists, such areas are often real forests on which they depend. The scope of this policy is unclear as of yet. According to Soumitra Ghosh from the National Forum of Forest Peoples and Forest Workers, the Minister of Forests has spoken about 30 million ha, and some official documents talk about 20 million ha.[5] Activists have been very worried about the Green India Mission, foreseeing it will start many TP conflicts and problems.

The government document outlining the policy in India has included, however, many of the critical points related to TPs, and if the policy is executed as drafted, the most severe problems could potentially be minimized. However, this is as of yet a big 'if', as most, if not all, TP-promoting government policies and corporate projects outline similar safety measures as in the Green India Mission, whilst failing to execute these in practice. On page 12, the Green India Mission document refers to the much higher productivity of tree crops in Brazil and Indonesia in comparison to India, and suggests the conventional TP techniques for covering the gap and increase India's "potential." The techniques include genetic manipulation and cloning; tree nurseries; and improvement of "investment climate," signifying government subsidies in different form, including "all costs of planting" on government lands and "supply of seedlings at the site at nominal cost and training" in private lands. The officially acknowledged coverage area of the new Indian TP program is 1.5 million ha. A large part of the new TPs will be used to gain carbon credits. India is the world's second largest producer of carbon credits, and "carbon sinks" and other climate change-mitigation projects in the rapidly emerging climate and emission markets are becoming a growth strategy for India and many other poor Southern countries. It needs to be emphasized that according to my interviews, there is at least one massive protest somewhere in India per week that includes the resisting of ITP expansion (e.g. interview with Ville-Veikko Hirvelä, Siemenpuu, Helsinki, November 2012). Within this setting, these new land use changes predicted by

Contemporary global resource exploitation 117

the Green India Mission will likely lead to the rise of new grievances and thus conflicts.

Nevertheless, as also contentious agency has its role to play, and corporate agency varies depending on many issues, some TP projects in the pipeline will be scrapped because of resistance and/or the depressed global economic situation, overproduction and low prices of pulp, for example. Plantation expansion has been much affected by pulp prices and by timber costs; now new trends are "carbon sink" and energywood TPs which could significantly shape the dynamics, even though pulp will continue to be very important because there is a broad transition from petrochemical (e.g. plastic) to biodegradable packaging. Although in December 2011 pulp prices were still above pre-2008 prices, they were coming down rapidly, with a decline of over US $100 per ton since January 2011: in the USA, prices stood at about $830 per ton in July 2012 (see FOEX Indexes, www.foex.fi). Insofar as prices rise, as they have done, those who got in early in land markets will be happy with their established corporate enclaves. With many new large-scale pulp projects in the pipeline, overcapacity, along with slowing growth, is likely to continue to threaten pulp prices, but pulp prices alone do not determine expansion. Pulpwood plantations can be transformed into charcoal or other energywood projects, as happened with Celmar, a 1990s failed pulp project in Brazil's Maranhão. Therefore, this being a flex commodity, boom-bust market cycles as drastic as in cacao or other edible crops will not likely be seen (although, being a vulnerable monoculture, destruction of plantations might be experienced due to epidemic diseases or uncontrollable fires, these being a growing risk as the size of monocultures and climate disruptions increase).

How?

State-industry-resistance interaction and investment location

Where TPs expand is explained by a variety of issues, and is understandable only in the global interdependent context where forestry capitalists, states and civil society groups interact. State dynamics help to explain how, where and what plantations are established. The state role has been discussed thoroughly in the literature. The research has emphasized that most governments eased the corporate-driven globalization process from the beginning with subsidies to large-scale plantations (e.g. Silva 2004; Bull _et al._ 2006; Clement _et al._ 2009; Patterson and Hoalst-Pullen 2011; Redo _et al._ 2012), weakened environmental regulation and territorial titling (Clapp 1995; du Monceau 2008; Miola 2009; Pakkasvirta 2010; Gautreau and Vélez 2011), liberalized financial markets (Stewart _et al._ 2011) and/or violent methods such as dispossession (Marchak 1995; Carrere and Lohmann 1996; Kay 2002), if governments shared an electoral-institutional-ideological alliance with the industry. However, also notable exceptions exist, including, for example, the political

118   *Contemporary global resource exploitation*

economic dynamics in ALBA countries in Latin America (field research, 2004–11), Thailand (Barney 2004), Vietnam (Sikor 2012) and India (Saxena 1994; Dauvergne and Lister 2011: 173), which have not provided privileged land access to globally leading pulp and paper companies. Instead, STPs or state-owned ITPs have been created in some of these countries.

Whether ITPs or STPs are created depends mostly on whether capital comes in search of land, not labor (ITPs created), or both land and labor (STPs created) (see Clapp 1998 for a study of Chile in this respect). The reasons to establish STPs are many, such as the desire by corporations to alleviate risk of resistance by incorporating smallholders into forestry. One reason may also be to draft socially and/or environmentally oriented policies, for example in states with deeper democracy, outside of corporate capture, and/or states seeking to diversify rural incomes and environmental services via STP promotion.

Although the main reasons for TP expansion are placed on the pushing side, the resistance has been found also to play a role. In some places resistance has become a major force in impacting where or what type of expansion takes place. An early example is Thailand in the 1980s and early 1990s (Hall 2002). In Thailand in 1992, militarized expansion of eucalyptus plantations was discontinued because of resistance. Expansion would have required the displacement of 250,000 families. Instead, paper firms from Japan withdraw from Thailand and invested in Australia. Thai firms responded to the toughening political and regulatory context by investing in neighboring countries with lower levels of regulation and resistance (Hall 2002). The 1992 Re-Afforestation Act, an outcome of increasingly strong eucalyptus activism, led to a complete halt on new corporate plantation (ITP) concessions since 1992 (Barney 2004).

The industry moves are thus based on state support and societal resistance responses. For example, Finnish paper companies started to avoid Indonesia after global criticism by powerful NGOs regarding environmental destruction in the 1990s. Instead they shifted focus to South America, particularly Uruguay as it provided a less conflictive setting than the more productive, yet more resistance-orientated context of many Brazilian states.

When faced with resistance capable of challenging land control, this uncertainty about long-term corporate access to land is one of the most major concerns for ITP promoters. In interviews for this study, executives gave more importance to the resistance movement than the movement leaders themselves. When resistance is too strong, plantation firms choose instead to expand in political environments with greater land access security and less dense rural populations, such as in Australia and Uruguay. Hall (2002), studying ITPs as pollution havens, notes that the main reason for selecting political systems where corporate land tenure is protected more strongly is not merely land control per se. More important is that greater security of tenure raises the possibility to inflict environmental damage, environmental damage being a required outcome for establishing ITPs for Hall (2002).

Contemporary global resource exploitation 119

Low population density is commonly understood to diminish the prospects and strength of resistance over water use and pollution issues by impacted populations. Evidence from a comparative study of expansion in Brazil in the previous chapters of this book, however, suggests that ITP expansion even in high rural density contexts has been rapid and massive, given that large land masses have been appropriated easily and cheaply. Although demographics matter, more important is politics. Low land prices, natural conditions, supportive state policies and incentives remain the key reasons for plantation location, particularly in contexts of low visibility, low impact, or absence of conflictive resistance.

"Political forests": the centrality of land control in ITPs

Forestry plantations started to be developed most extensively after World War II. In this period, argue Vandergeest and Peluso (2006), the FAO became a central organization promulgating a type of forestry empire, which accompanied the older ideal German forestry model that has replaced natural forests with managed timber stands ever since its nineteenth-century inception. These empires still interact with local ecologies and political economies. The result has been dramatic expansion in tree plantations and restriction of old forestry practices in most areas of the world, particularly if states have promoted industrial forestry as a key developmental policy. For example, forestry played a major role in the post-World War II national political economies and states of Southeast Asia, leading to tree plantation expansion (Fox *et al.* 2009). The expansion happened in an agrarian political-economic setting based on the creation of what Peluso and Vandergeest (2001) call "political forests" – a term by which they emphasize how "forests" are politically constructed and might not even have forest in them, with "forest" demarcation serving more the political needs of land control than the ecological concerns of forest preservation or use, with this notion applying globally. In fact, tree monocultures have often replaced high-biodiversity natural forests, although officially expanding on "degraded" lands (Sargent and Bass 1992).

The elites have gained most from this consolidation of "degraded" forests under state control, in the form of land concessions, subsidies and rents, argue Barr and Sayer (2012) in a discussion of the Asia-Pacific. Timber provides rent incentives for the elites in a similar way to oil (Ross 2001). The elites have directed the ITP-created timber rents to political and economic activities allowing even greater expansion of the rent-yielding area (thus further expanding ITPs) and power outside the forestry sector. The rent incentive has led in Indonesia to what Barr and Sayer (2012) call perverse outcomes, wherein naturally or already commercially valuable forest or timberland is destroyed and replaced with TPs.

Most worryingly, according to researchers, the conversion of land to TPs is irreversible in many Southern contexts, e.g. in Uruguay (Carámbula *et al.* 2011) and Chile (Nahuelhual *et al.* 2012). In Chile, the conversion to

120   *Contemporary global resource exploitation*

plantation forestry is absolute and irreversible: once established, corporate areas are required to remain permanently under plantation forestry by Chile's law DL 701 (Nahuelhual *et al.* 2012). In Uruguay, the government has given very strict investor guarantees to foreign companies such as Stora Enso, assuring that they will receive land for establishing a sufficient number of plantations for the needs of their pulp mill investment (Bacchetta 2012).

Job creation and livelihoods

The establishment of ITPs is accompanied by job-creation discourse, this being a major factor granting public legitimacy (general acceptance making expansion possible, in the broad sense and generally). The jobs offered by TP expansion depend on the TP investment type. If the trees are destined for large-scale pulp mills, jobs have been more precarious and temporary than in construction wood-destined forestry areas, studies in Brazil (Gonçalves 2001) and Uruguay (Carámbula and Piñeiro 2006) suggest. The literature on relations (including conflict) between TP owners and labor is large (Gerber and Veuthey 2010), and would require a review of its own, being away from the focus of this chapter on expansion dynamics. Such studies are an essential accompaniment to the current expansion's many political impacts, such as the cutting of autonomy and power from ITP-critical trade unions, as happened in Brazil when Aracruz and Votorantim were merged to form Fibría (Kröger 2012b), and the impacts of these changes on ITP legitimacy. Some notes can be made.

Governments feel they need to boost export-based commodity production to join the global economy, saying this would create jobs. For example, the government officials of Laos have started to give more large-scale land concessions to companies after the 2000s neoliberal period. Yet, in some cases peasant land has been bulldozed at night without warning: most forest and perennial cropland is transformed into plantation land very quickly, even in one night.

In Brazil, people displaced by these activities have formed camps and some of them have started to work as wage workers for the plantations, while struggling to gain their own land (field research, 2004–11); meanwhile in Laos, companies have in-built planning for such camps on future plantations, to get access to and control cheap labor close to land. Indigenous people living in forests have had to shift from an economy where they produce 90% of their own food and buy only 10%, to an economy in which they must buy 90% of their own food and can gather only 10%. This has led to a violent process of proletarianization, in which land is turned into capital and people into labor, according to Baird (2011).

In some cases, for example in Southeast Asia, plantation companies have not even wanted the peasants they have expelled to become their workers: instead, they have imported laborers they see as more fit for plantation work (Kenney-Lazar 2011). In most cases, possible compensation for land loss has

Contemporary global resource exploitation 121

been paid only if dispossessed groups have mobilized, as a retroactive way to smooth the resentment, and not as an a priori strategy to try to remove people from their lands peacefully.

Thus, the conditions under which pulp plantations may complement, rather than threaten, livelihoods of local communities are extremely limited, argue Pirard and Mayer (2009) in a study of Indonesia. They claim that at least one-fifth of land should be left to intensified local agriculture and agroforestry instead of plantations. Company operations should be carried out with care and constant consultation with impacted populations, not too hastily and carelessly. Priority should be given to local employment. The minimum conditions should also include careful determination of plantation sites and more transparent government licensing of plantation concessions and pulp mills, recognizing local and customary rights (ibid.). The abovementioned minimum conditions Pirard and Mayer (2009) find essential for ITPs and large-scale pulpwood TPs to support local livelihoods are very tight – in fact, so tight that it might be impossible to fulfill them by ITPs.

Smallholder versus industrial tree plantations

This section discusses the smallholder-industrial tree plantation politics in different agrarian dynamics. In some contexts STPs are the main route of TP expansion, in other contexts it is ITPs. Contract eucalyptus farming on smallholders' lands has come to be the mainstay of fiber provision for Thailand's pulp industry (Boulay and Tacconi 2012). This TP investment pace and style was secured by contentious agency, including strong protests since the 1980s. Now pulp mills are small in Thailand and there is real competition between them to secure fiber. Barney (2004) notes that about 65% of all eucalyptus in Thailand is cultivated by smallholders (over 30,000 households, with on average 5ha to 8 ha plantations), with some companies such as Phoenix Pulp and Paper buying 100% of their fiber from local outgrowers. Establishment of large-scale corporate eucalyptus plantations has been made impossible in Thailand with the resistance against eucalyptus based also on environmental reasoning (Puntasen *et al.* 1992). However, smallholders are currently increasingly interested in planting eucalyptus as a cash crop (Boulay and Tacconi 2012).

Tree planting may therefore also promise benefits to smallholders, besides the elites and corporations, although potentially it would undermine livelihood security (Barr and Sayer 2012) as subsistence food cultivation areas would turn into timber production. The potential is seen in smallholder TPs whose plantations do not present a harmful rent base for the elites. Leys and Vanclay (2010) see potential in STPs if undertaken by people themselves, for example by forming cooperatives able to influence decision making, particularly regarding sale prices. The bargaining power of smallholders in Thailand was very good, according to Barney (2004), but this was largely due to the impossibility of expanding corporate plantations and the creation of a

122   *Contemporary global resource exploitation*

competitive cash crop market for eucalyptus. This suggests the promoters of ITPs and STPs are in a zero-sum game over producing smallholder or corporate-benefiting agrarian structures, including timber markets.

Failures of STP schemes are common, illustrated, for example, by Barney's (2008) discussion of the failed attempt to transform subsistence-oriented peasants into smallholder arboreal entrepreneurs in Laos. Stable institutions, secure tenure and enabling policies are necessary preconditions for STPs even potentially to improve livelihoods, argue Kassa *et al.* (2011) in a detailed study of Ethiopia. Smallholders are typically in an unfavorable bargaining position, not being well enough informed about wood markets or about the growth of their wood stock, even in Vietnam, which is considered a relative STP "success story" (Schnell *et al.* 2012). The grand STP program of Indonesia has failed dramatically (Obidzinski and Dermawan 2010). Government policies led to financial unfeasibility of community and smallholder tree plantation activities.

Failures in livelihood provision are linked to environmental degradation, which has taken place also in the "success" context of Vietnam (McElwee 2009). In most cases the environment suffers because of TPs even though smallholders would gain economically. McElwee (2009) argues that the Vietnamese STP program focused on establishing tree plantations rather than supporting natural regeneration, which explains why important sources of non-timber forest products have been replaced with monocrop exotic TPs. The most vulnerable populations have been negatively impacted, even though some people would have gained from the conversion of supposedly "bare" hills composed of shrubs, into tree plantations. McElwee argues that exotic tree plantations targeting individual households in Vietnam have supplied often only low-quality and low-value timber and fuelwood, and suggests that natural regeneration targeting villages would be a better forest policy by supplying a diversity of forest products. STPs targeted at the poor in Vietnam have often disadvantaged the poorest as these developmental schemes have been embedded in unequal local power and economic relations (Sikor and Nguyen 2007), although the situation might have improved in recent years (Sikor 2012).

Even the smallholder tenure TPs that improve smallholders' rights have their problems. In some places with predominant national smallholder-policy "success," such as Vietnam, the livelihoods of those not earning tenure have actually been damaged by smallholder tenure as they have become even poorer or more marginalized (Barr and Sayer 2012). Most problematically, as plantation forestry is dominated by forest industry power, the majority of smallholder farmers seeking buyers or contracts for selling their plantation wood face a negotiating opponent with a strength and self-interest that far outstrips that of families, leaving these typically with highly unfavorable terms or, worse, timber flows accompanied by coercion. In some political-economic settings, it is better for one's livelihood and quality of life to be a subsistence farmer whose production is not overtly tied to commodity markets.

Contemporary global resource exploitation   123

In any case, in general more safety measures are needed for TP timber markets to work for development. Cossalter and Barr (2005) argue that the lack of mechanisms ensuring mutual accountability typically leaves smallholders or other outgrowers in a very disadvantaged position. Outgrower schemes have also created a class of wealthy middle farmers sidelining with companies and criticizing the resistance against ITP expansion (Kröger and Nylund 2012). Such outgrower expansion is currently becoming a main ITP expansion tactic as conflicts and land prices are booming.

For these reasons – as most political contexts in the global South are dominated by pro-ITP government-industry alliances and protected only in a limited way, if at all, by progressive state actor-social movement agency – most smallholder and other plantation forestry schemes endowed with developmental expectations will continue to create future resentment. In any case, environmental concerns of TPs are sidelined in these development debates.

Environmental impacts

The environmental impacts of TP expansion have been studied extensively in peer-reviewed journal articles. Tree plantations typically cause severe damage to the soil, water flows and ecosystems (Jackson *et al.* 2005). TPs have a higher water use compared to pastures and agricultural crops, which is a main reason for local grievances by farmers (Stewart *et al.* 2011). Water usage by eucalyptus is dramatic and environmentally dangerous particularly in plantations set in prior pasture or agriculture areas and managed under large-scale cutting practices (Jackson *et al.* 2005; Stape *et al.* 2008; Jobbágy *et al.* 2012). Pine plantations increase evapotranspiration and decrease stream flow; pines are also invasive, impacting negatively on surface water runoff, grazing resources and biodiversity, and exacerbating the problem of wildfires (van Wilgen and Richardson 2012). The greatest possibility of negative trade-off between tree plantations and reduced water yields is in regions where water resources are threatened by climate change (Calder *et al.* 2007). Water use and pollution are the key concerns of impacted populations both in the South and the global North, such as in Tasmania (Flaten 2011). Tree plantations reduce average stream flow and groundwater recharge, but may also have some minor environmental planning benefits in some environments (van Dijk and Keenan 2007). Yet, commonly, no corporation or state research institution systematically monitors the impact of tree plantation expansion.

Forest destruction and loss of unique biodiversity (including also natural grasslands) has accompanied expansion (Nosetto *et al.* 2008: 1; Little *et al.* 2009: 162). According to Nahuelhual *et al.* (2012), TP expansion, for example in Chile, has been a direct cause of deforestation and biodiversity loss. The biodiversity loss experienced by the conversion of shrubs to TPs applies

124   *Contemporary global resource exploitation*

across the globe, also in global North contexts like New Zealand (Nagashima *et al.* 2002).

Government forest policies linked directly with land tenure security have had tremendous impact on changes in forestland cover. In Brazil, the new Forest Code approved in 2012 allows for the consideration of the conversion of "degraded forest" (which might be primary forest) or recently logged primary or secondary forest into a tree plantation such as pulpwood eucalyptus as reforestation. This change in the legislative setting will drive further TP expansion in Brazil, as plantations are associated not only with stronger land control and ownership rights, but also with "green development" – according to the official view – within the new "bio-economy." On the other hand, in China, under the Sloping Land Conversion Program, farmers were offered long-term property rights on areas in which they planted trees (Barr and Sayer 2012), to give environmental benefits such as flood control. Both in China (Grossjean and Kontoleon 2009) and in Brazil (Puppim de Oliveira 2008) increased tenure and land use control rights were the most important factor leading to conversion, planting or maintenance of land cover.

Some tree plantations might also give some benefits. Land tenure of plantations is seen in the literature as making a difference. Smallholder and communal forestry are seen as better solutions than state or corporate forestry. However, according to Palo and Lehto (2012), both of the "social," public forms of forest land tenure (communal and state control) are more problematic than private ownership (particularly semi-natural) forests, because in state-owned forests (and TPs) administrative orders typically force stumpage prices under the respective market prices, leading to deforestation or overuse. Higher stumpage prices would naturally benefit smallholders, but not necessarily the environment if TPs were to replace high-biodiversity areas or cause soil and stream flow damage.

The genetic variety in trees as well as other species is vanishing rapidly with the drive to establish TP monocultures. Exotic tree species, particularly numerous pine species, are often invasive aliens from plantations into nearby nature: the sustained functioning and the provision of important ecosystem services of conservation or water production areas have been mostly negatively impacted (Richardson 1998). Most impacts are detrimental to the invaded systems and threaten sustained functioning and the provision of important ecosystem services. The invasive spread of alien trees from plantations into adjoining areas of natural vegetation has meant that the negative effects are being felt in areas set aside for conservation or water production (ibid.).

Corporations prefer exotic species monocultures, introduced species being thus related to agrarian structures. Public and smallholder plantation ownership correlates with a lower percentage of exotic species TPs. For example, India with 70% public ownership had only 13% of exotic plantations (FAO 2010), but in Chile with 70% corporate ownership (Del Lungo *et al.* 2006), 100% of plantations were exotic (FAO 2010). These points suggest that agrarian political economy explains also a large part of the environmental impacts of TPs.

Contemporary global resource exploitation 125

The rest of this chapter will focus in more detail on these and other political issues underlying the resistance to TPs.

Underlying fault lines of tree plantation resistance

Several explanatory fault lines of and explanations for resistance are identified in the TP literature and are discussed below one by one, besides the internal movement mobilization and interactive political dynamics-linked reasons discussed earlier.

The role of exotic tree species in conflicts

Table 5.2 combines data from FAO (2010) on the percentage of exotic plantations of all plantations across the globe, and compares this with the largest existing research on global tree plantation conflict spread (Gerber 2010).

Table 5.2 Countries with over 800,000 ha of forestry plantations, % of introduced species, and conflict existence

	'000 ha	% exotic	ITP conflict existed until 2009*
South Africa	1,763	100	x
China	77,157	28	x
Republic of Korea	1,823	67	
India	10,211	13	x
Turkey	3,418	2	
Bulgaria	815	5	
France	1,633	36	
Germany	5,283	8	
Hungary	1,612	41	
Norway	1,475	18	
Portugal	849	99	
Russian Federation	16,991	0	
Slovakia	959	2	
Spain	2,680	37	
Sweden	3,613	18	
United Kingdom	2,219	64	
United States of America	25,363	2	
Australia	1,903	53	
New Zealand	1,812	100	
Argentina	1,394	98	x
Brazil	7,418	96	x
Chile	2,384	100	x
Uruguay	978	100	x

Source: (Elaborated by the author, including all countries that reported data on % of introduced/exotic species were included, FAO 2010; * Gerber 2010)

126 *Contemporary global resource exploitation*

Table 5.2 illustrates a sharp division of conflicts based on the global political economic location of a country; the percentage of exotic TPs in a country matters in relation to the global positioning of that country. Conflicts were situated in the global South (e.g. Brazil, South Africa). Non-conflictive TP settings were either in the global North (e.g. New Zealand, UK), or had a very limited percentage of exotic species (e.g. Russia, Turkey). If a plantation was in the global South, there was a clear correlation between high exotic species percentage and conflict. China and India, with low percentages of exotic plantations, are exceptions in the table, but then again these are large countries and a preliminary survey of research implies that in the areas where exotic TPs expand, conflicts exist, while in the areas where domestic species are planted, conflicts are far less common. However, more research needs to be done on these two countries, both because of a lack of English-language sources on these increasingly important TP expansion countries, and because of the interesting anomaly they present in the table, illustrating that they have a mixed TP political line, combining both corporate exotic ITPs and domestic species STPs and public TPs, among other initiatives.

Yet, the table makes it clear that in general, plantations that are causing conflicts and are the most important to examine consist of introduced species. Planting of locally existing trees does not lead to grievances as often, as this generates fewer environmental or landscape changes. Non-exotic species plantations are typically not fenced, are not treated with fertilizers or herbicides, and tolerate the growth of other species as well (such as mushrooms, berries and fruits). Agrotoxins are typically forbidden in countries with more rigorous forest legislation, making their TPs more like natural forests. The plantation of exotic species is typically accompanied by large-scale patterns of land use change and social division of labor, making introduced species (of all types, not only trees) the most dangerous threat to the continuation of rural communities in general (Beckford 1972), also in tree plantation areas (Clapp 1998; Gerber and Veuthey 2010).

Comparing the conflict occurrence data in Gerber (2010) and the FAO research notes on the division of tree plantation ownership between smallholders, corporations and the state in different countries (del Lungo *et al.* 2006: 25), one could deduce that conflicts concentrate disproportionally to areas where corporate ownership dominates over smallholder ownership. For example, 90% of plantations were corporate in Brazil, whereas in Vietnam smallholder plantations represented 64% in 2005. Brazil is rife with conflicts (Kröger 2011), as is Indonesia (Gerber 2010), but in Vietnam there is an absence of conflicts (Sikor 2012).

The role of national political dynamics: "war-like" and "democratic" conflict settings

The political dynamics between different actors attempting to influence plantation expansion pace and style vary depending on moral economies and

Contemporary global resource exploitation 127

ethics in rural areas. The above discussion highlights that the reason behind the natural resource conflicts studied here is not their technical quality per se (such as the use of exotic tree species), but corporate resource exploitation that decides to expand exotic monocultures in a detrimental way to local nature and populations, these ways ranging from more to less violent. There are political dynamics wherein extreme physical violence is used against resistance, such as the Mapuche resisting pulpwood in southern Chile, southern Chinese villagers resisting Stora Enso, and Indonesian conflicts; and then there are dynamics in which more subtle mechanisms are present and physical violence mostly absent, such as in the Uruguayan pulpwood expansion. Most cases lie somewhere between the extremes.

Usefully for the general study of violent plantation politics, Cramer and Richards (2011) review the literature on the agrarian dimensions in violent conflicts, arguing that the set of social relations and political dynamics shaped by and shaping commodity production should be placed at the center of inquiry in understanding the agrarian roots of violence. They draw, for example, on Nugent and Robinson (2010), who examine variations in the background, composition and strategies of elites, and in their analytical approach to land laws and the mobilization of labor explain the existence of violence as these affect paths to different smallholder or large-scale commercial plantation settings. Cramer and Richards (2011) urge researchers to look at the social and political dynamics to distinguish the features of war-like plantation conflict settings.

Cases of tree plantation violence can be conceptualized as developmental conflicts, caused by primitive accumulation defined by "civilizing" frontier rhetoric and high modernist discourses accompanying the war-like, secretly oppressive, or in other ways violent enclosure of "peripheral," "bare," "degraded," "unused," "unproductive" and "empty" lands by most powerful elites. In these contexts, the ethical answers are given undemocratically and from outside, this capitalist politics typically leading into lopsided economic and unsustainable environmental outcomes (see Gibson-Graham 2006). Authoritarian regimes with military-dominated territories involve war-like political dynamics in which the resistance is blocked from the use of state institutions and framed as terrorists, such as in Chile. In the more benign "democratic"-type settings the state can be used by forces of resistance when sympathizers are being placed within the state system. In the former case, conflicts are often "deeper," i.e. suffering is greater; in the latter, the conflicts are often "wider," i.e. more people are involved and physical signs of conflict, such as semi-permanent occupation of ITP lands, is experienced.

The classic example of "war-like" expansion dynamics has been Indonesia. The country has been the scene of some of the most severe human rights violations connected with ITPs and the army has been extensively involved. The financing of the military and police forces by ITP companies is a common phenomenon, and has created private security forces that treat activists and local populations who resist plantation expansion as terrorists and

128 *Contemporary global resource exploitation*

criminals. Noor and Syumanda (2006) have called ITP expansion in Indonesia "forestry militarism." In most cases it should be stressed that military action is secondary, even in Indonesia. The principal ordering of territories in accordance with the imperatives of ITP expansion is carried out through corporate-influenced legislative maneuvers, including tax incentives, zoning, territorial titling, policy plans and other guarantees of expansion. Nevertheless, since "political capital linked to memories of wartime affiliations have crucial spatial and place-based connections," Baird and Le Billon (2012: 290) highlight that the ethics of social relations crafted by war-like setting histories have to be assessed. This is critical for understanding where and what, by whom, how and for what reason land deals are negotiated in (post-)violent plantation expansion areas, such as Laos or Cambodia.

In "democratic" conflict settings, with progressive state institutions and actors monitoring breaches of law, ITP expansion has come under increased scrutiny. Some movements are not fortunate enough to have democratic institutions or the indirect support of sympathetic state actors in their conflicts. They may surely at any time try to embed in the state to gain sympathizers or supportive institutions and policies, but if barred they might turn to revolutionary mobilization. TP politics has examples of abrupt changes in settings. At any moment, "democratic" dynamics of ITP politics can turn "war-like," for example, a military *coup d'état*. A "war-like" setting can also turn into a "democratic" one. The consequences of enduring cycles of violence are severe and the Mapuche case in Chile is a case in point.

Forestry militarism: war-like conflicts in Chile

The indigenous Mapuche population is in a deep conflict with Arauco, Forestal Mininco and the Chilean state. Treated as terrorists, the Mapuche are persecuted under anti-terrorist laws, and organizers of demonstrations are often given hefty prison sentences. Yet, even the Federal Bureau of Investigation (FBI) and other US intelligence agencies aver that there are no terrorists in Chile, nor armed wings of the Mapuche community (Varela 2011). What the accusations represent, rather, according to the Mapuche interviewed by the author in fall 2011, is an effort to render the politically contentious strategy of protests against plantation expansion illegal. These "war-like" dynamics deserve a deeper look. The below information on the Mapuche in Chile is based on the author's interview on October 19, 2011, with Mijael Carbone Queipul, the political leader of the Temucuicui community, and the leader of the five-year old Alianza Territorial Mapuche organization that attempts to unite different Mapuche, and personal communication with other Mapuche leaders.

A mere one hundred and twenty years ago, the Mapuche had complete sovereignty over their lands. In the years since, most Mapuche – who now number about 1.5 million – have turned from indigenous to peasant culture. Mapuche territory has been a target for colonization by non-indigenous

Contemporary global resource exploitation 129

peoples, particularly since the 1950s. In the 1970s, the Pinochet dictatorship introduced a further threat by bringing in pulp companies. The tree plantation cover of the landscape in the pulping area grew from 5.5% in 1975 to 42.4% by 2007 (Nahuelhual *et al.* 2012), one of the largest concentrations of ITPs globally. Both the companies and other colonizers have illegally grabbed Mapuche land at zero or low cost, driving the populations out, and planting pine or eucalyptus. The Mapuche do not even have a say over who can set up a camp on their land: pulp companies drive their badly paid workers into tent "cities" on Mapuche territory. One result is a constant traffic of worker and pulp company trucks through villages, accompanied by heavily armored police vehicles. Access to water has also been affected because of the acidification of lakes next to pine plantations. ITP expansion has destroyed or strongly curtailed traditional economic-cultural activities: for example, fire-using agriculture is forbidden due to fear of fire spreading to TPs, and access to collect important non-timber forest products is fenced by ITPs (du Monceau 2008). Most Mapuche have not received money or any other benefits from the ITP plantation companies, according to Mijael Queipul, a local leader, except a fraction of Mapuche close to the mills who, he said, had been co-opted by the company.

Mapuche territory has become extremely militarized. Police monitor the population with helicopters and strategically placed cameras, photographing protesters and ransacking households at random. Police also burn crops, claiming that the Mapuche have an armed wing in the mountains fed by villagers. Amnesty International considers Mapuche leaders arrested on terrorism charges to be political prisoners.

In spite of all the state intimidation, however, there have been many protests of up to seven thousand people, ranging from road blocks to occupation of ITP lands, building of houses and planting of food crops on felled eucalyptus or pine plantations, hunger strikes, marches in cities, and other demonstrations that have stopped the transportation of wood to pulp mills. Land occupations and conflicts occur mostly in outlying large-scale production areas seized a few decades ago from the Mapuche, not in the areas closest to the pulp mills of Arauco and Mininco. This is for two reasons. First, areas near the mills are almost completely planted with ITPs, leaving few people in the vicinity, of whom none are Mapuche. Second, the Mapuche prefer not to stage direct anti-company protests that could eventually rebound on company workers.

Queipul sees Mapuche resistance, including nonviolent resistance of police evictions during land occupations, as necessary and fruitful. Mapuche have regained some land from pine monocultures, in one case 2,000 ha purchased from Mininco by CONAI (Chilean National Commission for the Environment), on which a community settlement is being built. From about one thousand communities, one hundred or so have recovered some land, thus slowing down ITP expansion. This is a considerable resistance feat, bearing in mind the difficult circumstances.

130   *Contemporary global resource exploitation*

In general, despite protests against ITP companies remaining constant since the days of Pinochet, the underlying pattern of ITP expansion has changed relatively little. Plantations are expanding into the *cordilleras*, which are also Mapuche territories, and the social democratic government of Michelle Bachelet continued to use anti-terrorist laws to quell Mapuche mobilization between 2006 and 2010. Mapuche lands and resources remain officially state owned, with no recognition of indigenous rights; President Bachelet even went to the trouble of securing an exception for Chile in the International Labour Organization (ILO) indigenous people's code (the exception attempt made by Bachelet on August 8, 2008 would have limited the applicability of Article 35 of the ILO Convention in Chile). In this sense, ethnic lines and lack of information on these war-like dynamics by the Chileans in cities delimit the applicability of democracy and ethical reasoning. While CONADI (the Chilean Indigenous Development Corporation, theoretically responsible for promoting indigenous affairs) was created in 1993 in return for the support given by the Mapuche to the democratization and anti-Pinochet movement which later took political power, the agency has become completely politicized and captured by political parties' private interests, according to the Mapuche leaders. Leading politicians including the current President Sebastián Piñera, who, according to Queipul, is said to "own half of southern Chile," are seen as eager for ITPs and other market projects to annex the remainder of Mapuche lands. According to Queipul, "the Chilean state wants to see us in a museum [only]". What unites the war-like ITP contexts of Chile and Indonesia, for example, is that timber extraction is rendered in these political economies principally as a key rent base for the elites.

Differing state-resistance movement relations in ITP resistance

Even considering the elite dominance, what is striking in this conflict is that the Mapuche groups presented by Queipul have no support within the government or the state, not even from the indigenous affairs institute CONAI, unlike in Brazil, where at least some state actors and politicians and institutes are sympathetic and open to the grievances of ITP-affected populations. There's a strong elite also in Brazil; the social spaces and structural politics are not so different. Thus, I suggest answers have to be sought from within resistance composition, strategies and agency.[6] There have been many Mapuche groups, with diverse strategies ranging from alliance with political parties to radical protesting: this disunity led to some inter-Mapuche conflicts (du Monceau 2008). Furthermore, although resistance in Chile has achieved some government land restitution programs, these have marginalized the Mapuche further and increased their dependency (ibid.). This is a striking difference from the Brazilian government land restitution gained by ITP resistance. The Mapuche have no parliamentary representative and plan widescale abstention from voting, because not even left-wing governments have been their friends. This suggests the Mapuche have had a very weak or non-existent embedded autonomy in relation to the state-industry alliance. The main Mapuche objective now is to "reconstruct the Mapuche Nation as an autonomous territory, and to slow down the entry of transnational companies, making use of the land in their control." Contentious agency-promoting strategies have had their weaknesses here; corporate agency has been very strong. By creating these "war-like" dynamics, the government-elite alliance has attempted to curb both embedded autonomy and resistance protests, to bar the access of contentious agency to the state-remediated political games of contentious politics, electoral politics, and institutional and structural politics to influence TP expansion. Nevertheless, as stronger willingness for contentious agency exists now within the displaced Mapuche, they are using the strategies of organizing and politicizing, campaigning and networking to deepen their capacity for resistance.

The new political organization of the Mapuche, Alianza Territorial Mapuche, has already had success in uniting previously separate groups around this objective, although according to the Mapuche leaders themselves, they still have much to learn about the best ways of making people aware of the situation and of the importance of protesting. "We are waiting to be strong enough to confront the government face to face," said Queipul, who sees little reason to accept the "developmental path" offered by the government. Contentious agency is very visible in these "war-like" struggles. In November 2012 the consequences of this new will had already started to break the public silence, as Elena Varela's (2011) critical film on Mapuche activists' imprisonment was allowed to be sold by the authorities, this allowing even the possibility for a rare glimpse of the dynamics for the majority in the cities.

"We want to say to the world that not even prison will silence us. We will fight until we have rights." Queipul insists that groups that wish to support the Mapuche struggle come to visit their territory before starting co-operation. This stand brings to mind the politics of Zapatistas. These more radical and culturally more encompassing alternative approaches seem to be correlated with stronger clashes with the established powers. Queipul considers ITPs "a silent extinction of the Mapuche," comparing native people with native plants, and the companies and the state with exotic outsiders. "We have not been so egoistic with our Mother Earth" as the companies or states have, he explained, noting that Mapuche have their own medicine and sustainable, alternative economy and do not need TPs. Queipul added that the Mapuche are not against development, "but against the destruction of Mother Earth." This framing of the issues, together with the growth of the community-based Alianza, positions the Mapuche as a radically antagonistic counter-force to developmentalist state policies important for the ruling elite.

Thus, the conflicts continued to deepen: in early 2012, news reports told of over 50,000 ha of plantations of pulp companies burned down. The companies and the government accused the Mapuche of starting the fires.

132 *Contemporary global resource exploitation*

The Mapuche said the accusation was absurd and argued that the companies themselves started the fires deliberately because their plantations had caught a monoculture disease, destroying the plantations. The companies wanted to gain fire insurance payments instead of losing stock to the disease (Tweedie 2012). The war continues and Mapuche families are being randomly persecuted by the armed forces of Chile, for example by setting homes on fire (ibid.) and jailing leaders. If the general public continues to get more information on these ethical issues and be touched by them, in the sense of the new public frame boosting and directing general contentious agency to this issue, conflicts will become wider, increasing the likelihood of changing the course of development more than silence. The type of heterodox framing will be essential here. A comparison of the different discourses and class-ethnic lines in Brazil and Chile allows a return to the key question of the grievance relationship to mobilization that was touched upon in prior chapters.

Comparison of class- and ethnic territorial-based resistance

The ethnic territorial rights-based discourse evident in Mapuche leaders' accounts deserves some study, illustrating another key fault line in TP resistance. According to du Monceau (2008), who has produced the most extensive study on the Mapuche-ITP conflicts, the Mapuche struggle has moved from class-based to ethnic identity-based mobilization. In the broader sense, this is a consequence of the neoliberal turn in the economy. In contrast to the Mapuche leaders interviewed, du Monceau (2008) argues that even the Mapuche have joined the very neoliberal land-governing practices offered to them by NGOs and the state. They are lured to plant exotic pine and eucalyptus in STPs, which replace traditional livelihoods and landscapes with rapidly expanding, water- and soil-degrading TPs. Meanwhile, they are tied to global markets and to the institutional bureaucracy of developmental programs (ibid.). Nevertheless it seems that after 2008 this might no longer be so much the case, as communities see that STPs do not improve their situation.

The key difference between ITP resistance in Brazil and Chile is that in Brazil there is a united, class-based front that demands land and equalization of class cleavages, while in Chile there are ethnic identity-based groups with no united front. These latter groups express their demands in terms of territory and rights (du Monceau 2008). Chilean anthropologist José Bengoa (2006; cf. Roux 2012) has noted a general shift from class-based land claims to territorial demands revolving around ethnic collective rights. Identity- and class-based claims on land are not the same thing, and the shift engenders heavy consequences both politically and theoretically. Edelman (1999) criticized the over-emphasis of the post-1980s Latin American "new social movement literature" on (postmodern) identity-based rather than classic material grievance-stimulated counter-movements, arguing convincingly that material

Contemporary global resource exploitation 133

changes are still more important in increasing mobilization potential than identity construction. This claim is supported by the empirical finding that the land- and class-based Brazilian ITP resistance has been much more successful than the territory- and ethnicity-based Chilean resistance.

When the class-based, landed producer status of a peasant group (including indigenous communities), traditionally organized to bargain with the state, is turned into a manager of culture-based territory, this can atomize groups by identity distinction although not necessarily resulting in real autonomy. The territory right discourse fits well within the "Green economy" and in the plans of its proponents. It is much easier to deal with ethnic territory-based resistance than with class- and land-based movements. The former can be integrated more easily into a cross-class capitalist alliance, for example as STP producers. The incorporation of indigenous people can carry the added benefit of legitimizing the forestry business because their cultural identity can provide a new value internationally, in the (ethical) "bio-economy." If the principal goal of a group is to gain ethnic identity recognition, they may well set their land-use autonomy to a second position if offered economic integration as employees or "producers of carbon credits," for example, by the powerful. This impacts the economic outcomes of corporate resource exploitation.

The comparative analysis in Barney (2004) suggests that resistance groups in Thailand with less racialized ethnic territorial claim making than in Malaysia were more successful than their Malaysian counterparts in barring corporate plantations where territory/ethnicity/right claims superseded land/ class claims more typical of Thailand. In contexts where common property rights and communal land tenure are central legal categories, the resistance has had to withhold arguments founded on these bases. This has proven tricky, because corporations, highly modernist states, and most expert econo- mists and foresters who plan industrial forestry largely overlook communal ownership forms. These are culturally very different notions from forestry capitalism's still-in-vigor dominant culture, the basis of which is assuming that private ownership, sustained yields and private initiative are the corner- stones of any possible development (Nylund and Kröger 2012). Particularly groups with weaker symbolic capital, such as the Afro-Brazilian Quilombo communities, have been in a difficult position to ascertain their territorial/ identity/right claims against high modernist-state-pulp industry alliances. In comparison, landless peasants placing their argumentation on class and land claims have been more successful. Yet, as Chapter 3 demonstrated, also the ethnic territory right claim-based movements, such as the Brazilian indigen- ous movements, can change strategies by making class-based land claims via protesting, made smoother if a broader peasant-resistance network exists. This suggests that the basis of resistance argumentation, in other words strategies and contextual group dynamics, has to be carefully studied. More compara- tive research is required on the land/territory, class/ethnicity cleavage and its influence on resistance to land grabbing.

134 *Contemporary global resource exploitation*

Concluding remarks

This chapter has outlined the broad political lines in tree plantation expansion and resistance around the world. A review of the existing literature suggests that there is a larger academic discussion on tree plantations in Southeast Asia than in South America or other regions such as Africa, which is currently experiencing even more ITP expansion than Asia. In all regions, TP expansion, environmental impacts and developmental consequences have been studied much more than TP conflict dynamics, and therefore the emphasis in this book placed on explaining resistance fills a gap in the knowledge.

State-industry-civil society interaction has determined investment locations. Corporate land control is central for expanding ITPs. To ensure this, class and socio-ecological relations have had to be modified. Enclosures of Southern lands have accompanied most expansion, securing cheap timber commodity flow to the North. Developmental and environmental consequences of these expansion mechanisms have been dire; these have been somewhat different in smallholder and corporate-dominated markets. STPs and ITPs are in a zero-sum game over molding agrarian political economic structures such as land tenure systems and local timber markets.

Agrarian structures and state-industry-resistance relations are essential for explaining whether TPs are established and of what type (smallholder or industrial). TPs expand by smallholder tree plantations where significant agrarian reform has taken place and scattered, family-based ownership is maintained (such as Finland), or where reform is taking place, for example by a combination of direct action land reform and supportive state policies blocking the intrusion of powerful corporations (such as in Thailand and Vietnam). Industrial tree plantations boom in places where corporate land access is eased by the retained rural existence of colonial plantation economies and/or land-holding elites, such as in Brazil. ITPs have also boomed in "war-like" settings with state interference/paramilitary violence supporting key forestry capitalists for which timber extraction is a key rent base, such as in Indonesia and Chile.

The emergence of "green economy" where flex trees are planted is changing the dynamics. The practice in all TPs is to use ever faster-growing trees in shorter cycles. Many existing pine plantations, for example, which have a relatively slow rotation, are being converted to faster hybrid, cloned or genetically modified eucalyptus variants, better adapted to cold. This development and global warming open up previously unsuitable lands for ITP expansion – and conflict. The same TPs can be used in ever more numerous ways, including as pulpwood, energywood, or as "carbon sinks," and the processing plants of plantation wood such as modern pulp mills can become important energy producers. The rapidly changing global economy and nature require flexibility and rapid adaptability: thus flex tree plantations have inbuilt survival skills as they increase the range of possible timber uses. They will continue to expand, forming entire landscapes of "phony forests" of single species.

Contemporary global resource exploitation 135

As non-food land use changes, TP establishment should be integrated more fully into the debate on land grabbing. TPs should be studied by both agrarian political economy and by forest sciences, including forest policy and conflict studies, and any other industry-specific literature to understand the supply chains in which TP timber is used. Such cross reading of literature is very helpful for social scientific environmental research as it allows more comprehensive explanations. The global review suggests that even though there is a need for many more studies to accompany the ever more rapid expansion, we already have a growing, and empirically and theoretically rigorous literature on which future studies on tree plantations can be built.

The spread of contentious agency in industrial forestry conflicts was studied globally to spot also possible general industry- and investment-specific trends across very different political contexts. Resistance revolves mostly around introduced species. Eucalyptus, acacia and pine trees are the tree species most often involved in conflict. Eucalyptus is the most prominent tree species in ITP conflicts. Even though there are some differences in corporate practice and the occurrence of resistance, the large-scale ITP model fosters conflicts of interest everywhere. The will to resist increases as the ITP projects mature and people stop believing company promises.

The chapter revealed that the study of global natural resource politics, such as industrial forestry expansion and resistance, has to be located in local-global agrarian dynamics between particular sets of companies, states and civil society responses, all actor categories illustrating considerable and interdependent variance in agency. For example, because of the resistance to ITPs in Thailand in the 1980s, and growing domestic criticism of exporting pollution to poorer countries, Japanese pulp firms have developed a strategy of expanding in environments with sparser population density and stronger tenure assurance, such as Australia (Hall 2002, 2003) or in Brazil in the area in Minas Gerais where Cenibra is currently located (Gonçalves 1991, 2001). This move has placed the Japanese companies in areas without conflict. ITP politics continues to be contentious, but another set of companies is being engaged in the conflict-avoiding path. Resistance and conflict do not emerge automatically according to the gravity of impacts or problems, but instead depend on the intensity of grievances felt by impacted populations, their mobilization capacities and the political setting. The concluding chapter summarizes the book's findings on the mobilization against corporate resource exploitation at this historical global conjuncture, synthesizing lessons from the cases already discussed and from other counter-movement examples across industries engaged in large-scale investment projects.

Notes

1 FAO (n.d.) *Definitions Related to Planted Forests*, www.fao.org/docrep/007/ae347e/AE347E02.htm.

136 *Contemporary global resource exploitation*

2 However, in FAO (2010) Mexico is presented as having had no tree plantations at all in 1990; in FAO (2011) the figure for 1990 Mexico is 350,000 ha. When asked about the discrepancy, an FAO official responded in email communication that 350,000 ha seems like a mistake, but could not give a definite answer on why there was a mistake, or if this was a mistake. If the figure is zero, then the TP growth in Mexico has been even higher than 815%.
3 Pulp Mill Watch, China, www.pulpmillwatch.org/countries/china/.
4 See also: www.firstpeoplesfirst.in/admin/pdf/116The%20Indian%20CDM%20% 282%29.pdf.
5 Email communication, February 27, 2012.
6 Why has not a similar institution to the Public Ministry, which the broad resistance in Brazil helped to create in the 1980s, been created also in post-dictatorship Chile?

Conclusion
The role of resistance in natural resource politics

This book assessed the hypothesis that corporate resource exploitation can be impacted more effectively when the resistance is formed by, utilizes and promotes contentious agency. The hypothesis provided the opportunity to contribute to and challenge some parts of social scientific theory, especially theories in the social movement literature. McAdam, Tarrow and Tilly (2001, 2008) suggest that the analysis should be dynamic, surveying the intersections between resistance, authorities and opponents. A substantial part of the existing literature studying social movement outcomes has focused on studying target responses (e.g. company or state counter-strategies) to movement mobilization (e.g. Luders 2010). Soule (2009), studying the impact of contention on corporate policies, suggested studies need to identify which strategies work and under what circumstances, calling for assessments of the relative and joint impacts of various factors on how economic outcomes are impacted by activists' demands. I have attempted to provide a dynamic theoretical framework and empirical examination to answer these calls. My focus has been on contributing to the understanding of the causal relations between specific quality and combination of movement and corporate strategies in differing natural resource politics dynamics on the slowing down of extraction expansion.

The hypothesis proved to be robust. Based on the systematic analysis of empirical evidence across pulp investments in Brazil and other tree plantation expansion across the globe, the findings strongly support the hypothesis. This resistance to land grabbing achieved widely divergent outcomes across tree plantation expansion areas and these differences are explicable in light of the joint-effect strategy analysis that was developed. The new theory of when and how contentious agency can impact, even reverse the expansion of corporate resource exploitation, helps to explain in detail the reasons behind the variation in natural resource policy. Expansion, especially variation in expansion outcomes, is explained not only by corporate agency promotion, but also by the dynamics this process has with the promotion of contentious agency and the state support that mediates between and influences expansion and conflict.

The contentious agency of social movements explains much of the variation in extraction expansion outcomes. The strategies promoting contentious agency the impacts of which were studied were: a) organizing and politicizing

138   *Conclusion*

a social movement; b) campaigning by framing issues in a heterodox way; c) pioneering, disruptive, massive and re-symbolizing protests; d) networking with allies; and e) embedding with the state apparatus whilst maintaining autonomy. The creation of a virtuous cycle among these strategies, a process in which each one of them reinforces the others, entails crucial benefits for movements, even in difficult circumstances. This process sustains a high level of mobilization and resistance, which are preconditions for changing the current resource extraction expansion. The specific impact of these strategies is defined in the political games, dynamics and combinations in which used.

Corporate and contentious agency in a given political system reveals the causal dynamics leading to particular resource exploitation paces and styles. By comparing combinations of strategies in different contexts, various times, across different movements and against counterfactuals by a fine-tuned analysis of state-business-social movement dynamics, the book shows the importance of contentious agency in natural resource politics.

This is a contribution to the existing literature. Despite a large body of research, "we still have little systematic understanding of the consequences of social movements," claims political scientist Marco Giugni (2004: 2). Researchers like Paul Burstein claim that collective action by movements is largely unsuccessful in changing public policy (Tilly and Tarrow 2007: 128). However, many earlier cases demonstrate that some protest activities have had crucial impacts on policies. Giugni (2004: 2) gives the examples of street demonstrations that helped bring down Eastern European communist regimes and the 1995 Greenpeace action against Shell, which depressed sales and prompted important changes within Shell. Indeed, many social movement scholars believe protests are efficacious, but few investigate in detail whether this is the case, as they concentrate instead on the origins of the movement (Andrews 2004: 2).

The bulk of the earlier social movement research (e.g. Tarrow 2011), including that on economic outcomes (e.g. Soule 2009), has also retained a rigid, and in my view arbitrary, division of internal and external movement factors influencing mobilization and outcomes. A novelty here has been to use and develop the concept of Peter Evans (1995) on embedded autonomy. This means to study state-business movement interaction as taking place via relational political games, in which movements and companies embed the state and maintain autonomy to different degrees in different contexts. This provides a more accurate description of the events, and enabled episodes to be explained better, uniting agency and structure and avoiding their rigid separation. Embedded autonomy is one of the heuristic tools I call "strategies," following the urge of McAdam *et al.* (2001) to create studies based on mechanisms, processes and dynamics. Contentious agency is a process created by concatenated strategies and in dynamic interaction with corporate agency.

Both "external" and "internal" movement action was considered via the dynamic heuristic devices of "strategies" used in "political games." These are particular settings of "strategic action fields," the study of which Fligstein and

Conclusion 139

McAdam (2011) suggest should become central in social sciences. Strategic action fields – such as political games where resource use is determined – vary across contexts and depending on the social actors involved: the settings of natural resource politics created by them thus have specific rules, typically varying across and within nation-states.

Theoretical-methodological contributions

In the field of social movements and conflict scholarship, this book presented an original methodological contribution, providing analysis and organization of data gathered by means of participant observation and in-depth interviews through qualitative comparative analysis (QCA). The principal methodological contribution was to show that the QCA technique can be used to disaggregate systematically the causal relations between particular sets of social movement strategies and economic outcomes. By triangulation and causal process tracing, the analyst can discover the specific qualities of strategies that are most effective in political games. To this end, for example the discussion of the importance of pioneer initiatives to the functioning of protesting offered a more precise and detailed assessment of protest act quality importance in influencing economic outcomes. The methodology also enabled detailed explanations about the qualities important in organizing and politicizing, campaigning, networking and embedding strategies.

Above all, I emphasized that protests must be understood relationally, answering the calls (McAdam *et al.* 2001; Silva 2009; Luders 2010); the QCA methodology coupled with ethnographic case studies and process tracing was a very helpful methodology within this theoretical framework. Future research should apply the theoretical framework developed here to other political systems, industries and conflicts to assess whether the movement strategies identified here are effective tools in all cases.

The major findings were very important and exciting: namely, that disruptive protests combined with embeddedness within sub-national and municipal legislatures and courts (even if this is indirectly by the latter adapting the former's heterodox frame), while maintaining autonomy, have contributed to a movement achieving its goals, even in the face of worsening political opportunities.[1] This notion of embedded autonomy in particular challenges strands of the literature – namely, Piven and Cloward's *Poor People's Movements* (1978), and political opportunity-based explanations of movements (including the MST) (Ondetti 2008), as well as more anarchistic, horizontal and anti-state tendencies of contemporary activism.

The book provides a framework for assessing the importance of contentious agency in political games. For example, when people join the MST and embrace its strategies, they can generate a new sense of individual and collective agency, a landless movement member habitus. This does not happen automatically or everywhere, but is conditioned by an interaction of personal

140   *Conclusion*

histories and the relational territorial, symbolic and social spaces where habitus is located, formed and changes (Bourdieu 1990, 1991, 1998), impacted by local moral economies (Wolford 2010a). Transformation to contentious agency is most likely to happen in the contextual setting of encampment time; the period when individuals can become movement members, and live in an alternative space. When a landless activist (encampment member, settler or MST leader) wins land by collective actions, for example by campaigning against large-scale pulp projects, this can create contentious agency instead of passivity or conventional agency.

The results from the comparison of cases supported the hypothesis that contentious agency (promoted by the usage of strategies a–e) probably leads to a more abrupt slowing of plantation expansion (greater areas, reversal of expansion by difficult-to-change decisions and policies). It also shows that contentious agency and strategies promoting it can be replicated to influence economic outcomes. Transformations to investment pace and style were initiated when contentious actors became socially and territorially very close to each other. Bourdieu (1991) theorized that changes in the positioning of actors in social and territorial spaces leads into similar transformations in the symbolic space. Industrial forestry cases illustrated how the theory works in practice: the replication of contentious strategies can be seen as a significant change in central elements in the symbolic space of the investment-impacted populations. Furthermore, the symbolic space transformation by the change in strategy led to a simultaneous formation of contentious habitus.

The strategies can exist in all political systems, but their activeness, specific contents, combinations and outcomes are likely to vary. For example, the contributions to those struggling to become state actors in the political system by movements and companies – a tactic of state embedding that was studied – is also generalizable. However, it takes specific forms depending on the political system: where electoral politics does not exist it takes another form, such as a fight for political alliances and sympathies by offering gifts to those who fight for the state actor positions. Still, the tactic is the same and its scope helps to assess how the contributions of corporations to the state actors in the political system influence the economy and vice versa.

Due caution is required to generalize the research framework and findings. Taking into consideration local varieties and specificities in contention and capitalism, the framework can be applied wherever there are corporate resource exploitation-based conflicts, such as plantation-based investments, agro-combustible complexes, large dams, open-pit mines and agribusiness endeavors. Nevertheless, each industry should receive particular analysis, because of diverging markets, commodity uses, conflict dynamics and sector-specific differences. The common lesson to be drawn is that movements do matter – in a specific way, depending on the strategies and political games in which they are engaged in influencing investment outcomes. This should be taken into consideration in planning new large-scale projects, resistance to them or reform.

Beyond dynamics of contention

In their *Dynamics of Contention*, McAdam *et al.* (2001) did not make a causal claim between mechanisms and their outcomes, but merely noted the qualities and existence of several mechanisms occurring across very different political systems and contexts in similar ways. In this sense, the findings based on the empirical evidence assessed here support making two broad arguments going beyond the prior claims.

The qualitative comparative analysis implies, first, that particular strategies lead to particular outcomes. Second, contentious agency, particularly the quality of it, exists and is significantly important even in very negative "political opportunity structures" where "political threats" are huge. These were disaggregated and more clearly specified to identify the causal qualities in different circumstances (this having been suggested in the latest literature, for example by Luders 2010); "opportunity structures" turned from "external" into dynamic by assessing them as government-industry alliances and corporate agency. "Political opportunities," if seen as external and not disaggregated, Luders (2010: 11) noted, "limit the analytical reach of a theory of movement outcome." Thus the book delved deeper into investigating the specific strategies and their encounters that ensure contentious and corporate agency for social actors. Focus was on resistance. A local social movement organization that built on strategies a–e was more likely to succeed than one that did not. Contentious agency turns passive people into active citizens who question and transform power relations.

Cultural change caused by movement and corporate strategies, not much studied in the *Dynamics of Contention*, was also integrated into the framework and analysis. Prior investigation of movement outcomes, for example in Luders (2010: 38), has also not accounted for cultural change, for which reason assessment may be leaving out important information (as Luders also contends) and be presenting the reality in too simplified terms. When cultural change is integrated into explanation, the divisions between movements, their targets, third parties and "public opinion," are rendered fluid, intermeshed, overlapped and embedded by social actions. In the real world, relations are dynamic, not divided into "external" and "internal" "variables." The theoretical refinements in this book, including the inclusion of relational and cultural change analysis, has proven valuable as the empirical findings that resulted contradict many important prior claims and call for further inquiry and reflection.

Contentious agency boosts significant cultural changes – changes that can be traced back to social movement strategies. This was demonstrated, for example, by the study of how the strategies used by many local groups of the Brazilian landless movement were replicated by the indigenous groups in conflict with eucalyptus expansion in Espírito Santo, this resulting in the indigenous resistance turning into more radical means – and, causally, greater movement success (other factors remained constant here).

142 *Conclusion*

I suggest that social movement studies need to give much more emphasis to strategies because, as the research findings in Brazil alone (see the end of Chapter 3) imply, the variation in outcomes is impossible to explain by political opportunity alone. Indeed, such a research design limitation would have generated the arbitrary result that plantation expansion was slowed in 2007 and 2008 in some pulp holdings, whilst political opportunities were highly beneficial for plantation expansion and highly negative for agrarian reform movements.

The qualitative comparative analysis suggested that pioneering, nonviolent, disruptive, massive and symbolic protests have been particularly important. The strategies used by movements, if even studied, are seldom specified in the general movement literature (Luders 2010): they are treated as similar, although qualitative differences render them very different political tools. Thus, I disaggregated movement and business strategies to assess what were the minimal requirements across differing contexts for them to have resulted in slowing down expansion. For example, the protests in Brazil criticizing pulpwood plantation that were studied (note the likely sector and country specificity here) had to involve at least 300 people, be physically non-violent, be reported in the main media and be pioneering: stringent requirements. It was found that the more truly pioneering the acts were, the more beneficial outcomes were for the movement.

Refinements on prior theorizing were undertaken, following calls for this. For example, the strategies of "campaigning by heterodox framing" and "pioneering protesting" provide a more detailed explanation of how movements work towards their desired goals than the "innovative collective action" mechanism offered by McAdam *et al.* (2001). Pioneering acts and campaigning by heterodox framing do not produce simply "innovative shifts in the locus, forms, and meaning of collective action" (ibid.: 48); because of their distinctiveness in comparison to other episodes of contention in the applicable political system, and simultaneous use of other supporting strategies, they are also central in significantly influencing economic outcomes.

Contentious agency and its economic outcomes in land grabbing conflicts

The contemporary resource conflicts are a symptom of larger transformations and pressures in the globalized political economy: the race for the last resources (Klare 2012). Besides the rapid expansion, the ill-fitting style of investment has increased conflict potential. Corporate resource exploitation focuses on increasingly large-scale investment projects in ever-more distant places (Bunker and Ciccantell 2005). Differences exist between investments depending on the natural conditions, the political system, the culture of corporate social responsibility and other managerial techniques. From the viewpoint of those dispossessed and displaced, these enclosures are broadly similar in their destructive impacts on their livelihood, lifestyles and nature.

Conclusion 143

Resistance comes in many forms: or not at all. Opportunities are always there: I have shown that local people can resist expansion, even in the middle of a very active corporate agency including a tight state alliance, depending on the exercise of contentious agency. Contentious agency matters: a systematic comparison of pulp investments in Brazil shows that state actors have adopted a more critical pulp investment stance in places where the critics have provided an alternative, heterodox frame, conceptualized investments in a new way and embedded the state. Conflicts are then eased when the state actors take a more balanced policy line that takes into consideration the social movements and the local populations and not simply the corporations.

Successful movements manage to set up alternative social, symbolic and territorial spaces, frame political lines, urge society to question the status quo, build ties and demand changes from politicians, and enforce the proper functioning of state institutions. These dynamics are extremely important when the goal is to slow or reverse large-scale investment projects. The project of building contentious agency makes a big difference particularly when one observes where episodes of contention, such as conflicts over land grabbing, turn from local discontent into transnationally acknowledged conflicts, as was the case in the pioneering April 2004 Veracel eucalyptus plantation occupation by the MST.

Contentious agency matters particularly prior to major investment, in blocking the project advancement, but is the key to any potential success afterwards for movements to attain their stated goals. If organized civil society actors do not demand policy continuity, the rule of law and constitutionality, the excesses of corporate resource exploitation are unlikely to be regulated and democracy is likely to be weakened. This is especially true in political systems where the policy process is slow, marked by strong private interests and unresolved structural hierarchies. Such systems include the capitalist global system and many national political systems. The state-forest industry alliance, the ties of which were shown to be tight in Brazil and other industrial forestry expansion countries, indicates that global capitalism and the states and governments giving the green light on large-scale land deals, are increasingly interconnected and mutually dependent. Simultaneously, the growing contentious agency by social movements and sympathetic state actors and the slowing and reversal of corporate resource exploitation suggests that global capitalism is in conflict with the views, actions and policies of a growing number of municipalities, state parliaments, local judiciary and local state institutions, not to mention local populations. Land grabbing is not the only megatrend of the past five to ten years; the other key process in this global historical conjuncture is the growing trans-local resistance to this process by impacted populations to varying degrees and strategies of resistance.

The ongoing resistance to paper investments even against the most adverse odds in the global South astounded Marchak (1995: 331):

144   *Conclusion*

> Despite its transnational organization, the plethora of transnational agencies backing it, the global consulting and engineering corporations urging it forward; despite military regimes and client-state governments; despite jail terms for opponents and exile for some; the global forest industry has failed to silence environmental activists.

In spite of the media war, government support and credit favoring ITP expansion, the resistance in many places has managed to achieve greater support, has fostered an extensive network of allies and embedded autonomy within the state apparatus, and/or has built a stronger social movement organization. In Brazil, the MST has managed the construction and transmission of a heterodox framing of pulp and eucalyptus in the maturing investment areas through its protest actions. After the resistance has challenged the experts, state officials are starting to realize that rural populations also have rights to their traditional homelands, including the right to define, participate and gain from development. This can be explained by contentious agency promotion.

Resistance has been transnationalizing. In the April 2004 Veracel occupation, the MST showed it had taken a new line of political action. Now the Brazilian landless movement frames transnational corporations as its principal adversary. This framing correlates with the reality, which is important, as the world has actually become much more transnational. The new stance brings the issues that concern the movement, e.g. eucalyptus expansion, to the attention of a far larger global audience than the old framing, through which the MST saw its principal adversary as national traditional large-scale farmers and the Brazilian state. By protests against multinational corporations, mobilization can bring the debate into the transnational arena; it can attract the attention of transnational investors, government and civil society actors. Protests against more starkly Brazilian companies, such as Fibria, do not gain nearly as much international attention as protests against joint ventures such as Veracel or foreign direct investments such as the Stora Enso Rio Grande do Sul pulp investment project. Furthermore, in struggling at a transnational level, the social movement can attack and defend itself in numerous spheres in comparison to limiting itself to national contention. The new transnational corporation-challenging, and rights- and livelihood-promoting stance of the MST seems to have worked well for the movement, even though and particularly considering the very difficult political context of general decline in agrarian reform support by government and endemic agribusiness- and elite-based rent-seeking favoring policies.

In all cases where plantation expansion was slowed, state actors have executed orders in the form of court decisions or institutional support for the movements instead of the paper industry. The MST and its allies' role in these decisions has been one of a long-term outsider criticizer that constantly spreads contention and keeps alternatives on the table. The findings of a cross-contextual and temporal analysis covering expansion and resistance

Conclusion 145

attempts since the 1990s showed that continuing resistance bears fruit eventually – if certain strategies are utilized in a specific manner. The seeds of contention can bear fruit any time, even after a substantial delay, as state institutions, especially in the global South, often take a long time to handle bureaucratic issues like legal cases. For example, the decision by a Federal Court demanding that Veracel uproot about half of all its eucalyptus plantations, tens of thousands of hectares, came 15 years after the suit was filed (execution is still withheld as the company has filed a complaint).

An end to the reckless investment might loom because of growing resistance. I have given empirical evidence that resistance to industrial forestry investment is spreading generally, although not unilaterally, and shown how and why. Carrere and Lohmann foresaw spreading contention in their 1996 book *Pulping the South*. They argued that "well-informed and well-organized citizens at local, national and transnational levels can find common ground and put a halt to the global advance of the currently-dominant model of tree plantations and paper manufacture," and that they were "already starting to do so" (Carrere and Lohmann 1996: 253). ITPs are still business as usual in most parts of the world. However, as shown in Chapter 5, business has not continued as usual in those investment areas where contentious agency has been active, including parts of Brazil, Thailand, and ALBA countries in Latin America and Vietnam. The latter half of 2008 was an historic moment when popular resistance, for example in Brazil, Peru and Venezuela, against pulp investments started to gain new sympathy from some legislators as well as judges and public prosecutors. These dynamics of contention were a surprise to many in the paper industry.

State-business-social movement dynamics are multi-faceted. Even though the state-paper industry alliance is very strong, the Brazilian state – or any state – is a site of conflicting interests. Indeed, as this research shows, Brazil is not only the stronghold of agribusiness; it is also the country where the rising transnational natural resource flow is vehemently criticized.

Democracy-promoting contentious agency

I will next discuss the role of contentious agency in promoting democratic development and thereafter relate the cases studied within research on the rise of the broader counter-movement against corporate resource exploitation.

The concept of contentious agency aims to contribute to the debate over the possibility of substantial social and economic change. Consolidation of democracy is a macro-process that helps explain the slowing of accumulation by dispossession, because democracy delimits a process that promotes corporate agency at the expense of society. However, even within a democratic polity, molding an orthodox investment model towards sustainable investment requires that someone provide alternative framings for development. Movements can channel the wishes of the people influenced by expansion. In such a situation, movements promote the power of democracy within the economy.

146   *Conclusion*

By offering alternative frames, well-organized social movements can both deepen democracy and push for regulation and more sustainable, equitable and publicly accepted investment and development policies. Those criticizing developmentalist and economistic investment projects and industrial policies have strengthened democracy because they push for the redefinition of institutions, rights and mechanisms that produce high levels of inequality and violence.

Contentious agency is a medicine for empowerment. Considering that democracy entails one vote per person and the setting is such that contenders do not have as much power in a given realm as those they are challenging, the promotion of contentious agency can extend democracy in the given realm if used for such a goal. Contentious agency could be used to promote not only national but also global democracy. However, to validate these claims, the new theory of contentious agency promotion should be tested by a transnational, global democracy analysis in which contentious and corporate agency are analyzed primarily on a transnational, not a national, level. Given the current state of global governance regimes, such studies could focus on the transnational spaces or potential spaces for the promotion of global democracy, such as the WSF, the UN system, the Bretton Woods institutions, and also on internet communities and networks as well as other less actor- and physical space-bounded dynamic terrains.

Also a note to companies, based on the findings here and elsewhere in the literature. It would be wiser for companies to behave in a more socio-environmentally responsible way as this would increase earnings as reputation would improve (Vogel 2005; cf. Soule 2009). Socially responsible investment does not harm returns but may increase these; on the other hand, there's also evidence that protest events are associated with negative stock price returns (King and Soule 2007) and financial performance. One reason is that there are financial benefits associated with good reputation (Soule 2009). Repeated and very disruptive protests were seen as particularly detrimental to the perception of a company's responsibility by the financial markets (ibid.). This suggests wise companies avoid protests by being responsible from the beginning. Responsible investment includes democratic decision making on the style of business together with the impacted populations. This was found unlikely to happen if people did not demand to be heard.

Global mobilization against corporate resource exploitation

How are these findings able to shed light on perhaps the most important question facing humanity currently, posed at the onset of this book? What is the possibility for resistance to check and reverse the disastrous pace and style of our current resource extraction and consumption and in what way? The conclusions above provided some answers to these questions and I will now relate these to the possibilities of scaling-up the local resistance to a transnational level, by making connections to other cases. This will help to open up

Conclusion 147

pathways for future research that would aim to understand mobilization against destructive corporate resource exploitation.

The building of transnational alliances between social movements and resistance against capitalist resource exploitation has taken place for decades and even centuries. Now this process is meeting with the last race for non-renewable resources. In general in contemporary world politics, argues Teivainen (2012), it has become very difficult to ignore the challengers of transnational capitalism, such as critical think tanks, NGOs, movements and other actors. I have argued this includes the populations displaced by large-scale projects. In most investment areas the displaced people have absolutely nowhere to go to continue to live the life they had. Where will those driven out from their forests by open-pit mines, phony forests, roads, railroads, airports, dams and factories go? When land all around is grabbed, where will they find nature where their "primitive" cultural ways, much more sustainable than those of the "civilized" world, can be continued? Scott (2012) calls this period the final enclosure of non-state spaces. These peripheral spaces have been hitherto typically neglected as useless, territories where marginalized people were relegated. Suddenly, in the past decade or so, these spaces have been understood to have great economic importance for the resource needs of mature capitalism (Scott 2009). As their lands are grabbed in the race for what's left, these non-state people are forcefully inserted into pre-defined spaces and into the midst of natural resource politics where outcomes are determined by largely state-remediated political games.

What role can the dispossessed have in turning the race for what's left, the final enclosure of the last non-renewable resources by the powerful, the dominant phenomenon of the contemporary global historical conjuncture? Could we start to see the whole situation as something more than a zero-sum game for the world's last resources and land? Such a race exists only insofar as we depend on the current economic model of growth based on the wasteful and limitless increase of consumption. I have argued that people can forge social movements based on contentious agency that radically challenges the dominant understanding of development, and demand deeper and more direct democracy and an altogether different basis for maintaining our livelihoods. This can create sustainable socio-ecological relations. Securing space, territory and land for the development of a mosaic of sustainable alternatives requires concrete resistance to the insatiable turning of nature relations into a transnational commodity flow.

When to act? Whereas the "political opportunity" framework argues that large-scale crises and other political openings can be capitalized on by movements for significant benefits (see Tarrow 2011), some scholars, including Harmes (2012) argue for the need to focus less on waiting for the clues that we are in a large crisis, and instead develop a strategy for promoting incrementally significant changes on an issue-by-issue basis even in the absence of any clues that pose "opportunities" or "threats." He argues that such approaches help in changing the rules of the game more beneficial for

148 *Conclusion*

resistance. I have tried to show how this is possible in natural resource politics, with a study of the differing sets of strategies boosting contentious agency impact on local investment outcomes. Such an approach can yield better results, because without the capacity created by political organizing and a willingness to act, the resistance will miss the opportunities opening for it.

Crises such as the multifaceted one we are in now (Gills 2010) are situations of both danger and possibility. Innovative framing of these in the current historical conjuncture is required. Bunker and Ciccantell (2005) emphasize the need to demystify the discourses falsely claiming that large-scale resource extraction and export could lead to local development. They suggest accurate historical comparisons and analyses pinpointing flaws in seemingly coherent technical analysis, alongside diffusion of this heterodox framing as efficiently as possible, by transnational networking involving all sorts of specialists and impacted populations around the world. Harmes (2012) suggests that the progressives could learn more from the tactics of the industrial lobby and think tanks, starting also to use crisis situations by prepared rapid responses to promote their ideas, for example by political marketing techniques producing detailed and issue-specific policy briefs, use of communications "war rooms" and political advertising. As the race for resources gets tougher, we are likely to see such professionalization take place, given its potential to reap more rapidly the desired and visible outcome of discontinuing an unwanted project.

Transnational contentious agency plays an increasingly important role. One looking at the task list of the entities visiting the WSF quickly gets a broad picture of the magnitude of mobilization efforts against corporate resource exploitation. For the radical peasants, who are increasingly transnationally organized by such movements as La Vía Campesina, a world economy run by corporations is not a destiny. Other examples include the advocacy work of the Transnational Institute, FIAN (Food First Information and Action Network), the World Rainforest Movement and other transnational actors agglomerating distinct but united grassroots forces.

In general, transnational ties of social movements have favored these in their struggle against large-scale investments (Khagram 2004). However, transnational ties can be also partly detrimental to the resistance, particularly in the context of rising nationalism. The studied ITP conflicts revealed that the more deeply rooted a given social actor is in national politics, such as an industry or a social movement, the more likely it is to attain its goals. In Brazil, India and Russia, for example, transnational ties of resistance movements, such as indigenous groups and environmental NGOs, have been systematically misrepresented to the public by those in favor of large-scale investments in order to cash in nationalist sentiments, utilize the force of nationalism in opposing all alternative development projects and to represent their supporters as "manipulated by outsiders." This has also been the case in pulp conflicts, where Aracruz Celulose, for example, advertised itself as "100% Brazilian," and represented the resistance of the indigenous as manipulated and directed by the interests of competing companies and groups in Europe and the USA.

It is useful for the resistance to "follow the money." As Chapter 2 showed, most of the financing for pulp projects in Brazil comes not from transnational circles, such as the World Bank, but from the National Development Bank (BNDES). In order to resist pulp investment in Brazil, it has made much more sense for the resistance to operate principally in the realm of Brazilian politics. The transnational ties of the opponents in conflicts can be used in opponent framing to harness the maximum amount of public nationalistic support and global attention. For example, the MST has deliberately focused its protests against transnational corporations, against outsiders such as Stora Enso. It has increasingly avoided national companies like Fibria, starting dialogue with these, putting most effort into the struggle against transnational or globalizing capital. On the other hand, in 2011–12 the government had smoothed the discussions between national companies and the resistance, and the national pulp capital had become slightly more dialogue-prone than the foreign companies such as Stora Enso, having a more aggressive expansion line. Corporate agency quality interacts with contentious agency.

The heavily local quality of action present in the ITP conflicts is not an exception. Much of the collective action, planning and the activists are local even in theoretically transnational advocacy campaigns (Keck and Sikkink 1998). Yet, actions via transnational networking could prove to be crucial to promote dialogue and transformation. Advocacy and visibility promotion could effectively lead to transparency, government regulation and towards greater corporate social responsibility. Transnational advocacy in the rubber tappers' case in the end of the 1980s was fundamental in pressuring the Brazilian state to change its Amazon policy and examine the problems more closely (Keck 1995). Parallel pressure on the states of origin of the corporations in question, on the receiving state and corporations by the local people and their national allies is required for truly lasting solutions, because the problems of today are transnational.

Globalization changes the possibilities of resistance everywhere. Expansion of transnational movements such as Vía Campesina are cases of local and national contention turning into transnational activism, a case of upward scale shift (see Tarrow 2005; Reitan 2007; Borras 2010) and frame extension in which significant national movements, such as the MST, shift objects and claims upward from targeting their state to targeting transnational resource-exploiting corporations to transform the transnational resource flow.[2]

Particularly dire in this counter-hegemonic globalization, argues Harmes (2012), is the need better to promote heterodox ideas among national politicians and the broad public, two occasions on which the broad progressive front has so far not achieved as much change to the status quo. I have focused on empirically assessing the efficacy of strategies by which national politicians and states could better be influenced, as well as analysis on the way contentious agency can be used to develop alternative social space, territory and symbolic

150   *Conclusion*

systems that keep on influencing the broader public as they spread. The MST settlements, in many cases impacting their neighborhood and spreading the metaculture of replication, which allows greater autonomy and contentious agency and delimits the local tradition and know-how destroying capitalist dissemination of consumerism, are a case in point.

The globally rising mobilization against corporate resource exploitation shows the importance of material- instead of more purely identity-based counter-movements. The resurgence of material-based mobilization, visible in the 1990s to 2000s anti-neoliberal mobilization wave in Latin America criticizing resource-corporatizing endeavors such as water privatization in Bolivia, showed that the new social movement literature had misjudged that identity politics would have overtaken material interests (Silva 2009: 10).[3] Sawyer (2004) argues it was the resistance to devastating oil exploration and counter-agrarian neoliberal reform in Ecuador by the affected indigenous organizations in the 1990s and 2000s that built a large counter-movement against transnational resource exploitation in that country. Later this led to a leftist government and a radically new state. The new state had different political game rules. The indigenous people in Ecuador used the same strategies identified in this book as central for blocking investment, including protests (ibid.). The difference from the Brazilian context was that instead of state embedding whilst protesting, the main contention focus was upon developing a new configuration of a plurinational state, which the Ecuadorian resistance succeeded in bringing about. Not disconnected with this outcome, the Ecuadorian legal cases against Chevron's oil operations in the Amazon have been a central example in the new thrust to give multinational companies liability for the damage they have done, including fining them. This has been made possible by the anti-state-focused protesting strategy of the broad resistance mobilization in Ecuador, which managed to replace the existing state, and change the configuration and rules of the political game where transnational resource extraction policies are determined.

This example of comparative resistance suggests that contentious agency and the resistance outcomes determined by its interaction with state-capital alliances can also flow from the building of a new state institution structure. The strategy of radical new state-seeking protest can typically ensure deeper outcomes for movements, if succeeding (think of the Arab Spring revolutions, for example: it would had made little difference just reforming the dictatorships). On the other hand, to try to find potential powerful swing actors within the state and even industry to change the institutions or the policy is a safer and possibly more lasting and thus impactful route, because the radical anti-state mobilization against existing rules can backslash and lead to the destruction of the hard-built resistance organizations. Embedded autonomy has many advantages that revolution attempts lack.

I argue that both the embedding of existing games and new state-creating strategies are better than waiting for a large crisis before acting. For example, waiting for a significant crisis has resulted in the loss of many good

Conclusion 151

opportunities since the end of the 1990s, when the dislocations and hardships of failing neoliberal policies started to be experienced across the globe in different places (Harmes 2012). Harmes makes an important point by noting that the current slower occurring and developing global crisis, involving, for example, climate disruptions and somehow controlled financial meltdowns – not leading to such major recessions as in the 1930s – has produced less radical counter-movements and transformations in the establishment than the crisis of the 1930s. Major, abrupt crises are more prone to cause radical alternatives to be marched in, than slowly stirring discontent, which passes largely unnoted and is thus even normalized. It is the sharpness in relative worsening of local situations, such as land use, that matters most in the framing of relative grievances, which cause mobilization where resistance capacity and willingness to act lead to the use of strategies a–e, for example.

Large-scale corporate resource exploitation projects, which often produce deep crises and local impacts, have a greater potential – resistance capability permitting and willingness existing – to cause more radical mobilization and fostering of contentious agency than more invisible, unidentifiable, slower and more gradual dislocations and hardships (even if these would in the end mean an even greater total dispossession than abrupt changes). As with all power and according to Foucault's (1994) general theorizing on power relations, rapid increases in visible corporate power and material flows carry the *potential* of resistance. Considering the inbuilt potential for resistance – particularly in the projects invested in by those who are most powerful – and the mobilizing importance of material interests typically more important than identity-based issues, the ever larger-scale and locally ever more damagingly impactful resource extraction projects carry perhaps the most potential for building a new large-scale countermovement.

The race between nation-states and corporations for the last non-renewable resources, and to secure the best areas of nature for the production of renewable resources in the emerging "green capitalism," is a clearly deepening path, increasing conflict potential and impacts. As industrial capitalism and civilization relies on material resources, the networked trans-local resistance against large-scale resource exploitation carries a very high potential of forming the core of the second major Polanyian counter-movement – the second great transformation. Natural resource politics is becoming ever more central in explaining world politics, as people even in the global North will eventually have to understand the natural limits to consumption growth. Contentious agency plays the central role here.

One example of the successes of movements resisting the destructive investment model comes from Peru. Under the state support of the Alan García government lessening the legislation protecting the Amazon, CMPC, a Chilean pulp and paper company, announced plans to invest in the Amazon, to cut forest, plant trees and to build a pulp mill. Following the plan, in August 2008 "more than 3,000 indigenous and *campesino* protestors from various parts of the Amazon region declared an indefinite national strike against the

152 *Conclusion*

new legislation" (WRM 2008), a strategy that resulted in the Peruvian Congress repealing the legislative decrees the government had signed to help extractive corporations into the Amazon on August 22, 2008. This led to the discontinuation of expansion even before it had started in the Peruvian Amazon – at least for a while – which might just be enough to secure long-term discontinuation if contentious agency is retained.

The promise of global resistance turning into a widespread phenomenon powerful enough to turn into a process stripping corporations from easy entry all over lies in sustaining strategies promoting contentious agency in the streets, forests, fields, palaces and offices. Multiple abrupt crises and environmental havoc can help to secure a broad counter-movement, but ultimately it depends on activism. We are witnessing how corporate agribusiness and other operations enclose the remaining fertile land and other resources faster than ever. In order to survive, people have to challenge destructive natural resource exploitation by increasing contentious agency that defends right livelihood. The industrial forestry-resistance cases that have led to the slowing or even discontinuation of plantation expansion imply that if contentious agency expands, social movements can at least slow, and even reverse these investments. The extent to which the same lesson can be applied in the different industries that maintain global capitalism is to be answered by other studies.

Notes

1 In the study of political economic conflicts, "political opportunity structures" are influenced strongly by state-industry alliance; as corporate agency defines these to large extent, its study is essential to understand what the resistance faces.
2 McAdam *et al.* (2001: 331) define scale shift as "a change in the number and level of coordinated contentious actions to a different focal point, involving a new range of actors, different objects, and broadened claims."
3 See *Peasants Against Globalization* by Marc Edelman (1999) for an elaborated discussion on the problematic over-emphasis of identity over material interests in the new social movement theory.

References

Abers, R.N. (2000) *Inventing Local Democracy: Grassroots Politics in Brazil*, Boulder, Colorado: Lynne Rienner.

ABRAF (2011) "Anuário estatístico da ABRAF 2011 ano base 2010" [Yearly Statistics of ABRAF, Based on Year 2010], Brasília: ABRAF.

Abu-El-Haj, J. (2007) "From Interdependence to Neo-Mercantilism: Brazilian Capitalism in the Age of Globalization," *Latin American Perspectives* 34(5): 92–114.

Alvarez, S., Dagnino, E. and Escobar, A. (eds) (1998) *Cultures of Politics/Politics of Cultures: Re-Visioning Latin American Social Movements*, Boulder, Colorado: Westview Press.

Andrews, K. (2004) *Freedom is a Constant Struggle: The Mississippi Civil Rights Movement and its Legacy*, Chicago: University of Chicago Press.

Arrighi, G. (1994) *The Long Twentieth Century*, London: Verso.

Arrighi, G., Aschoff, N. and Scully, B. (2011) "Accumulation by Dispossession and its Limits: The Southern African Paradigm Revisited," *Studies in Comparative International Development* 45(4): 410–38.

Arruda, M., Souza, H. and Afonso, C. (1975) *Multinational Corporations and Brazil*, Toronto: Latin America Research Unit.

Asselin, V. (2009) *Grilagem: Corrupção e violência em terras do Carajás* [Illegal Land Grabbing: Corruption and Violence in the Lands of Carajás], 2nd edn, Imperatriz: Ética.

Avritzer, L. (1994) *Sociedade Civil e Democratização*, Belo Horizonte: Del Rey.

Avritzer, L. and Wampler, B. (2004) "Participatory Publics: Civil Society and New Institutions in Democratic Brazil," *Comparative Politics* 36(3): 291–312.

Bacchetta, V. (2012) "La soberanía a la deriva," *Ecoportal.net*, September 13.

Baird, I. (2011) "Turning Land into Capital, Turning People into Labor: Primitive Accumulation and the Arrival of Large-Scale Economic Land Concessions in the Lao People's Democratic Republic," *New Proposals: Journal of Marxism and Interdisciplinary Inquiry* 5(1).

Baird, I. and Le Billon, P. (2012) "Landscapes of Political Memories: War Legacies and Land Negotiations in Laos," *Political Geography* 31: 290–300.

Barney, K. (2004) "Re-encountering Resistance: Plantation Activism and Smallholder Production in Thailand and Sarawak, Malaysia," *Asia Pacific Viewpoint* 45(3): 325–39.

——(2008) "Local Vulnerability, Project Risk, and Intractable Debt: The Politics of Smallholder Eucalyptus Promotion in Salavane Province, Southern Laos," in Snelder and Lasco (eds) *Smallholder Tree Growing for Rural Development and Environmental Services*, Springer, 263–83.

154 References

Barr, C. and Sayer, J. (2012) "The Political Economy of Reforestation and Forest Restoration in Asia-Pacific: Critical Issues for REDD+," *Biological Conservation*, in press.

Barros, G. (2005) "País caminha para a anarquia, diz Ermírio," *Folha de S. Paulo*, May 19, www1.folha.uol.com.br/folha/brasil/ult96u60966.shtml (accessed August 11, 2009).

Barros, J. (2008) "O papelão da Suzano no Piauí" [The Fiasco of Suzano in Piauí], Rede Ambiental do Piauí, www.portaldomeioambiente.org.br/pma/index.php?option=com_content&view=article&id=717.

Beckford, G. (1972) *Persistent Poverty: Underdevelopment in Plantation Economies of the Third World*, London: Zed Books.

Bengoa, J. (2006) *La comunidad reclamada: identidades, utopías y memorias en la sociedad Chilena actual*, Santiago: Catalonia.

Benson, M. and Rochon, T. (2004) "Interpersonal Trust and the Magnitude of Protest: A Micro and Macro Level Approach," *Comparative Political Studies* 37: 435–57.

Berterretche, J. (2010) "Brasil petista: social-liberalismo com vocação 'desenvolvimentista'," *Desacatobrasil*, October 15.

BNDES (2009) "Desembolso anual do sistema BNDES" [Annual Lending by the BNDES System], www.bndes.gov.br/estatisticas.

Boff, L. (1993) *Ecologia, mundialização, espiritualidade*, Petrópolis: Atica.

Boito, A. (2007) "Estado e burguesia no capitalismo neoliberal," *Revista de Sociologia e Política* 28: 57–73.

Borras, S.M. (2001) "State-Society Relations in Land Reform Implementation in the Philippines," *Development and Change* 32: 545–75.

——(2010) "The Politics of Transnational Agrarian Movements," *Development and Change* 41: 771–803.

Borras, S.M., Franco, J., Gómez, S., Kay, C. and Spoor, M. (2012) "Land Grabbing in Latin America and the Caribbean," *Journal of Peasant Studies* 39(3–4): 845–72.

Boulay, A. and Tacconi, L. (2012) "The Drivers of Contract Eucalypt Farming in Thailand," *International Forestry Review* 14(1): 1–12.

Bourdieu, P. (1990) *In Other Words: Essays Towards a Reflexive Sociology*, Cambridge: Polity Press.

——(1991) *Language and Symbolic Power*, Cambridge: Polity Press.

——(1998) *Practical Reason: On the Theory of Action*, Cambridge: Polity Press.

——(2000) *Pascalian Meditations*, Cambridge: Polity Press.

Bracelpa (2009) "Área total reflorestada em 31/12/2007" [Total Area Reforested on January 31, 2007], www.bracelpa.org.br/bra/estatisticas/pdf/anual/reflo_01.pdf.

——(2010) "Relatório Anual 2009/2010" [Annual Report 2009/2010], www.bracelpa.org.br/bra2/sites/default/files/estatisticas/rel2009.pdf.

Brandão, C. (2007) "Tempos e espaços nos mundos rurais do Brasil" [Times and Spaces in the Rural Worlds of Brazil], *Ruris* 1(1), www.ifch.unicamp.br/ceres/037-64-carlos_rodrigues.pdf.

Bresser-Pereira, L. (2010) "The Global Financial Crisis and a New Capitalism?" *Journal of Post Keynesian Economics* 32(4): 499–534.

Bull, G.Q., Bazett, M., Schwab, O., Nilsson, S., White, A., Maginnis, S. (2006) "Industrial Forest Plantation Subsidies: Impacts and Implications," *Forest Policy and Economics* 9(1): 13–31.

Bunker, S. and Ciccantell, P. (2005) *Globalization and the Race for Resources*, Baltimore: The Johns Hopkins University Press.

References 155

Caldeira, R. (2008) "My Land, Your Social Transformation: Conflicts within the Landless People Movement (MST), Rio de Janeiro, Brazil," *Journal of Rural Studies* 24: 150–60.

Calder, I., Hofer, T., Vermont, S. and Warren, P. (2007) "Towards a New Understanding of Forests and Water," *Unasylva* 58(4): 3–10.

Carámbula, M., Menéndez, V. and Piñero, D. (2011) *La expansión de capital forestal en el agro Uruguay*, conference proceeding, VII Jornadas Interdisciplinarias en Estudios Agrarios y Agroindustriales, University of Buenos Aires.

Carámbula, M. and Piñeiro, D. (2006) "La forestación en Uruguay: Cambío demográfico y empleo en tres localidades," *Revista Agrociencia* X(2): 63–75.

Cardoso, F. and Faletto, E. (1979) *Dependency and Development in Latin America*, Berkeley: University of California Press.

Carrere, R. (2005) "Annex," in Granda, *Carbon Sink Plantations in the Ecuadorian Andes: Impacts of the Dutch FACE-PROFAFOR Monoculture Tree Plantations Project on Indigenous and Peasant Communities*, www.wrm.org.uy/countries/Ecuador/face.html.

——(2009) "Brasil: duro questionamento à maquiagem FSC de plantações de eucaliptos e advertência perante seu avanço no Piauí," *WRM Bulletin* 144.

Carrere, R. and Lohmann, L. (1996) *Pulping the South: Industrial Tree Plantations and the World Paper Economy*, London: Zed Books.

Carter, M. (2009) "The Landless Rural Workers Movement and Democracy in Brazil," final draft version, April 17, 2009, Land Action Research Network, www.landaction.org/spip/spip.php?article436 (accessed July 14, 2009).

Carvalho, J. (1997) "Mandonismo, coronelismo, clientelismo: Uma discussão conceitual," *Dados* 40.

Castro, E. *et al.* (2007) "Perfis dos jovens participantes de eventos dos movimentos sociais rurais: construções de um ator politico," Paper presented to the XIII Congresso Brasileiro de Sociologia, Recife.

Cerioli, P.R. and Broilo, E. (2003) *Ocupando a Bíblia*, 2nd edn, Caderno de educação, 10, Veranópolis: ANCA.

Claessens, S., Feijen, E. and Laeven, L. (2007) "Political Connections and Preferential Access to Finance: The Role of Campaign Contributions," *Journal of Financial Economics* 88: 554–80.

Clapp, R.A. (1995) "Creative Competitive Advantage: Forest Policy as Industrial Policy in Chile," *Economic Geography* 71(3): 273–96.

——(1998) "Regions of Refuge and the Agrarian Question: Peasant Agriculture and Plantation Forestry in Chilean Araucania," *World Development* 26(4): 571–89.

Clement, F., Orange, D., Williams, M., Mulley, C. and Epprecht, M. (2009) "Drivers of Afforestation in Northern Vietnam: Assessing Local Variations Using Geographically Weighted Regression," *Applied Geography* 29(4): 561–76.

Collier, R.B. (1999) *Paths Toward Democracy: The Working Class and Elites in Western Europe and South America*, Cambridge, UK: Cambridge University Press.

Collier, R.B. and Handlin, S. (eds) (2009) *Reorganizing Popular Politics: Participation and the New Interest Regime in Latin America*, University Park, PA: Penn State University Press.

Cossalter, C. and Barr, C. (2005) *Fast-growing Plantation Development and Industrial Wood Demand in China's Guangxi Zhuang Autonomous Region*, A Report Prepared for the Guangxi Forestry Bureau and the World Bank, Center for International Forestry Research, Bogor, Indonesia.

156 References

Cossalter, C. and Pye-Smith, C. (2003) *Fast-Wood Forestry: Myths and Realities*, Jakarta: Center for International Forestry Research.

CPT (2011) "Síntese Terra – 2009/2010," April 7, www.cptnacional.org.br/index.php? option=com_jdownloads& Itemid=23&view=finish&cid=211&catid=37.

Cramer, B. and Kaufman, R. (2010) "Views of Economic Inequality in Latin America," *Comparative Political Studies:* doi:10.1177/0010414010392171.

Cramer, C. and Richards, P. (2011) "Violence and War in Agrarian Perspective," *Journal of Agrarian Change* 11(3): 277–97.

Dagnino, E. (2002) *Sociedade Civil e Espaços Públicos no Brasil*, São Paulo: Paz e Terra.

Dagnino, E., Olvera, A.J. and Panfichi, A. (eds) (2006) *A disputa pela construção democrática na América Latina*, São Paulo: Paz e Terra.

Dalton, R., Recchia, S. and Rohrschneider, R. (2003) "The Environmental Movement and the Modes of Political Action," *Comparative Political Studies* 36: 743–71.

DaMatta, R. (1992) *Carnivals, Rogues, & Heroes: An Interpretation of the Brazilian Dilemma*, Notre Dame: University of Notre Dame.

Dauvergne, P. and Lister, J. (2011) *Timber*, Cambridge: Polity Press.

del Lungo, A., Ball, J. and Carle, J. (2006) *Global Planted Forests Thematic Study: Results and Analysis*, Planted Forests and Trees working paper 38, Rome: FAO, www.fao.org/forestry/site/10368/en.

de'Nadai, A., Overbeek, W. and Soares, L. (2005) *Promises of Jobs and Destruction of Work: The Case of Aracruz Celulose in Brazil*, London: WRM.

Diniz, E. and Boschi, R. (2004) *Empresários, Interesses e Mercado – Dilemas do Desenvolvimento no Brasil*, Belo Horizonte: Editora UFMG.

Doctor, M. (2007) "Lula's Development Council: Neo-Corporatism and Policy Reform in Brazil," *Latin American Perspectives* 34: 131–48.

Drèze, J. and Sen, A. (2002) *India: Development and Participation*, Oxford: Oxford University Press.

du Monceau, M.I. (2008) *The Political Ecology of Indigenous Movements and Tree Plantations in Chile: The Role of Political Strategies of Mapuche Communities in Shaping their Social and Natural Livelihoods*, University of British Columbia, doctoral dissertation.

Eakin, M. (2001) *Tropical Capitalism: The Industrialization of Belo Horizonte, Brazil*, New York: Palgrave.

The Economist (2010) "Nest Egg or Serpent's Egg?" August 5.

Edelman, M. (1999) *Peasants Against Globalization: Rural Social Movements in Costa Rica*, Stanford: Stanford University Press.

Eesley, C. and Lenox, M.J. (2006) "Firm Responses to Secondary Stakeholder Action," *Strat. Mgmt. J.* 27: 765–81.

Evans, P. (1979) *Dependent Development: The Alliance of Multinational, State and Local Capital in Brazil*, Princeton, NJ: Princeton University Press.

——(1995) *Embedded Autonomy: States & Industrial Transformation*, Princeton, NJ: Princeton University Press.

——(2008) "Is an Alternative Globalization Possible?" *Politics & Society* 36: 271–305.

Falleti, T. and Lynch, J. (2008) "From Process to Mechanism: Varieties of Disaggregation," *Qual Sociol* 31: 333–39.

FAO (2001) "Forest Distribution by Country," www.iucn.org/about/work/programmes/ forest/fp_resources/fp_resources_forest_cover.cfm (accessed August 12, 2009).

——(2010) *Global Forest Resources Assessment 2010.*

References 157

——(2011) *State of the World's Forests 2011.*

Fase, Greenpeace and Ibase (1993) *Dossiê Veracruz [Veracruz Dossier]*, Rio de Janeiro: Fase.

Fearnside, P. (1998) "Plantation Forestry in Brazil: Projections to 2050," *Biomass and Bioenergy* 15(6): 437–50.

——(1999) "Plantation Forestry in Brazil: The Potential Impacts of Climatic Change," *Biomass and Bioenergy* 16(2): 91–102.

Fernandes, B.M. (1996) *MST: formação e territorialização*, São Paulo: Hucitec.

——(2009) "The MST and Agrarian Reform in Brazil," *Socialism and Democracy* 23(3): 90–99.

Fernandes, B., Welch, C. and Constantino, E. (2010) "Agrofuel Policies in Brazil: Paradigmatic and Territorial Disputes," *Journal of Peasant Studies* 37(4): 793–819.

Ferreira, S. (2009) "'Donos do Lugar': A Territorialidade Quilombola do Sâpe do Norte – ES" ["Lords of Place": The Quilombolo Territoriality in Sâpe do Norte, Espírito Santo], PhD dissertation, UFF, Niterói.

Fingerl, E. and Filho, J. (1998) "The Brazilian Pulp and Paper Industry Investment Requirements," BNDES, www.bndes.gov.br/english/studies/r_03_98i.pdf.

Finnish Forest Industries Federation (2009) "The Forest Cluster – A Network of Expertise and Business Activities," Helsinki: Forest Industries Statistics Service.

Flaten, K. (2011) "Tree Plantation Expansion: Impacts on Rural Communities in the Central North of Tasmania," *ISP COLLECTION*, Paper 1078.

Fligstein, N. and McAdam, D. (2011) "Toward a General Theory of Strategic Action Fields," *Sociological Theory* 29: 1–26.

Foucault, M. (1994) *Dits et écrits. T. IV, 1980–1988*, Paris: Gallimard.

Fox, J. (1993) *The Politics of Food in Mexico: State Power and Social Mobilization*, London: Cornell University Press.

Fox, J., Fujita, Y., Ngidang, D., Peluso, N., Potter, L., Sakuntaladewi, N., Sturgeon, J., Thomas, D. (2009) "Policies, Political-Economy, and Swidden in Southeast Asia," *Human Ecology* 37(3): 305–22.

Franklin, A. (2008) *Apontamentos e Fontes para a História Econômica de Imperatriz*, Imperatriz: Ética.

Freire, P. (2000) *Pedagogia da Indignação: Cartas Pedagógicas e Outros Escritos*, São Paulo: UNESP.

Gamson, W. (1990) *The Strategy of Social Protest*, 2nd edn, Belmont: Wadsworth Publishing.

Gasques, J., Bastos, E. and Valdes, C. (2008) "Preços da Terra no Brasil" [Land Prices in Brazil], Rio Branco: SOBER, ageconsearch.umn.edu/bitstream/106106/2/587.pdf.

Gautreau, P. and Vélez, E. (2011) "Strategies of Environmental Knowledge Production Facing Land Use Changes: Insights from the Silvicultural Zoning Plan Conflict in the Brazilian State of Rio Grande do Sul," *Cybergeo: European Journal of Geography* 577.

Gerber, J. (2010) "Conflicts over Industrial Tree Plantations in the South: Who, How and Why?" *Global Environmental Change* 21(1): 165–76.

Gerber, J.-F. and Veuthey, S. (2010) "Plantations, Resistance and the Greening of the Agrarian Question in Coastal Ecuador," *Journal of Agrarian Change* 10: 455–81.

Ghosh, S., Hadida, Y. and Arindam, D. (2011) "Annexe 1: India's Imaginary Forest Carbon Sinks, Case 7: Forestry CDM Projects," *The Indian CDM: Subsidizing and Legitimizing Corporate Pollution*, Kolkata: Sasanta Dev, sanhati.com/wp-content/uploads/2011/12/cdmnagarikmancha.pdf.

158 References

Gibson-Graham, J.K. (2006) *A Postcapitalist Politics*, Minneapolis: Minnesota University Press.

Giddens, A. (1984) *The Constitution of Society: Outline of the Theory of Structuration*, Cambridge: Polity.

Gidwani, V. (2009) "Class," in Gregory et al. (ed.) *The Dictionary of Human Geography*, Chichester: Wiley-Blackwell, pp. 88–9.

Gills, B. (2010) "Going South: Capitalist Crisis, Systemic Crisis, Civilisational Crisis," *Third World Quarterly* 31(2): 169–84.

Giugni, M. (2004) *Social Protest and Policy Change: Ecology, Antinuclear, and Peace Movements in Comparative Perspective*, Lanham: Rowman & Littlefield Publishers.

Giugni, M., McAdam, D. and Tilly, C. (eds) (1999) *How Social Movements Matter*, London: University of Minnesota Press.

Gomes, E. (2004) "Reforming with the Reforms: Liberalization, Democratization and Corporatist Institutions in Brazil," paper presented to the International Studies Association Annual Meeting, Montreal.

Gonçalves, M.T. (1991) *Aspectos da economia e da política florestal de Minas Gerais nas décadas 1970 e 1980*, Belo Horizonte: BDMG.

——(2001) *Nós da madeira: mudança social e trabalhadores assalariados das plantações florestais nos Vales do Aço/Rio Doce de Minas Gerais*, doctoral dissertation, Rio de Janeiro: UFFRJ, CPDA.

Goodwin, J. and Jasper, J.M. (eds) (2004) *Rethinking Social Movements: Structure, Meaning, and Emotion*, Lanham, MD: Rowan & Littlefield.

Government of India (2010) *National Mission for a Green India*, Ministry of Environment and Forests, india.gov.in/allimpfrms/alldocs/15028.pdf.

Gramsci, A. (1971) *Selections from the Prison Notebooks*, New York: International Publishers.

Graziano, X. (2004) *O carma da terra*, São Paulo: A Girafa.

Grossjean, P. and Kontoleon, A. (2009) "How Sustainable are Sustainable Development Programs? The Case of the Sloping Land Conversion Program in China," *World Devel.* 37(1): 268–85.

Guidry, J. (2003) "Trial by Space: The Spatial Politics of Citizenship and Social Movements in Urban Brazil," *Mobilization* 8: 189–204.

Hall, D. (2002) "Environmental Change, Protest, and Havens of Environmental Degradation: Evidence from Asia," *Global Environmental Politics* 2(2): 20–28.

——(2003) "The International Political Ecology of Industrial Shrimp Aquaculture and Industrial Plantation Forestry in Southeast Asia," *Journal of Southeast Asian Studies* 34: 251–64.

Hammond, J.L. (1999) "Law and Disorder: The Brazilian Landless Farmworkers Movement," *Bulletin of Latin American Research* 18: 469–89.

——(2004) "The MST and the Media: Competing Images of the Brazilian Landless Farmworkers' Movement," *Latin American Politics & Society* 46: 61–90.

Harmes, A. (2012) "Crises, Social Forces and the Future of Global Governance: Implications for Progressive Strategy," in S. Gill (ed.) *Global Crises and the Crisis of Global Leadership*, Cambridge: Cambridge University Press, 216–32.

Hart, G. (2002) *Disabling Globalization: Places of Power in Post-Apartheid South Africa*, Berkeley, CA: University of California Press.

Harvey, D. (1983) *The Limits to Capital*, London: Verso.

——(2003) *The New Imperialism*, Oxford: Oxford University Press.

References 159

Hellman, J.A. (1992) "The Study of New Social Movements in Latin America and the Question of Autonomy," in A. Escobar and S.E. Alvarez (eds) *The Making of Social Movements in Latin America: Identity, Strategy and Democracy*, San Francisco: Westview Press.

The Hindu (2010) "Green India Mission document submitted to PM council," New Delhi, October 12, www.thehindu.com/sci-tech/energy-and-environment/article827050.ece.

Hobson, B. (2003) "Introduction," in idem. (ed.) *Recognition Struggle and Social Movements: Contested Identities, Agency, and Power*, Cambridge: Cambridge University Press.

Hochstetler, K. and Keck, M.E. (2007) *Greening Brazil: Environmental Activism in State and Society*, London: Duke University Press.

Hornborg, A. (2001) *The Power of the Machine: Global Inequalities of Economy, Technology, and Environment*, Lanham, MD: Altamira.

Hornborg, A., McNeill, J.R. and Martínez-Alier, J. (eds) (2007) *Rethinking Environmental History: World-System History and Global Environmental Change*, Oxford: Altamira.

IBGE (2006a) "Confronto dos Resultados dos Dados Estruturais dos Censos Agropecuários 1970–2006" [Summary of the Results of Structural Statistics in Agricultural Census], www.ibge.gov.br/graficos_dinamicos/censo_agro/default.htm.

——(2006b) "Censo agropecuário 2006. Tabela 1.1 – Utilização das terras nos estabelecimentos, por tipo de utilização, segundo a agricultura familiar, Brasil – 2006" [Census of Agriculture. Land Use in Establishments by Type of Use, According to Family Farming], Rio de Janeiro: IBGE.

Jackson, R.B., Jobba, E.G., Avissar, R., Roy, S.B., Barrett, D.J., Cook, C.W., Farley, K.A., le Maitre, D.C., McCarl, B.A. and Murray, B.C. (2005) "Trading Water for Carbon with Biological Carbon Sequestration," *Science* 310: 1944–47.

Jepson, W.E. (2006) "Private Agricultural Colonization on a Brazilian Frontier, 1970–80," *Journal of Historical Geography* 32(4): 839–63.

Jobbágy, E., Baldi, G. and Nosetto, M. (2012) "Tree Plantation in South America and the Water Cycle: Impacts and Emergent Opportunities," in T. Schlichter and L. Montes (eds) *Forests in Development: A Vital Balance*, Springer, 53–63.

Joly, C. (2007) "Especialização produtiva do território e o circuito espacial produtivo de celulose em Eunápolis – BA" [Specialization of the Territory and Spatial Productive Circuit of Pulp in Eunápolis – BA], master's thesis, USP, São Paulo.

Juvenal, T. and Mattos, R. (2002) "O setor de cellulose e papel. BNDES 50 anos – histórias setorais" [The Paper and Pulp Sector. BNDES 50 Years – Sectoral Histories], Rio de Janeiro: BNDES, www.bndes.gov.br/SiteBNDES/export/sites/default/bndes_pt/Galerias/Arquivos/conhecimento/livro_setorial/setorial04.pdf.

Kassa, H., Bekele, M. and Campbell, B. (2011) "Reading the Landscape Past: Explaining the Lack of On-Farm Tree Planting in Ethiopia," *Environment and History* 17(3): 461–79.

Kay, C. (2002) "Chile's Neoliberal Agrarian Transformation and the Peasantry," *Journal of Agrarian Change* 2(4): 464–501.

Keck, M.E. (1995) "Social Equity and Environmental Politics in Brazil: Lessons from the Rubber Tappers of Acre," *Comparative Politics* 27: 409–24.

Keck, M.E. and Sikkink, K. (1998) *Activists Beyond Borders: Advocacy Networks in International Politics*, Ithaca, NY: Cornell University Press.

Kenfield, I. (2007) "Taking on Big Cellulose: Brazilian Indigenous Communities Reclaim their Land," *NACLA Report on the Americas*, November/December.

160   *References*

Kenney-Lazar, M. (2011) *Dispossession, Semi-proletarianization, and Enclosure: Primitive Accumulation and the Land Grab in Laos*, paper presented at the international conference on global land grabbing.

Khagram, S. (2004) *Dams and Development: Transnational Struggles for Water and Power*, Ithaca: Cornell University Press.

King, B. (2008) "A Political Mediation Model of Corporate Response to Social Movement Activism," *Administrative Science Quarterly* 53: 395–421.

King, B. and Pearce, N. (2010) "The Contentiousness of Markets: Politics, Social Movements, and Institutional Change in Markets," *Annual Review of Sociology* 36: 249–67.

King, B. and Soule, S. (2007) "Social Movements as Extra-institutional Entrepreneurs: The Effect of Protests on Stock Price Returns," *Administrative Science Quarterly* 52: 413–42.

Kingstone, P. (1999) *Crafting Coalitions for Reform: Business Preferences, Political Institutions, and Neoliberal Reform in Brazil*, Pennsylvania, PA: The Pennsylvania State University Press.

Kingstone, P. and Ponce, A. (2010) "From Cardoso to Lula: The Triumph of Pragmatism in Brazil," in W. Hunter, K. Weyland and R. Madrid (eds) *Leftist Governments in Latin America: Successes and Shortcomings*, Cambridge: Cambridge University Press, 98–123.

Klare, M. (2012) *The Race for What's Left: The Global Scramble for the World's Last Resources*, New York: Metropolitan Books.

Koopmans, P.J. (2005) *Além do eucalipto: o papel do extremo sul* [After Eucalyptus: the Role of the Extreme South], Teixeira de Freitas: CDDH.

Kröger, M. (2005) *The Intercultural Encounter between the Brazilian Landless Workers Movement (the MST) and Veracel Celulose: A Power Analysis*, master's thesis, University of Helsinki, Latin American Studies.

——(2010) *The Politics of Pulp Investment and the Brazilian Landless Movement*, doctoral dissertation, University of Helsinki, Political Science, Acta Politica No. 39.

——(2011) "Promotion of Contentious Agency as a Rewarding Movement Strategy: Evidence from the MST-Paper Industry Conflicts in Brazil," *Journal of Peasant Studies* 38(2): 435–58.

——(2012a) "The Expansion of Industrial Tree Plantations and Dispossession in Brazil," *Development and Change* 43(4): 947–73.

——(2012b) "Neo-mercantilist Capitalism and Post-2008 Cleavages in Economic Decision-making Power in Brazil," *Third World Quarterly* 33(5): 887–901.

——(2013) "Grievances, agency and the absence of conflict: The new Suzano pulp investment in the Eastern Amazon," *Forest Policy and Economics*, Forest Policy and Economics 33: 28–35.

Kröger, M. and Nylund, J.-E. (2012) "The Conflict over Veracel Pulpwood Plantations in Brazil: Application of Ethical Analysis," *Forest Policy and Economics* 14(1): 74–82.

Kudlaviz, M. (2011) "Dinámica agrária e a territorialização do complexo celulose/papel na microrregião de Três Lagoas/MS" [Agrarian Dynamics and Territorialization of the Pulp/Paper Complex in the Micro-region of Três Lagoas/MS], master's thesis, UFMS, Geography.

Kuisma, M., Henttinen, A., Karhu, S. and Pohls, M. (1999) *The Pellervo Story: A Century of Finnish Cooperation, 1899–1999*, Helsinki: Pellervo.

Lander, I. (2012) "Stop the Biomass Blackout: Say no to the UK's Destructive Bioenergy Policies," *The Ecologist*, February 7.

References 161

Lazzarini, S. (2011) *Capitalismo de laços: Os donos de Brasil e suas conexões*, Rio de Janeiro: Elsevier.

Lehmann, D. (1990) *Democracy and Development in Latin America: Economics, Politics and Religion in the Post-War Period*, Philadelphia: Temple University Press.

Lerrer, D. and Wilkinson, J. (2012) *Impact of Restrictive Legislation and Popular Opposition Movements on Foreign Land Investments in Brazil: The Case of the Forestry and Pulp Paper Sector and Stora Enso*, paper presented at the International Academic Conference on Land Grabbing II, Cornell University, October 17–19.

Lessa, C. (2010) "Empresa Privada e o Projeto Nacional" [Private Company and the National Project], *Valor Econômico*, December 22 (Opinion).

Lewicki, R., Gray, B. and Elliot, M. (2003) *Making Sense of Intractable Environmental Conflicts: Concepts and Cases*, Washington: Island Press.

Leys, A.J. and Vanclay, J.K. (2010) "Land-use Change Conflict Arising from Plantation Forestry Expansion: Views Across Australian Fence-Lines," *International Forestry Review* 12(3): 256–69.

Li, T.M. (2007) *The Will to Improve: Governmentality, Development, and the Practice of Politics*, London: Duke University Press.

——(2011) "Centering Labor in the Land Grab Debate," *Journal of Peasant Studies* 38(2): 281–98.

Lichbach, M. (1998) "Contending Theories of Contentious Politics and the Structure-Action Problem of Social Order," *Annu. Rev. Polit. Sci.* 1: 401–24.

——(2008) "Modeling Mechanisms of Contention: MTT's Positivist Constructivism," *Qual Sociol* 31: 345–54.

Little, C., Lara, A., McPhee, J. and Urrutia, R. (2009) "Revealing the Impact of Forest Exotic Plantations on Water Yield in Large Scale Watersheds in South-Central Chile," *Journal of Hydrology* 374: 162–70.

Luders, J.E. (2010) *The Civil Rights Movement and the Logic of Social Change*, Cambridge: Cambridge University Press.

Lyytinen, J. and Nieminen, T. (2009) "Stora Enso's Jackpot," *Helsingin Sanomat*, August 30.

Macedo, M.E. (2005) "Entre a 'violência' e a 'espontaneidade': reflexões sobre os processos de mobilização para ocupações de terra no Rio de Janeiro," *Revista Mana* 11/2: 473–97.

Mancuso, W. (2007) "O empresariado como ator político no Brasil: balanço da literatura e agenda de pesquisa," *Revista de Sociologia e Política* 28: 131–46.

Marchak, P. (1995) *Logging the Globe*, Montreal: McGill-Queen's University Press.

Martínez-Torres, M. and Rosset, P. (2010) "La Vía Campesina: The Birth and Evolution of a Transnational Social Movement," *Journal of Peasant Studies* 37: 149–75.

Martins, J.S. (2003) *O sujeito oculto: ordem e transgressão na reforma agrária*, Porto Alegre: Editora da Universidade/UFRGS.

McAdam, D., Tarrow, S. and Tilly, C. (2001) *Dynamics of Contention*, Cambridge: Cambridge University Press.

——(2008) "Methods for Measuring Mechanisms of Contention," *Qualitative Sociology* 31: 307–31.

McAllister, L. (2008) *Making Law Matter: Environmental Protection and Legal Institutions in Brazil*, Stanford: Stanford University Press.

McCarthy, J.D. and Zald, M. (1977) "Resource Mobilization and Social Movements: A Partial Theory," *American Journal of Sociology* 82: 1212–41.

162 References

McElwee, P. (2009) "Reforesting 'Bare Hills' in Vietnam: Social and Environmental Consequences of the 5 Million Hectare Reforestation Program," *AMBIO: A Journal of the Human Environment* 38(6): 325–33.

McMichael, P. (1992) "Rethinking Comparative Analysis in a Post-developmental Context," *International Social Science Journal* 133: 351–65.

——(2008) "Peasants Make their Own History, but not Just as they Please," *Journal of Agrarian Change* 8: 205–28.

Medeiros, L. and Leite, S. (eds) (2004) *Assentamentos rurais: mudança social e dinâmica regional*, Rio de Janeiro: Mauad.

Medeiros, M. (2005) *O que faz os Ricos ricos: O outro lado da desigualdade brasileira*, São Paulo: Editora Hucitec.

Melucci, A. (1998) "Third World or Planetary Conflicts?" in S. Alvarez *et al.* (eds) *Cultures of Politics, Politics of Culture: Re-visioning Latin American Social Movements*, Boulder: Westview.

Meszaros, G. (2007) "The MST and the Rule of Law in Brazil," *Law, Social Justice & Global Development* 2007/1: 1–24.

Meyer, D. (2004) "Protest and Political Opportunities," *Annu. Rev. Sociol.* 30: 125–45.

Meyer, D. and Tarrow, S. (eds) (1998) *The Social Movement Society: Contentious Politics for a New Century*, Lanham: Rowman & Littlefield Publishers.

Miller, S. (2007) *Environmental History of Latin America*, Cambridge: Cambridge University Press.

Miola, I. (2009) *Paper Law: The Contradictory Legal and Political Responses of the Global North and South to the Transnationalization of the Pulp and Paper Industry*, master's thesis, Oñati International Institute for the Sociology of Law.

——(2010) "Between Strictness and Flexibility: How Law Enables the Globalization of the Pulp and Paper Industry," *El Norte – Finnish Journal of Latin American Studies* 5, www.elnorte.fi/archive/2010–15/2010_5_elnorte_miola.pdf.

MMA (2005) "Temas Conflituosos Relacionados à Expansão da Base Florestal Plantada e Definição de Estratégias para Minimização dos Conflitos Identificados" [Conflictive Themes Related to the Expansion of Planted Forest Base and Defini-tion of Strategies to Minimize the Identified Conflicts], Brasília: Ministry of the Environment (MMA).

Moore, J. (2011) "Ecology, Capital, and the Nature of Our Times: Accumulation & Crisis in the Capitalist World-Ecology," *Journal of World-Systems Research* XVII: 108–47.

Mueller, A.P. (2000) "The Ghost That Haunts Brazil," www.neoliberalismo.com/Archivo-01/ghost.htm.

Munck, R. (2007) *Globalization and Contestation: The New Great Counter-movement*, London: Routledge.

Myllylä, S. and Takala, T. (2011) "Leaking Legitimacies: The Finnish Forest Sector's Entanglement in the Land Conflicts of Atlantic Coastal Brazil," *Social Responsibility Journal* 7(1): 42–60.

n.a. (2007) *Industrial Forest Plantations Programme*, organized by the University of Helsinki, Departments of Forest Ecology, Forest Economics and Forest Resource Management in collaboration with Pöyry, Indufor, Stora Enso, CIFOR and the Finnish Ministry of Foreign Affairs, August 7–23.

NACLA (North American Congress on Latin America) (2007) "Taking on Big Cel-lulose: Brazilian Indigenous Communities Reclaim their Land," *Report on the Americas*, Nov./Dec.

References 163

Nagashima, K., Sands, R., Whyte, A.G.D., Bilek, E.M. and Nakagoshi, N. (2002) "Regional Landscape Change as a Consequence of Plantation Forestry Expansion: An Example in the Nelson Region, New Zealand," *Forest Ecology and Management* 163(1–3): 245–61.

Nahuelhual, L., Carmona, A., Lara, A., Echeverría, C. and González, M. (2012) "Land-cover Change to Forest Plantations: Proximate Causes and Implications for the Landscape in South-central Chile," *Landscape and Urban Planning* 107(1): 12–20.

Neef, A. (2012) "Land Grabbing in Cambodia: Narratives, Mechanisms, Resistance," presentation at Cornell University, Global Land Grabbing Conference II, October 18.

Neri, M. (ed.) (2008) *A Nova Classe Media*, Rio de Janeiro: FGV/IBRE, CPS.

Noor, R. and Syumanda, R. (2006) *Social Conflict and Environmental Disaster: A Report on Asia Pulp and Paper's Operations in Sumatra, Indonesia.*

Nosetto, M.D., Jobbágy, E.G., Tóth, T. and Jackson, R.B. (2008) "Regional Patterns and Controls of Ecosystem Salinization with Grassland Afforestation along a Rainfall Gradient," *Global Biogeochem. Cycles* 22, GB2015.

Nugent, J.B. and Robinson, J.A. (2010) "Are Factor Endowments Fate?" *Revista de Historia Economica/Journal of Iberian and Latin American Economic History* 28: 45–82.

Nylund, J. (2009) "Forestry Legislation in Sweden," Report No. 14. Uppsala: The Swedish University of Agricultural Sciences, Department of Forest Products.

Nylund, J. and Kröger, M. (2012) "Cleavage in the Understanding of Sustainability: Sustainable Pulp Industry versus Sustained Local Livelihood," *Scandinavian Journal of Forest Research* 27(2): 229–40.

Obidzinski, K. and Dermawan, A. (2010) "Smallholder Timber Plantation Development in Indonesia: What is Preventing Progress?" *International Forestry Review* 12(4): 339–48.

Oliveira, A. (2011) "É uma mentira dizer que no Brasil a terra é produtiva" [It is a Lie to Say that in Brazil the Land is Productive], special interview with Ariovaldo Umbelino by Márcia Junges, *IHU Online*, January 10.

Oliveira, A.O. (2010, officially [published in reality 2012]) "A questão de aquisição de terras por estrangeiros no Brasil – um retorno aos dossiês" [The Question of Land Acquisitions by Foreigners in Brazil – A Return to the Dossiers], *Agrária* 12: 3–113.

Ondetti, G. (2006) "Repression, Opportunity, and Protest: Explaining the Takeoff of Brazil's Landless Movement," *Latin American Politics & Society* 48: 61–94.

——(2008) *Land, Protest, and Politics: The Landless Movement and the Struggle for Agrarian Reform in Brazil*, University Park: Penn State University Press.

Pakkasvirta, J. (2010) *Fábricas de celulosa: historias de la globalización*, Buenos Aires: La Colmena.

Palo, M. and Lehto, E. (2012) *Private or Socialistic Forestry? Forest Transition in Finland vs. Deforestation in the Tropics*, New York: Springer.

Patterson, M.W. and Hoalst-Pullen, N. (2011) "Dynamic Equifinality: The Case of South-central Chile's Evolving Forest Landscape," *Applied Geography* 31(2): 641–49.

Peet, J.R., Robbins, P. and Watts, M. (eds) (2010) Global Political Ecology, London: Routledge.

Peluso, N.L. and Vandergeest, P. (2001) "Genealogies of Forest Law and Customary Rights in Indonesia, Malaysia, and Thailand," *J. Asian Stud.* 60(3): 761–812.

164 References

Peluso, N.L. and Watts, M. (2001) *Violent Environments*, Ithaca: Cornell University Press.

Perreault, T. and Valdivia, G. (2010) "Hydrocarbons, Popular Protest and National Imaginaries: Ecuador and Bolivia in Comparative Context," *Geoforum* 41: 689–99.

Piketty, M., Wichert, M., Fallot, A. and Aimola, L. (2009) "Assessing Land Availability to Produce Biomass for Energy: The Case of Brazilian Charcoal for Steel Making," *Biomass and Bioenergy* 33(2): 180–90.

Ping, L. and Nielsen, R. (2010) "A Case Study on Large-Scale Forestland Acquisition in China," *Right and Resources*, www.rightsandresources.org/documents/files/doc_1800.pdf.

Pirard, R. and Mayer, J. (2009) "Complementary Labor Opportunities in Indonesian Pulpwood Plantations with Implications for Land Use," *Agroforestry Systems* 76(2): 499–511.

Piven, F.F. and Cloward, R. (1978) *Poor People's Movements: Why They Succeed, How They Fail*, New York: Vintage Books.

Pochmann, M., Guerra, A., Amorim, R. and Silva, R. (eds) (2006) *Atlas da Nova Estratificação Social no Brasil: Classe Média, Desenvolvimento e Crise*, São Paulo: Cortez Editora.

Polanyi, K. (2001 [1944]) *The Great Transformation: The Political and Economic Origins of Our Time*, Boston: Beacon Press.

Polletta, F. (2002) *Freedom is an Endless Meeting: Democracy in American Social Movements*, Chicago: Chicago University Press.

Power, T. and Doctor, M. (2004) "Another Century of Corporatism? Continuity and Change in Brazil's Corporatist Structures," in H. Wiarda (ed.) *Authoritarianism and Corporatism in Latin America – Revisited*, Gainesville: University Press of Florida.

Puntasen, A., Siriprachai, S. and Punyasavatsut, C. (1992) "Political Economy of Eucalyptus: Business, Bureaucracy and the Thai Government," *Journal of Contemporary Asia* 22(2): 187–206.

Puppim de Oliveira, J. (2008) "Property Rights, Land Conflicts and Deforestation in Eastern Amazonia," *Forest Policy and Economics* 10(5): 303–15.

Ragin, C. (1987) *The Comparative Method: Moving Beyond Qualitative and Quantitative Strategies*, Berkeley: University of California Press.

——(2009) "Fuzzy Set/Qualitative Comparative Analysis," www.u.arizona.edu/~cragin/fsQCA/index.shtml (accessed December 30, 2008).

Rangel, L.N. (2010) "'Encampment Time': An Anthropological Analysis of the Land Occupations in Brazil," *Journal of Peasant Studies* 2010/2: 285–318.

Redo, D., Mitchell, T., Clark, M. and Andrade-Núñez, M. (2012) "Impacts of Internal and External Policies on Land Change in Uruguay, 2001–9," *Environmental Conservation* 39: 122–31.

Reitan, R. (2007) *Global Activism*, London: Routledge.

Reuters News (2009) "Preço da terra no Brasil recua com saída de compradores" [Land Price Drops in Brazil due to the Exit of Buyers], January 21.

Richardson, D.M. (1998) "Forestry Trees as Invasive Aliens," *Conservation Biology* 12: 18–26.

Robinson, W. (2008) *Latin America and Global Capitalism: A Critical Globalization Perspective*, Baltimore: The Johns Hopkins University Press.

Rose, R. (2005) *The Unpast: Elite Violence and Social Control in Brazil 1954–2000*, Athens, OH: Ohio University Press.

Ross, M.L. (2001) *Timber Booms and Institutional Breakdown in South East Asia*, Cambridge: Cambridge University Press.

References 165

Rothman, F. and Oliver, P. (2002) "From Local to Global: The Anti-dam Movement in Southern Brazil, 1979–92," in J. Smith and H. Johnston (eds) *Globalization and Resistance: Transnational Dimensions of Social Movements*, Lanham: Rowman & Littlefield.

Roux, H. (2012) *Land Access or Celebrating Territory: A Political Choice on the Redefinition of Rural Social Categories*, IRSA, conference paper, Lisbon, August 3.

Sadek, M. and Cavalcanti, R. (2003) "The New Brazilian Public Prosecution: An Agent of Accountability," in S. Mainwaring and C. Welna (eds) *Democratic Accountability in Latin America*, Oxford: Oxford University Press.

Santana, C. (2011) "Conjuntura crítica, legados institucionais e comunidades epistêmicas: Limites e possibilidades de uma agenda de desenvolvimento no Brasil," in R. Boschi (ed.) *Variedades de capitalismo, política e desenvolvimento na América Latina*, Belo Horizonte: Editora UFMG, 121–63.

Santos, R. (2011) *O Projeto Grande Carajás e seus reflexos para a cultura extrativista no Maranhão*, Imperatriz: Ética.

Sargent, C. and Bass, S. (eds) (1992) *Plantations Politics: Forest Plantations in Development*, London: Earthscan.

Sassen, S. (2010) "A Savage Sorting of Winners and Losers: Contemporary Versions of Primitive Accumulation," *Globalizations* 7(1): 23–50.

Sauer, S. and Leite, S. (2012) "Agrarian Structure, Foreign Investment in Land, and Land Prices in Brazil," *Journal of Peasant Studies* 39: 873–89.

Sawyer, S. (2004) *Crude Chronicles: Indigenous Politics, Multinational Oil, and Neoliberalism in Ecuador*, London: Duke University Press.

Saxena, N.C. (1994) *India's Eucalyptus Craze: The God that Failed*, London: Sage.

Schenck, K. (2011) *Vattenfall in Liberia – African Timber for Climate Friendly Bioenergy in Germany*, PowerPoint presentation, WRM meeting Montevideo, September 21.

Schneider, B. (2009) "A Comparative Political Economy of Diversified Business Groups, Or How States Organize Big Business," *Review of International Political Economy* 16(2): 178–201.

Schneider, S. and Niederle, P. (2010) "Resistance Strategies and Diversification of Rural Livelihoods: The Construction of Autonomy Among Brazilian Family Farmers," *Journal of Peasant Studies* 37: 379–405.

Schnell, S., Kleinn, C. and Álvarez, J. (2012) "Stand Density Management Diagrams for Three Exotic Tree Species in Smallholder Plantations in Vietnam," *Small-Scale Forestry*, in press, DOI:10.1007/s11842-012-9197-z.

Schwartz, S.B. (1984) "Colonial Brazil, c. 1580–c. 1750: Plantations and Peripheries," in L. Bethell (ed.) *Colonial Latin America*, Cambridge: Cambridge University Press, 423–99.

Scott, J.C. (1998) *Seeing Like a State: How Certain Schemes to Improve the Human Condition Have Failed*, London: Yale University Press.

——(2009) *The Art of Not Being Governed*, New Haven: Yale University Press.

——(2012) *The Art of Not Being Governed: An Anarchist History of Upland Southeast Asia*, London: Yale University Press.

Seligmann, L.J. (2005) "Ethnographic Methods," in Daniel Druckman (ed.) *Doing Research: Methods of Inquiry for Conflict Analysis*, London: Sage.

Sen, A. (2005) *The Argumentative Indian*, London: Penguin.

Seufert, P. (2012) *The Human Rights Impacts of Tree Plantations in Niassa Province, Mozambique*, FIAN.

166   References

Sherman, D.J. (2011) "Critical Mechanisms for Critical Masses: Exploring Variation in Opposition to Low-Level Radioactive Waste Site Proposals," *Mobilization* 16(1): 81–100.

Sigaud, L. (2005) "As condições de possibilidade das ocupações de terra," *Tempo Social* 17: 255–80.

Sigaud, L., Rosa, M. and Macedo, M. (2008) "Ocupações de terra, acampamentos e demandas ao estado: uma análise em perspectiva comparada," *Dados* 51: 107–42.

Sikor, T. (2012) "Tree Plantations, Politics of Possession and the Absence of Land Grabs in Vietnam," *Journal of Peasant Studies* 39(3–4): 1077–101.

Sikor, T. and Nguyen, T.Q. (2007) "Why May Forest Devolution not Benefit the Rural Poor? Forest Entitlements in Vietnam's Central Highlands," *World Dev.* 35: 2010–25.

Silva, E. (2004) "The Political Economy of Forest Policy in Mexico and Chile," *Singapore Journal of Tropical Geography* 25: 261–80.

——(2009) *Challenging Neoliberalism in Latin America*, Cambridge: Cambridge University Press.

Silver, B. (2003) *Forces of Labor: Workers' Movements and Globalization since 1870*, Cambridge: Cambridge University Press.

Silvestre, L. (2008) "Justiça condena Veracel Celulose por desmatar 96 mil ha de Mata Atlântica" [Justice Sentences Veracel Celulose for Deforesting 96,000 ha of Atlantic Forest], *Brasil de Fato*, August 14, 4.

Siqueira, C. (2012) "Eldorado investe R$ 600 mi para iniciar fabricação," *O Estado de São Paulo*, July 13.

Snow, D. and Benford, R. (1992) "Master Frames and Cycles of Protest," in A. Morris and C. McClurg-Mueller (eds) *Frontiers In Social Movement Theory*, New Haven: Yale University Press.

Socio-Environmental Forum of the Extreme South of Bahia and Alert against the Green Desert Network (2010) "Armed Security Force of Fibria (Aracruz) Kills Local Villager in Bahia," press release, March 23.

Sohngen, B., Mendelsohn, R. and Sedjo, R. (2001) "A Global Model of Climate Change Impacts on Timber Market," *Journal of Agricultural and Resource Economics* 26(2): 326–43.

Soule, S. (2009) *Contention and Corporate Social Responsibility*, Cambridge: Cambridge University Press.

Souza, I. and Overbeek, W. (2008) *Violações socioambientais promovidas pela Veracel Celulose, propriedade da Stora Enso e Aracruz cellulose: Uma história de ilegalidades, descaso e ganância* [Socioenvironmental Violations Committed by Veracel Celulose, Property of Stora Enso and Aracruz Celulose: A History of Illegalities, Neglect and Greed], São Paulo: CEPEDES/Expressão Popular.

Stape, J., Binkley, D. and Ryan, M. (2008) "Production and Carbon Allocation in a Clonal Eucalyptus Plantation with Water and Nutrient Manipulations," *Forest Ecology and Management* 255(3–4): 920–93.

Stewart, H.T.L., Race, D.H. and Curtis, A.L. (2011) "New Forests in Changing Landscapes in South-East Australia," *International Forestry Review* 13(1): 67–79.

Tarrow, S. (1998) *Power in Movement: Social Movements and Contentious Politics*, 2nd edn, Cambridge: Cambridge University Press.

——(2005) *The New Transnational Activism*, Cambridge: Cambridge University Press.

——(2011) *Power in Movement: Social Movements and Contentious Politics*, 3rd edn, Cambridge: Cambridge University Press.

References 167

Taylor, M. (2008) *Judging Policy: Courts and Policy Reform in Democratic Brazil*, Stanford: Stanford University Press.

Teivainen, T. (2002) *Enter Economism, Exit Politics: Experts, Economic Policy and the Damage to Democracy*, New York: Zed Books.

——(2003) *Pedagogía del poder mundial: Relaciones internacionales y lecciones del desarrollo en América Latina*, Lima: CEPED.

——(2012) "Global Democratization without Hierarchy or Leadership? The World Social Forum in the Capitalist World," in S. Gill (ed.) *Global Crises and the Crisis of Global Leadership*, Cambridge: Cambridge University Press, 181–98.

Teixeira, F. and Guerra, O. (2000) "50 Anos da Industrialização Baiana: do enigma a uma dinâmica exógena e espasmódica" [50 Years of Bahian Industrialization: From Enigma to an Exogenous and Spasmodic Dynamics], *Bahia Análise & Dados* 10: 87–98.

Tilly, C. (1999) "Conclusion: From Interactions to Outcomes in Social Movements," in M. Giugni, D. McAdam and C. Tilly (eds) *How Social Movements Matter*, London: University of Minnesota Press.

Tilly, C. and Tarrow, S. (2007) *Contentious Politics*, Boulder: Paradigm Publishers.

Tweedie, M. (2012) *Mapuche Leader Condemns Arson Attack on Family Home*, January 9, ilovechile.cl/2012/01/09/mapuche-leader-condemns-arson-attack-parents-home/44225.

UNEP (2012) *Global Environment Outlook* (GEO-5).

Urban, G. (2001) *Metaculture: How Culture Moves Through the World*, Minnesota: University of Minnesota Press.

USDA (2005) "USDA's Foreign Agricultural Service and Global Trade Information Services Data," www.ers.usda.gov/AmberWaves/November06/Features/Brazil.htm.

Vandergeest, P. and Peluso, N.L. (2006) "Empires of Forestry: Professional Forestry and State Power in Southeast Asia, Part 2," *Environment and History* 12: 4359–93.

van Dijk, A. and Keenan, R. (2007) "Planted Forests and Water in Perspective," *Forest Ecology and Management* 251(1–2): 1–9.

van Wilgen, B. and Richardson, D.M. (2012) "Three Centuries of Managing Introduced Conifers in South Africa: Benefits, Impacts, Changing Perceptions and Conflict Resolution," *Journal of Environmental Management* 106(15): 56–68.

Varela, E. (2011) *Newen Mapuche/The Strength of the People of the Earth*, a documentary film, Chile.

Vasi, I. (2009) "Social Movements and Industry Development: The Environmental Movement's Impact on the Wind Energy Industry," *Mobilization* 14: 315–36.

Vergara-Camus, L. (2007) *Neoliberal Globalization, Peasant Movements, Alternative Development and the State in Brazil and Mexico*, PhD dissertation, York University, Toronto, Department of Political Science.

Viana, O. (1922) *Populações Meridionais do Brasil: História-Organicação-Psychologia*, São Paulo: Monteiro Lobato & Cia. Editores.

Vogel, D. (2005) *The Market for Virtue*, Washington, DC: Brookings Institution Press.

Wacquant, L. (2008) *Urban Outcasts: A Comparative Sociology of Advanced Marginality*, Cambridge: Polity.

——(2013) "Symbolic Power and Group-making: On Pierre Bourdieu's Reframing of Class," *Classical Sociology* 13(2) (Spring).

Wallerstein, I. (2001) *Unthinking Social Science: The Limits of Nineteenth-Century Paradigms*, Philadelphia: Temple University Press.

Wampler, B. (2005) "Restructuring Brazil: Institutional Reform, Economic Liberalism, and Pluralism," *Latin American Research Review* 40: 242–52.

168 References

Watts, M. (2009) "Peasant," in Gregory et al. (ed.) *The Dictionary of Human Geography*, Chichester: Wiley-Blackwell, pp. 524–5.

Wittman, H. (2009) "Reworking the Metabolic Rift: La Vía Campesina, Agrarian Citizenship, and Food Sovereignty," *Journal of Peasant Studies* 36: 805–26.

Wolford, W. (2003) "Producing Community: The MST and Land Reform Settlements in Brazil," *Journal of Agrarian Change* 3: 500–20.

——(2010a) *This Land is Ours Now: Social Mobilization and the Meanings of Land in Brazil*, London: Duke University Press.

——(2010b) "Participatory Democracy by Default: Land Reform, Social Movements and the State in Brazil," *Journal of Peasant Studies* 37: 91–109.

Wright, E.O. (ed.) (2005) *Approaches to Class Analysis*, Cambridge: Cambridge University Press.

WRM (2007) "Armed Militia of VM – Vallourec Mannesmann – Cowardly Murdered Geraizero of the Canabrava Community," www.wrm.org.uy/countries/Brazil/armed_militia.html.

——(2008) "Victories of Peoples' Resistance in Peru and Brazil," *WRM Bulletin* 134.

Zald, M. (1996) "Culture, Ideology, and Strategic Framing," in D. McAdam, J. McCarthy and M. Zald (eds) *Comparative Perspectives on Social Movements: Political Opportunities, Mobilizing Structures, and Cultural Framings*, Cambridge: Cambridge University Press.

Zhouri, A. (2010) "'Adverse Forces' in the Brazilian Amazon: Developmentalism versus Environmentalism and Indigenous Rights," *The Journal of Environment & Development* 19(3): 252–73.

Zysman, J. (1994) "How Institutions Create Historically Rooted Trajectories of Growth," *Industrial and Corporate Change* 3: 243–83.

Index

abbreviations xiii-xiv
Abu,-El Haj, J. 97
acacia trees 135
"accumulation by dispossession" (ABD)
  38, 44–47; *see also* industrial forestry
Alert against the Green Desert Network
  49, 73
Alianza Territorial Mapuche
  organization in Chile 128, 131
Alliance for the Peoples of Our America
  (ALBA) 16, 73, 118, 145
alternative relationship to nature 64–65,
  122–123
Ambé, Elisangela 103–4
Amnesty International 129
Andrews, Kenneth 13, 138
Arab Spring 150
Aracruz Celulose (AC) 8, 39–41, 42,
  48–49, 73–75, 83, 90–92, 120, 148–49
  see also Fibria
Ascenção, Orlan 103
Associação Brasileira de Produtores de
  Florestas Plantadas (ABRAF) 94
Australia: paper/pulp firms 118, 135;
  tree plantations 114–15

Bachelet, Michelle 130
Bahia replication case 76
Baixa Verde camp (MST) 50
Barney, K. 110, 118, 121–22, 133
Bengoa, José 132
"Big Pulp" 42
"bio-economy" 1, 111, 124
Boff, Leonardo 63
Bolivia: water privatization 150; *see also*
  Alliance for the Peoples of our
  America
Bolse Familia program 95
book summary 2–3, 10–11

Borras. S. M. 61, 109
Bourdieu, Pierre 19, 20, 25, 27, 32, 33,
  67, 78, 140
Bracelpa (paper and pulp organization)
  10, 43, 56, 89–90
Brazil: Amazon policy 149; "capitalism
  of ties" 96; Celmar pulp project 117;
  Constitution (1988) 99; GDP 94; job
  creation 120; ITPs 110; land use 124;
  lawsuits 99; popular resistance 145;
  see also industrial forestry; MST
Brazilian Institute of Environment and
  Renewable Natural Resources
  (IBAMA) 103–4
Brazilian Rural Landless Workers'
  Movement *see* MST
BRIC (Brazil, Russia, India, China)
  countries 4

"campaigning by heterodox farming"
  65–66, 84, 140–142
campesino protestors in Peru 151
"capitalism of ties" 95–96
carbon credits (India) 116
"carbon sinks" 115, 134
Cardoso, Fernando Henrique 96–97
Carvalho, Adriana 103–4
Cenibra 135
Center for International Forestry
  Research (CIFOR) 42
Chevron oil 150
Chile: law DL 701 120; Mapuche people
  128–32; plantation forestry 119–20;
  Pinochet dictatorship 129; tree
  plantations 110, 123, 128–30
Chilean Indigenous Development
  Corporation (CONADI) 130
Chilean National Commission for the
  Environment (CONAI) 129, 130

170 Index

China: biomass 115; human rights 115; industrial tree plantations 115; land use 115, 124; Sloping Land Conversion Program 124
civil rights movement research, US 76
CMPC (Chilean pulp company) 151
Confederation of Agricultural Workers (CONTAG) 99
contentious agency, Brazilian landless movement and pulp conflict outcomes: autonomy with state 76–81; campaigning by heterodox framing 65–66; conclusions 84–85; strategies and economic outcomes 81–84; introduction 58–59; MST 59–61; networking with allies 71–76; organizing and politicizing 61–65; protesting 66–71; strategies and economic outcomes 81–84;
Coordination of Agrarian Development (CDA) 50–51
Crusius, Yeda 68–69, 90, 108
Cutrale (orange producer) 70

da Silva, Lula 75, 77, 90, 92–95, 97
da Silvo Neto, João Alves 76
Dahl, Robert 66
de Casmina, C and J 49
de Moraes, Antônio Ermírio 89
"Deep Brazil" 40
Dietrich, Mozar 79
dos Santos, Antonio Joaquim 49
du Monceau, M. I. 132
Duarte, José 102
Dynamics of Contention 141
Dynamics of Contention (DOC) research program 12, 27, 87

economics theory 23–26
Ecuador and natural resource exploitation 150
Ejército Zapatista de Liberación Nacional (EZLN) 73, 131
"embedded autonomy" 26, 61, 138
Environmental Impact Assessment (EIA) 103
Espírito Santo case 74–76, 83, 141
eucalyptus plantations: activism 118; Aracruz Celulose 74; conflict 135; destruction 100; dispossession; 39–41; expansion 37, 50, 54–55, 63, 68, 84; expansion in Espírito Santo 141; financial logic of expansion and exclusion 51–54; Imperatriz region

103; industrial forestry policy 36, 41–43; land issues 67; monoculture 55, 81; MST 52, 65, 79–80; oranges comparison 71; primitive land access 48–51; protests 2, 59–60, 74, 79, 89, 106; pulp investment model 67; resistance 135; state financing and pulp expansion correlation 43; states 43–48; Thailand 118, 121; Veracel Celulose 9, 53, 76,143, 145; Votarantim Celulose e Papel 89
Eucatex 49
European Union (EU): land leases 115
Evans, Peter 14, 33, 41, 61, 76, 100–101, 102, 138
exotic tree species: conflicts 125–26; environment; 124

favelas (shanty towns) 47, 52
Federal Bureau of Investigation (FBI) 128
Federation of Social and Educational Assistance (FASE) NGO 48, 73, 74
FIAN (Food First Information and Action Network) 148
Fibria 42, 55, 79, 106, 120, 144, 149
financial logic of expansion and exclusion: description 51–52; exclusion by rising land prices 53–54
Finland: paper companies 118; STPs 110, tree plantations 134
"flex" crop 109–10
"flex trees" 111
Fontelles, Claudio 93
Food and Agricultural Organization (FAO) 109, 112–14; 119, 124–26
Forest Stewardship Council (FSC) 49
formação (formation) 62
Foucault, Michel 20, 151
Franklin, Adelberto 104, 106
Freedom is a Constant Struggle 13
Freire, Paulo 33, 63
Fundação National do Índio (FUNAI) 87

Garcia, Alan 151
Genfors, Weine 10
Genro, Tarso 69
Gerdau, Jorge 96
German forestry model 119
Ghosh, Soumitra 116
Gibson-Graham, J. K. 18–19, 127
Giugni, Marco 13–14, 95, 138
global democracy promotion 144

global expansion of resource
exploitation (tree plantation conflicts):
conclusions 124–25; environmental
impacts 123–25; introduction 109–10;
smallholder versus industrial tree
plantations 121–23; tree plantation
resistance 125–33; why? 110–12;
global expansion of resource
exploitation (tree plantation conflicts)
how?: job creation and livelihoods
120–21; "political forests" – centrality
of land control in ITPs 119–20; state-
industry-resistance interaction and
investment location 117–19; where
and what? 112–17
global expansion of resource
exploitation (tree plantation conflicts)
where and what?: global "planted
forest" expansion 113; land use
changes 114–17
"global land grab" 4
globalization 149
GM (genetically modified): soybean 65;
trees 112
Gramsci, A. 20
"green capitalism" 1
"green development" 124
"green economy" 133–34
Green India Mission 116–17
"Green Revolution" 52, 111
Greenpeace (NGO) 48, 138
grigalem (illegal land grabbing) 40–41
grileiros (grabbers) 39
gross domestic product (GDP) 94,
112

Hanauer, Ana 65
Harmes, A. 149, 151
heterodox framing campaigns 65–66, 74,
144
Hirvelä, Ville-Veikko 109, 116

Ibase (NGO) 48
"ideal resistance model" 84
INCRA *see* National Institute of
Colonization and Agrarian Reform
INCRA-Suzano relationship 102
India: carbon credits 116; "carbon
sinks" 116, 134; exotic plantations
124; tree plantations 115–16; *see also*
Green India mission
Indonesia: pulp plantations and
livelihoods 121; STPs 122; "war-like"
expansion 127

industrial forestry in Brazil
(accumulation by dispossession):
conclusions 54–55; financial logic of
expansion and exclusion 51–54;
introduction 36–37; policy 41–43;
primitive land access: dynamics and
consequences 48–50; systematic
comparison across states 43–48; tree
monocultures and rural exclusion
37–41
industrial tree plantations (ITPs):
business as usual 145; conflicts 1, 135,
148–49; corporate concessions 118;
corporate controlled monoculture 20;
establishment 41, 120; expansion 111,
119; global capitalism 54; industry
power 55; land control 119–20; land
outsourcing 26; minimum conditions
121; MST 4; politics 128; pollution
havens 118; preferred locations 32;
protests 109; regulation 107;
resistance 67, 116, 123; state forest
lands 49; STPs 110, 118; "war-like"
settings 134
Institute of Agroforestry Development
(IDAF) in Espírito Santo 41
institutional game: structural and
institutional embedding: activists,
prosecutors meritocracy and rule of
law – resistance 97–101; power elite –
corporations 94–95; social equity and
social movement society – movements
95; state corporatism and
neoliberalism – corporations 96–97
International Labour Organization
(ILO) 130
International Monetary Fund (IMF) 91
"investment climate" 116

Japan pulp industry 135
Jarí 39, 42, 49
Joaquim dos Santos, Antonio 49

La Via Campesina movement 5, 17, 60,
62, 66, 69, 72, 148–49
latifundio farms 47
Laos: job creation and livelihoods 120;
STPs 120
Lazzarini, S. 95, 96–97
Letraviva 65, 92
Ley de Derechos de la Madre Terra
(Law of the Rights of Mother Earth)
in Bolivia 64
Li, Tania Murray 28, 38, 55

172 Index

Luders, J. E. 3, 5, 14, 70, 106, 137, 139, 141–42
Ludwig, Daniel 42
Luis, José 104–5

Maattomien ystävät (Finnish solidarity association) 9
MAB movement 104
McAdam, Doug 3, 5, 12–14, 25–27, 29, 33, 58, 71, 78, 137–39, 141–42
Mapuche people, Chile 128–30, 130–32
Marx, Karl 5, 28, 37–38
Meszaros, G. 60, 93, 98–99, 101
methodology and research 7–11
Mexico: tree plantations 113
Meyer, David and Tarrow, Sidney 95
Ministry of Agrarian Development 52
Ministry for the Environment (MMA) 39, 42, 73, 74, 91, 107
Mistica (drama) 62–63
mobilization and dynamics of contention: grievances in corporate plantation conflicts 29–30; material dimension in building mobilization 27–29
Moldan, Ludwig 10
Monsanto 65
Movement for Land Liberation (MLT) 50
Movimento dos Trabalhadores Rurais Sem Terra *see* MST
MST (Brazilian Rural Workers' Landless Movement): autonomy 14; camp 50; da Silva, Lula 92; democracy 17; electoral politics 93; embedded autonomy 76,-81, 139; eucalyptus plantations 52, 65, 79–80; heterodox framing campaigns 65–66, 74, 144; history 4, 52; ideals 99; institutional politics 98; "land" 20; legal services 99–100; Luis, José 104; members 139–40; mobilization 21, 95; paper industry conflicts 7; plantation expansion 144; politics 16; principal adversary 144; protests 66, 87, 89–90, 149; PT deputies 92; pulp conflict outcomes 10, 59–61, 62–66, 70, 72–78, 78–81, 83–84; research 8; resistance network 87; Rio Grande do Sul state 32; Rosa Luxemburgo camp 64; Sarney family 101; *sem terras* 22, 66, 75; state relations 97–98; Vale do Rio Doce 106; Veracel Celusose eucalyptus plantations occupation

143–44; violence guidelines 19; Wagner, Jacques 92
MST-INCRA-agribusiness dynamics 78–81
Mueller, Anthony P. 89
multinational corporations (MNCs) 39

National Agrarian Reform Program 99
National Development Bank (BNDES) 41–42, 88–89, 91, 149
National Forum of Forest Peoples and Forest Workers (India) 116
National Institute of Colonization and Agrarian Reform (INCRA) 41, 47, 53, 68, 70, 78–81, 84, 87, 102
National Network of Popular Independent Lawyers (RENAP) 99
networking with allies: contentious agency replication: eastern Brazil 74–76; description 71–73
non-governmental organizations (NGOs) 8–9, 48, 73, 81–82, 103, 109, 113, 118, 132, 145, 148
North American Congress on Latin America (NACLA) 39, 75, 90

O Globo 59, 96
objectively observable grievances 29
Ordem dos Advogados do Brasil (OAB) 99
organicidade (movement grid composed of people together) 62
Overbeek, Winnie 74

Partido dos Trabalhadores (PT) party 99, 103, 106
Pastoral Land Commission (CPT) 39
Pedagogy of the Oppressed 62
Peru: popular resistance; resistance to investment model 151–52
Phoenix Pulp and Paper 121
"phony forests" 134
pine plantations 123
pine trees 124, 135
Piñera, Sebastián 130
Pinochet dictatorship, Chile 129
"pioneering protesting" 142
"planted forests" (global expansion) 113
"planted semi-natural forests" 114
Polanyi, Karl/Polanyism 3, 5, 28, 41, 64, 98, 151
"political forests" (centrality of land control in ITPs) 119–20
political games concept 24, 26

Index 173

political games (resource exploitation pace and style): conclusions 107–8; electoral politics – state actors 90–94; institutional game – structural and institutional embedding 94–101; introduction 87–88; policy, ideology, space and games 88–90; private politics 101, 102–7
"political opportunity" framework 145
Poor People's Movements 139
Pöyry Forest Consulting 115
private politics: contentious strategies for movements 83; description 101; direct dialogue and negotiation 15; institutional politics 80; MST 66, 79; political games 26, 87, 101–7; process 31; pulp expansion frontier 102–7; state mediation 23–24
"private" pulp corporations 37
protests: description 66–67; MST 66, 87, 89–90, 149; pioneering protests 69–71; pulpwood expansion in Rio Grande do Sul 68–69; re-symbolizing 67–68; Red April 71
Public Ministry (Ministério Público) in Brazil 98, 100
Pulping the South 145

qualitative comparative analysis (QCA) 7, 58–59, 81, 139
Queipul, Mijael Carbone 128–30, 130–31
Quilombola communities 10, 40, 49, 133

Ramesh, Jairam 116
Re-Afforestation Act, 1992 118
Rede Nacional de Advogados e Advogados Populares (RENAP) 99
Redondo, José 102
relative grievances 29–30
Red April protests 71
REDD+ (UN programme for Reducing Emissions from Deforestation and Forest Degradation in Developing Countries) 112, 115–16
Reitan, Ruth 27, 149
resistance in natural resource politics: beyond dynamics of contention 141–44; contentious agency and its economic outcomes in land grabbing effects 142–45; democracy promoting contentious agency 145–46; global mobilization against resource

exploitation 146–52; introduction 137–39; theoretical-methodological contributions 139–40
The Rights and Resources Initiative 115
Rio Grande do Sul case 68–69, 83
Ripasa Celulose 49
Rossetto, Neuri 73, 77
Roussef, Dilma 88, 94, 96

Sampaio, Plinio (PT) 99
Santos, Wedson Souza 76
sem terras (MST members) 22, 64, 66, 68, 75
sem-teto (roofless) movement 75
Sen, Amartya 17
Silvestre, Luciana 74
Simula, Pertti 62
Sloping Land Conversion Program, China 124
smallholder-based forestry plantations (STPs): ethnic territory-based resistance 133; expansion 110; failures 122; industrial forestry expansion 110; ITPs 110; Mapuche people 132; politics 134; promotion 118; TP expansion 121
Smith, Adam 41
state land see *terra devoluta*
Stédile, João Pedro 92–93
Stora Enso 3, 8–9, 55, 72, 90, 115, 120, 127, 144, 149
Suzano de Papel e Celulose 49, 83, 101–3, 105–7

Tarrow, Sidney 12, 14, 33, 66, 95, 137–38, 147, 149
terra devoluta (state land) 41, 48, 50, 103
Terra Legal program 103
Thailand: eucalyptus plantations 118, 121; popular resistance 145; smallholders 121; STPs 110
The Economist 42, 95
The Hindu 116
theoretical bases 5–7
theory of contentious agency in natural resource politics: agency, development and democracy 17–19; agency, identity and emotions 19–20; conclusions 32–33; disaggregating processes and strategies 30–32; introduction 12–17; mobilization and dynamics of contention 27–30; political games and impact on natural resource exploitation 22–26; study of

174 *Index*

agency and control of space concepts 20–22

Tilly, Charles 12, 33, 68, 137–38

tree monocultures and rural exclusion: dispossession 39–41; primitive accumulation 37–39

tree plantations (TPs): corporate agency 111; economics 117; environmental impacts 123–25; establishment 134–35; exotic species 124; expansion 30, 55, 109, 113–16, 123, 134–35; global importance 110; jobs 120; land occupation 114; literature and resistance 25–33; monocultures 124; pulpwood 121; renewability 112; smallholder tenure 122; supply chains 135

tree plantations (TPs) – literature and resistance: class/ethnic territorial-based resistance comparison 132–33; economics 117; exotic tree species in conflicts 125–26; forestry militarism: war-like conflicts in Chile 128–30; national political dynamics: "war-like" and "democratic" 126–28; state-resistance movements in ITP resistance 130–32

United Nations Educational Scientific and Cultural Organization (UNESCO) 62

United Nations Environment Programme (UNEP) 110, 113

United Nations (UN) FAO *see* Food and Agricultural Organization

United States (US): civil rights movement research 76; lawsuits and corporate behavior 99; pulp prices 117

Urban, Greg 21

Uruguay: job creation 120; investment guarantees; Stora Enso 120; tree plantations 119

Vale do Rio Doce (CVRD) 48–49, 92, 106

Vallourec and Mannesmann (VM) 49

Varela, Elena 131

Vargas, Getulio 96

Veracel Celulose: case 8, 83; contentious agency replication 75–76; eucalyptus plantations 9, 59, 143–45; finance 51–53; *grilagem* 40; land access 48–51; MST 106, 143–45; occupation 66, 70, 80; 143–44; politics 90–91; pulp mill 44

Veracruz *see* Veracel Celulose

Viana, Oliveira 96

Vietnam: environment 122; smallholders 122; STPs 110, 122

virtuous circle of contentious agency 14–15

Votorantim Celulose e Papel (VCP) 42, 49, 79, 89, 91, 120 *see also* Fibria

Wagner, Jaques (PT) 91–92, 100

Wallerstein, Immanuel 95

Weber, Max 25

World Bank 38, 42, 91–92, 149

World Rainforest Movement (WRM) 49, 73, 109, 148, 152

World Social Forum (WSF) 73, 146

Zapatista Army of National Liberation 73, 131

Zogbi, Osmar 89

Zysman, John 32